Administering
the Community College
Learning Resources
Program

Administering the Community College Learning Resources Program

WANDA K. JOHNSTON

G. K. HALL & CO.
An Imprint of Macmillan Publishing Company
NEW YORK

Maxwell Macmillan Canada
TORONTO

Maxwell Macmillan International
NEW YORK   OXFORD   SINGAPORE   SYDNEY

G. K. Hall & Co.
An Imprint of Macmillan Publishing Company
866 Third Avenue
New York, NY 10022

Maxwell Macmillan Canada, Inc.
1200 Eglinton Avenue East
Suite 200
Don Mills, Ontario M3C 3N1

Macmillan Publishing Company is part of the Maxwell Communication Group of Companies.

Library of Congress Catalog Card Number: 93-23546

PRINTED IN THE UNITED STATES OF AMERICA

printing number
1 2 3 4 5 6 7 8 9 10

LIBRARY OF CONGRESS CATALOGING-IN-PUBLICATION DATA
Johnston, Wanda K.
  Administering the community college learning resources program /
Wanda K. Johnston.
    p. cm.
  Includes bibliographical references and index.
  ISBN 0-8161-1952-X.—ISBN 0-8161-1953-8 (pbk.)
  1. Community college libraries—United States—Administration.
  2. Instructional materials centers—United States—Management.
  3. Community colleges—United States—Administration. I. Title.
Z675.J8J64 1994
027.7—dc20   93-23546
                                                            CIP

The paper used in this publication meets the minimum requirements of American National Standard for Information Sciences—Permanence of Paper for Printed Library Materials. ANSI Z39.48–1984. ⊚™

Dedicated to
Dr. William Brace
for his inspiration and encouragement

Contents

Figures and Tables

Introduction

Since the first public community college opened its doors in 1901, 1,408 two-year college districts have been created in all fifty states. Of these, 968 were public community college districts. [Almanac 3] By 1991, 51 percent of all first time freshmen were enrolled in community colleges with the heaviest enrollments located in California, Texas, Illinois, Florida, New York, and Michigan. [Almanac 4–5] In each of these community colleges is a learning resources program (LRP) which provides the resources and services necessary to meet the informational and instructional needs of its students, faculty, administrators, and broader college community.

But what is a community college and the issues it faces? What is a learning resources program and how does it fit into the college as a whole? And how is a learning resources program administered? This book answers these questions for learning resources faculty, staff, and administrators who are planning or have already begun careers in community colleges and for others who work closely with community college learning resources programs.

The community college is an institution of higher education; however, it differs from the traditional college or university through its mission and governance. Although individual organizational patterns vary, most common is the public, independent, community college district located in a local community, controlled by a locally elected board of trustees, and supported in part by local tax revenues. Although state enabling legislation and external regulatory agencies influence the college, its specific mission and program reflect the priorities of its local community.

In most states, the mandate to the community college is to offer open-access to a comprehensive instructional program. For example, in Illinois, "community college districts shall admit all students qualified to complete any one of their programs including general education, transfer, occupational, technical, and terminal, as long as space for effective instruction is available. After entry, the college shall counsel and distribute students among its programs according to their interests and abilities." [Illinois 13]

George B. Vaughan, President of Piedmont Virginia Community College, summarized the community college mission with five constants: 1) It is an institution of higher education; 2) It mirrors society; 3) It emphasizes teaching instead of research; 4) It provides access to higher education regardless of race, age, or station in life; and 5) It provides a comprehensive instructional program supported by student advising, guidance, and counseling. [Vaughan 25–26] He then uses the metaphor of a large balloon, with an elastic skin capable of expanding and contracting, to describe the flexibility of the community college. In this metaphor, the five constants of the mission are "encapsulated within the balloon. Any number of external and internal forces react with the mission, creating tensions, and as a result the shape of the balloon is changed, but the skin never breaks." [Vaughan 26]

Continuing this metaphor, Vaughan predicts that "the successful college— the college that is true to its mission—will squeeze, push, and pull on the mission to make it conform to community needs, thus causing the balloon to take on a rather strange shape, especially from the perspective of those familiar only with traditional higher education." [Vaughan 27]

Consequently, community colleges share a common mission but are unique due to their responsiveness to a variety of external and internal influences. Similarly, learning resources programs share a common mission but are unique due to their responsiveness to their parent college's unique characteristics. All LRPs provide resources and services necessary to serve the informational, learning, and developmental needs of their students, faculty, administrators, and broader college community. Nearly always the LRP includes library, media, and telecommunication resources and services. Occasionally, it also includes specialized services such as the teaching resources center, microcomputer laboratories, staff development program, etc. All LRPs are responsive to their parent college's educational goals, curricula, student population, size and complexity, and special issues. Since each LRP is an integral part of the entire institution, no two are identical.

The LRP administrator is responsible for developing a learning resources program committed to the mission of the community college and to the priorities of his own college. The LRP administrator is a learning resources generalist, knowledgeable about all aspects of library, media, and telecommunications resources and services as well as a competent administrator. This administrator reports to the chief academic officer and holds the same administrative rank as others with similar campuswide responsibilities. He orchestrates college priorities, service needs, LRP staff and resources into a successful program with a vision of the future. Problem-solving, short- and long-range planning, human resources management, budget and alternative funding, public relations, and facilities planning are administrative skills the LRP administrator possesses. With his leadership, the learning resources program is an integral part of the college.

Thus, Part I reviews the historical perspectives as well as governance and funding influences affecting the community college movement, describes today's community college, and identifies current issues facing the community college. Part II provides an overview of the evolution, scope, and organization of the learning resources program and introduces it in terms of its current integration of resources and services responsive to the mission of its parent institution. Part III discusses the administration of the learning resources program including planning and evaluation, human resources management, budget and alternative funding, public relations, and facilities management.

In addition to this book, community college LRP staff should become familiar with two documents. First, included in Appendix I, is the "Standards for Community, Junior, and Technical College Learning Resources Programs." Approved by both the Association for Educational Communications and Technology (AECT) and the Association of College and Research Libraries (ACRL), the Standards "are intended to assist in evaluating and developing learning resources programs." [Standards 757]

Second is *Building Communities: A Vision for a New Century*, a report of the American Association for Community and Junior Colleges (AACJC) Commission on the Future of Community Colleges. This report reaffirms the mission of the community college by exploring the partnerships between the student and instructor, the curriculum taught, and the classroom interaction, the quality of campus life, partnerships beyond the campus, and leadership for the future. [Building 8]

This book is the result of the assistance of many people. Dr. William Brace, Professor in the Graduate School of Library and Information Science at Rosary College, provided the initial inspiration and encouragement for me to undertake the project. Appreciation for critiquing the manuscript is extended to Dr. Michael Murphy, President of St. Louis Community College at Florissant Valley, Carol Warrington, Director of Library Services at St. Louis Community College at Forest Park, and Pam Gaitskill, Director of Learning Resources at Prairie State Community College. A special "thank you" is extended to Sharon Fox, Alice McNeely, Larry Jenkins, and Nancy Flott who assisted with the manuscript for this book and to the many colleagues who contributed ideas and examples.

Selected Bibliography

"Almanac," *Chronicle of Higher Education* 38 (August 28, 1991): 3–5.

Building Communities: A Vision for a New Century. Washington: AACJC, 1988.

Illinois Public Community College Act With Additional Acts Affecting Districts. 1985 edition. St. Paul: West Publishing Company, 1986.

"Standards for Community, Junior, and Technical College Learning Resources Programs," *College & Research Libraries News* 51 (September 1990): 757–767.

VAUGHAN, GEORGE B. "The Community College Mission," *AACJC Journal* 58 (February/March 1988): 25–27.

PART I

THE PUBLIC COMMUNITY COLLEGE

1

Historical Perspectives

Since the first public junior college opened its doors less than a century ago, the community college movement has become the fastest growing single segment of higher education with 1,444 two-year colleges serving five million undergraduates across the United States in 1993. [Almanac 5] Between 1936 and 1993, the number of two-year colleges has grown steadily with the greatest growth in the public sector. By 1993, forty-five percent of all undergraduates were attending public and private two-year colleges. The number of public community colleges had grown from the first one, established in 1901 in Joliet, Illinois, to 999 serving 5.4 million undergraduates across the United States in 1993. [Almanac 5]

Today's community college is quite different from the first public community college, which was an extension of a high school. "There was a metamorphosis: Changes were rapid and were influenced by other models and ideologies of education. Propensity for change in the community college resulted primarily from: (1) a lack of certain academic traditions during its formative years; (2) the diversity of local communities that nurtured the colleges; and (3) the effectiveness of local, state, and national advocates in shaping a new institution. Over the generations, the philosophy and mission of many community colleges became increasingly equalitarian and utopian, guiding newly established colleges to respond quickly to economic and social trends of society. In doing so, the colleges cut themselves free from many of the traditions and constraints of other segments of education." [Tillery 4-5]

3

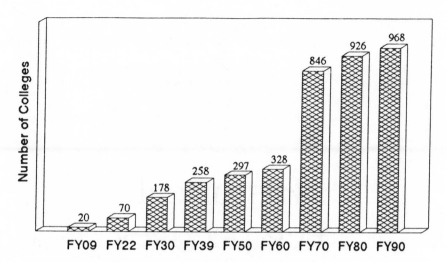

FIGURE 1.1   **Number of Public Two-Year Colleges Including Branch Campuses**   Source: National Center for Education Statistics. *Digest of Education Statistics 1990.* Washington, DC: U.S. Government Printing Office, 1991: 228. And Arthur M. Cohen and Florence B. Brawer. *The American Community College.* 2nd ed. San Francisco: Jossey-Bass, (1989): 10–11.

Tillery and Deegan follow this metamorphosis through four developmental generations. Following a foundation period (1862–1900) came the first generation, the extension of the high school (1900–1930); the second generation, the junior college (1930–1950); the third, the community college (1950–1970); the fourth, the comprehensive community college (1970–1985); and the current fifth generation which is still emerging. "Each of the generations was influenced by state and national leaders who interpreted or advocated roles and missions for the institution and who guided the development of new colleges." [Tillery 4] This chapter provides a historical perspective of the community college movement as it underwent the metamorphosis from an extension of a high school to today's comprehensive, public, community college.

Foundations of the Movement
(1862–1900)

The Morrill Act of 1862 provided a foundation for the public community college. With the intent of extending educational opportunities to the common people through the founding of land-grant colleges, proponents of this

Act introduced the concept of a "people's college" into the total system of free education. Specifically, each state received thirty thousand acres of public land for each congressman from the state. The revenue from the sale of this land were to be used toward establishing colleges with programs in agricultural and mechanical arts. [Monroe 6] The resulting sixty-eight land-grant colleges and universities taught both students and curricula which had been previously excluded from higher education. [Vaughan 11]

The Act of 1862, followed by the Act of 1890, provided the philosophical base for federal support to higher education in an effort to educate working people, pioneered the idea of communitywide service through agricultural and general education extension programs, and led to the development of a curricula emphasizing the practical vocations and the applied sciences of engineering and technology. "The land-grant institutions fought the battles regarding practical versus liberal education, who should go to college, and what courses and programs should legitimately be included as a part of higher education, and thus paved the way for similar battles later fought by community colleges." [Vaughan 11]

Another influence in the foundation of the community college was the elitist movement initiated in the early 1850s by Henry Tappan at the University of Michigan and followed by William Watts Folwell of the University of Minnesota. Both university presidents were concerned with the inferior quality of higher education in the United States compared with that in nineteenth century Germany. Consequently, they proposed an educational system emulating the German university system by separating the early, preparatory college years from the later, rigorous ones. Thus, universities would be reconstituted as research and training centers for an intellectual elite, and subsequently would improve America's economic position in the international community. The university presidents felt that Germany's development of "highly specialized universities had led directly to major German achievements in science and technology, which in turn had helped Germany become a leading industrial power. The importation of the German model of the university into the United States would therefore be a crucial step to improving America's economic position in the international system." [Brindt 24]

In addition, by purging the freshman and sophomore general education years from their institutions, these university leaders hoped to create "pure" universities restoring health and vitality to the American university and achieving for it, the elite status enjoyed by the German universities. "The first two years of college work, they felt, could be more appropriately handled in a reconstituted high school organized along the lines of the German gymnasium. Only the most academically adept graduates of the new six-year high school would proceed to the university." [Brindt 25] Little came of this movement due to tradition, alumni pressures, and the need for teaching positions for graduate students. [Monroe 8]

To implement this concept at the University of Chicago in 1890, William Rainey Harper secured permission from the Board of Trustees to separate instruction into two divisions known as the Junior College and Senior College and to award an "associate's degree" to students who completed work in the Junior College. [Monroe 9] His plan was to encourage many students to voluntarily terminate their educations at this point, so that only the gifted would continue on to the upper division and graduate work. [Brindt 25]

Not only did Harper seek to relieve the university of the lower undergraduate years, but also he hoped the Junior College at the university might serve as a model for the development of other junior colleges. In 1902, he outlined the benefits from the establishment of junior colleges. Specifically, the junior college would be a place where "many students who would not otherwise do so will undertake at least two years of college work." [Monroe 9] In addition, "professional schools could raise their standards, struggling liberal arts colleges might continue to survive as junior colleges, and the junior college at the university might serve as a model for high schools as they expanded their offerings to their own graduates." [Monroe 9] To create junior colleges, he proposed that weak four-year colleges become junior colleges, that two years of work be added to high schools creating junior colleges, and that new junior colleges become feeders to the universities. [Monroe 9]

Extension of High School (1900–1930)

Harper's influence encouraged J. Stanley Brown, the principal of Joliet Township High School, to expand the school's curriculum to include college-level courses. Students completing this advanced coursework were promised advanced standing at the University of Chicago. Thus, Joliet Junior College was established in 1901. Existing school facilities were used and teachers taught very much the same as they had high school courses.

Harper, David Starr Jordan of Stanford, and Alexis F. Lange of the University of California further expanded the junior college concept beyond the role of a feeder to the university by adding social and community services responsibilities. They proposed that in addition to providing the general education found in the college freshman and sophomore years, the junior college should "contribute to the stability of the social order by enabling the individual to discover the thing nature intended for him to do and by equipping him to occupy successfully and productively his proper niche in society." [Wagoner 7] Lange took this junior college idea further than Harper and Jordan by "emphasizing the integral relationship that should exist between the junior college and its surrounding community. Reflecting his alignment with progressive John Dewey, Lange maintained that the junior college as it matured should be part of the community, not isolated from it, and should strive to be as widely and directly useful to the community as possible." [Wagoner 8]

Lange and Jordan subsequently led the lobbying efforts culminating in the legal basis for junior colleges in California. In 1907, California passed legislation authorizing high schools to offer postgraduate education equivalent to the first two years of college. "This 1907 law was the first state legislation to authorize local junior colleges, although no funding was provided." [Vaughan 14] In 1917, legislation was passed providing state and local support for junior college students on the same basis as high school students. And in 1921, the California legislature authorized "the establishment of independent junior-college districts if such districts had a minimum high school population of 400 and a minimum assessed valuation of ten million dollars." [Monroe 11] This legislation provided for local control and access, equated junior college work with the first two years of university coursework, and extended public education two years beyond high school. The California legislature provided models for enabling legislation in other states. [Vaughan 14]

Most local community colleges were developed "through the efforts of a few concerned parents and citizens, some sympathetic school board members, and school administrators who had compassion for the less fortunate high school graduates in their communities." [Monroe 11] "By 1921, there were 207 junior colleges: 70 public and 137 private. The organization, control and financing varied from state to state and according to the parent organization. They were forged with a variety of governance structures and educational philosophies. These enterprises were outgrowths of the customs, legislation and needs of the community where they developed." [Plucker 28]

In 1920, at a meeting of junior college leaders, representing approximately seventy-five institutions, mostly private, the American Association of Junior Colleges (AAJC), later renamed the American Association of Community and Junior Colleges (AACJC), was organized. In 1921, when the AAJC adopted its first formal constitution, the junior college was defined as an "institution offering two years of instruction of strictly collegiate grade." [Wagoner 9] Five years later, AAJC expanded the definition to include occupational/technical education stating: "The junior college is an institution offering two years of strictly collegiate grade. This curriculum may include those courses usually offered in the first two years of the four-year college, in which case these courses must be identical, in scope and thoroughness, with corresponding courses of the standard four-year college. The junior college may, and is likely to, develop a different type of curriculum suited to the larger and ever-changing civic, social, religious, and vocational needs of the entire community in which the college is located. It is understood that in this case also the work offered shall be on a level appropriate for high school graduates." [Thornton 53]

In his 1925 seminal work, *The Junior College*, Leonard Koos advocated the ideal of a nationwide system of locally governed junior colleges which would eliminate the traditional barriers to advanced education—cost, distance, and class—and would provide democratic access to opportunity and knowledge. [Pedersen 51]

The Junior College (1930–1950)

The Great Depression affected the junior colleges negatively. State funding was reduced even though enrollments continued to grow. Youth and adults took advantage of occupational retraining at local junior colleges, while others prepared for new careers. "The Depression and war years resulted in a near moratorium on the founding of new colleges. Those that were established, however, continued to grow both in enrollments and in importance. Generation 2 began with 259 public two-year colleges and closed with 299." [Tillery 8]

In 1931, Walter Crosby Eells published his influential work, *The Junior College*, which stressed four functions which the junior college should perform. These included the democratizing function which extended educational opportunity to those intelligent enough to benefit, the transfer or preparatory function, the terminal program function, and the guidance activity function. The additional functions of adult education and community service were advocated for the junior college. [Wagoner 11]

The aftermath of World War II with the GI Bill of 1944 and the demands for educational access combined with the recommendations from the President's Commission on Higher Education revitalized the community junior college movement. The GI Bill was designed in part to thank American veterans for their service during the war as well as to delay their reentry into a workforce which might not be able to absorb them. Thus, the returning veterans "pressed colleges for entrance, viewing access as a right of entitlement rather than a privilege. Junior colleges, which had welcomed adult students during the war years, found by 1947 that veterans accounted for about 40 percent of their enrollment." [Wagoner 12] The GI Bill also set the precedent of federal financing of higher education for individuals and broke many social and economic barriers to education. [Vaughan 17-18]

The influx of huge numbers of new students raised questions regarding the future organization of higher education. Therefore, the 1947 President's Commission on Higher Education for American Democracy (the Truman Commission) was established. The Commission report repudiated any thoughts of higher education being restricted to the intellectual or economic elite. Instead the report promoted the necessity of education in a democratic world: "Equal education opportunities for all persons, to the maximum of their individual abilities and without regard to economic status, race, creed, color, sex, national origin, or ancestry, is a major goal of American democracy. Only an informed, thoughtful, tolerant people can maintain and develop a free society." [Monroe 14] Furthermore, the Commission concluded that "at least 49 percent of the population had the capacity to complete fourteen years of schooling and that at least 32 percent were able to complete an advanced liberal or professional education." [Brindt 69]

The Truman Commission recommended that the states create a network of community colleges which would bring higher education within easy access to the majority of Americans. "These community colleges would have no tuition, would serve as cultural centers for the community, offer continuing education for adults, emphasize civic responsibilities, be comprehensive, offer technical and general education, be locally controlled, and blend into statewide systems of higher education, while at the same time coordinating their efforts with the high schools." [Vaughan 19] Thus, the Commission report impacted the junior college movement by changing the name from junior college to community college and by legitimating the place of the community college within higher education. [Brindt 71]

The Community College (1950–1970)

Generation 3 is considered the golden era for the community college movement. State patterns of financing community colleges were well established and federal funding support, primarily through student financial aid and capital funding, increased. This resulted in the rapid establishment of community colleges and increases in enrollments. "After the G.I. Bill, and followed by the student aid bill in the early fifties, education became an entitlement. Transfer, vocational and terminal programs had become an accepted function of the junior college and a community service function was becoming recognized. Federal student aid through the National Defense Education Act of 1958 and the Higher Education Acts of 1965 and 1968 told students they could go to school if they wanted to, thereby expanding the potential student population." [Plucker 30]

Community colleges were growing more rapidly than any other segment of American higher education. Brindt noted that "during the last four years of the decade, new campuses opened at a rate of more than one a week. By the late 1960s, the junior colleges' share of total higher education enrollments had risen to nearly three in ten, up from one in six in 1955." [Brindt 84] Furthermore, he noted that "by 1970, public colleges enrolled more than 95 percent of all junior college students. By 1968, forty-nine of the fifty states had at least one public two-year college (Nevada was the lone exception). However more than two-thirds of all community college students were still enrolled in only seven states—California, New York, Illinois, Michigan, Florida, Texas, and Washington." [Brindt 84] Wagoner concluded this rapid growth was due to "the community college's apparent responsiveness to the needs or interests of individuals, their communities, and the larger society, combined with its low cost to those who sought its services." [Wagoner 13]

In the 1960 work, *The Junior College: Progress and Prospect*, Leland L. Medsker proposed that the comprehensive, multi-purpose community college should include "1) providing terminal curricula of two years and less in length; 2) providing curricula preparatory to advanced undergraduate education in four-year institutions; 3) providing general education for all students, terminal and preparatory; 4) aiding students to make educational and vocational choices that are consistent with their individual characteristics; and 5) offering a wide range of general and special courses for adults." [Medsker vii] Thus, the role of the community college would expand from the transfer preparatory and the terminal vocational functions to also include guidance or student personnel services, remedial functions, and adult education.

The Carnegie Commission on Higher Education was founded in 1967 to review the nation's system of higher education. In its report, *The Open-Door Colleges*, the Commission sought "to increase the proportion of college students in two-year, as opposed to four-year, institutions and to decrease the proportion of community college students enrolled in transfer programs." [Brindt 104] Specifically, the Commission recommended that two-year colleges were to expand in number to permit 95 percent of all Americans to be within commuting distance; that the colleges should be open-door, charging no or low tuition and admitting all applicants who were high school graduates or persons over the age of eighteen capable of benefiting from continued education; that the community college maintain its comprehensive model while stimulating the expansion of occupational education; and that community colleges develop independent districts and governing boards. [Brindt 105; Monroe 15]

The Comprehensive Community College (1970–1985)

By 1970, there was great confidence in the community colleges. "Their campuses were among the best in the land, and as community centers they served a large segment of the public. The faculty and administrators were well educated, and many of their leaders were graduates of major university leadership programs. Federal policies and groups, such as the Carnegie Commission for Higher Education, encouraged continued but disciplined expansion." [Tillery 16] Community colleges continued to grow in numbers and size.

"Between 1970 and 1977, the proportion of full-time students enrolled in occupational programs rose from no more than one-third to well over 50 percent—the largest and most rapid shift in the history of the junior college." [Brindt 116] This shift might be attributed to increased enrollments, especially of nontraditional students; to the diversification of vocational programs, including expansion into the workplace for upgrading employee skills or the establishment of worker retraining programs; to the rapid technological changes of the workplace, especially the impact of the high-technology industries; and to the disillusionment of the value of a baccalaureate degree.

The mission of the community college came under question as questions of who should be educated and who should pay for such education were raised. "The mix of students in community colleges sets Generation 4 apart from earlier periods. Participation rates of many underrepresented groups (reentry women, ethnic groups, the disabled, displaced workers) increased sharply in this generation. Student mix varied from region to region and from college to college, as did ways of using the comprehensive program in serving diverse students." [Tillery 22] Consequently, the concept of open door access was reviewed. "Substantial efforts were being made to (1) assess student readiness to learn; (2) guide students in course and program selection; (3) measure learning outcomes." [Tillery 20]

In 1970, "Generation 4 opened with generally stable financing of the comprehensive community colleges and with new state and federal financial aid programs for students. It ended amid taxpayer revolts in the several states and reductions in federal support. As a result, all but a few colleges have suffered enrollment losses or have reached plateaus in growth." [Tillery 19]

The Fifth Generation (1985–)

The growth years of the community college had come to an end. Community colleges instead began facing issues of "declining enrollments, financial cutbacks, challenges to the open-door philosophy and comprehensive mission, mounting criticisms from those external to the enterprise, and growing expressions of a loss of direction from within." [Wagoner 13]

Consequently, in 1986, the American Association of Community and Junior Colleges appointed the Commission on the Future of the Community

College to reaffirm the mission of the community college. The commission report, *Building Communities: A Vision for a New Century*, defined community "not only as a region to be served, but also as a climate to be created." [Building 7] The challenge of the Commission was "to embrace the institution's comprehensive mission. But the goal is not just outreach. Perhaps more than any other institution, the community college also can inspire partnerships based upon shared values and common goals. The building of community, in its broadest and best sense, encompasses a concern for the whole, for integration and collaboration, for openness and integrity, for inclusiveness and self-renewal." [Building 7] The report itself included sixty-three recommendations, but emphasized that each college must analyze its own situation, determine its own priorities, and put its own plan into action.

Generation 5 college leaders find themselves facing three major challenges. First is the renewal of the community college mission. This includes redefining the comprehensive program in terms of its academic, vocational/technical, and community service priorities and reassessing the college's responsibility to educational, social, and cultural equity. Second is the enhancement of the quality and productivity of college programs and services. In fiscally stringent times, efficiency and effectiveness are essential measures for public accountability as well as factors in the competition and/or linkage with other new and traditional educational providers. Third is management of change. Balances are sought between guardians of tradition and champions of change; between comprehensiveness and quality; between short-term expediency and long-term viability. Wise decision-making requires complete information while the time to gather it is diminishing, requiring cooperative efforts to pool collective information and make wise choices. As is discussed in Chapter 2, power, authority, and influence in the decision process are shifting to external constituencies, such as state legislatures and coordinating boards of higher education as well as local business and industry. These constituencies will assume a dual role in community college governance by providing resources for institution programs and by participating in the decision process.

The first community colleges fit vertically into the higher education world serving as extensions of high school or as the junior colleges of universities. During subsequent decades, the community college underwent a metamorphosis responding to the needs of diverse student populations and changing local communities. Generation 5 community colleges are facing challenging times. But, they should adapt successfully since "their physical plants are essentially in place; their faculties and managers are flexible and responsive to social change; their leaders have political sensibilities and skills in building consensus; and governance tensions are more a manifestation of vitality than of instability. Finally, the dominant value of the community colleges is right for the future: The Doors are open for those who want to learn." [Tillery 31]

Selected Bibliography

"Almanac," *Chronicle of Higher Education* 38 (August 25, 1993): 5.

BRINDT, STEVEN, and J. KARABEL. *The Diverted Dream: Community Colleges and the Promise of Educational Opportunity in America, 1900–1985.* New York: Oxford University Press, 1989.

Building Communities: A Vision for a New Century. Washington, DC: AACJC, 1988.

DEEGAN, WILLIAM L., and DALE TILLERY. "Toward a 5th Generation of Community Colleges," *AACJC Journal* 57 (April/May 1987): 36–40.

EELLS, WALTER CROSBY. *The Junior College.* Boston: Houghton Mifflin, 1931.

GLEAZER, EDMUND J. JR. *The Community College: Values, Vision, and Vitality.* Washington, DC: AACJC, 1980.

KOOS, LEONARD V. *The Junior College.* Minneapolis: University of Minnesota Press, 1924.

LORENZO, ALBERT L. "Anticipating Our Future Purpose," *AACJC Journal* 61 (February/March 1991): 42–45.

MEDSKER, LELAND L. *The Junior College: Progress and Prospect.* New York: McGraw-Hill, 1960.

MONROE, CHARLES R. *Profile of the Community College.* Washington, DC: Jossey-Bass, 1972.

PEDERSEN, ROBERT. "State Government and the Junior College, 1901–1946," *Community College Review* 14 (Spring 1987): 48–52.

PLUCKER, FRANK E. "A Developmental Model for the Community/Junior College," *Community College Review* 15 (Winter 1987): 26–31.

THORNTON, JAMES W. JR. *The Community Junior College.* 3rd edition. New York: John Wiley & Sons, 1972.

TILLERY, DALE, and WILLIAM L. DEEGAN. "The Evolution of Two-Year Colleges Through Four Generations." In *Renewing the American Community College,* ed. William L. Deegan and Dale Tillery. San Francisco: Jossey-Bass, 1985.

VAUGHAN, GEORGE B. *The Community College in America: A Pocket History.* Washington, DC: AACJC, 1982.

WAGONER, JENNINGS L. JR. "The Search for Mission and Integrity: a Retrospective View." In *Maintaining Institutional Integrity,* ed. Arthur M. Cohen. San Francisco: Jossey-Bass, 1985.

2

Governance and Funding

Vaughan's balloon metaphor, which described the external and internal factors affecting the developing mission of the community college, can be continued to describe the broader, complex forces affecting the entire community college system. [Vaughan 26–27] These broader forces include the continuing review of the community college mission, legislative and general public concerns about efficiency and effectiveness, and the funding required to support the comprehensive programs and to assure access for all who can benefit. [Martorana 40] This chapter reviews the external influences from national and regional, state, and local agencies which affect community colleges.

National and Regional Influences

A study of national influences is complicated by: "1) confusion as to national goals and lack of clearly defined expectations for higher education, 2) rapidly changing and vacillating leadership on the national level, and 3) the late arrival of the two-year college as a national priority." [Richardson 6] Higher education competes with defense, welfare, transportation, and public schools for political attention and support. Confusion in the public mind

14

regarding the role of higher education combined with funding issues has led to the frequent creation of committees and commissions assigned the task of defining the future of higher education and the role of the community college within it. Congress has contributed to this confusion through failing to define a unified and thoughtful national policy and failing to develop a reliable and consistent funding program regarding higher education.

During the past decade federal funding for higher education has supported four major purposes. Approximately one-third of total federal spending supports research. Another one-third supports student aid programs encouraging access to higher education and equality of educational opportunity for disadvantaged citizens. Around fifteen percent sponsors categorical programs administered through the Department of Education, as well as through the Department of Labor, Defense, Agriculture, and Commerce, and designed to encourage institutions to develop explicit programs tailored to current national priorities. And the balance of the funding is designated for both GI Bill and social security benefits. [Breneman 127–129]

Due to their missions and diverse student populations, community colleges generally receive more federal funds in the form of student assistance, including the GI Bill and social security education benefits, than from all other federal programs combined. Federal funding to serve postsecondary vocational education provides the next greatest portion of the funding. [Breneman 130–131] In 1985, two-year colleges were allocated $1.4 billion or only ten percent of the total amount designated for higher education appropriations, grants, and contracts. [El-Khawas 31]

Institutional and specialized accreditation exert additional external influences on the community college. "Accreditation is a nongovernmental, voluntary means of attesting to the quality of educational institutions and of assisting institutions to improve their programs." [Manning 261] Institutional accreditation evaluates not only educational activities of the institution, but also its governance and administration, financial stability, student personnel services, and institutional resources and accredits the institution as a whole. The Council of Postsecondary Accreditation includes six regional (Middle States, New England, North Central, Northwest, Southern, and Western) plus six specialized institutional accrediting associations. Their stated purpose is "to provide public confirmation that what the institution is doing is of acceptable quality and to assist each institution in improving its own activities." [NCA 1]

Specialized accreditation evaluates particular units or programs within an institution. Community colleges, because of their paraprofessional and technical career programs, have experienced increasing pressures from different specialized accrediting associations to conform to criteria prescribed by practitioners in the various fields. Examples include criteria set forth by the National League for Nursing and by the Engineering Council for Professional Development. To reduce the proliferation of professional accrediting agencies, the National Commission of Accrediting was formed by several hundred institutional members, the six regional accrediting associations, the American Association of Community and Junior Colleges, and other national organizations. [Richardson 13]

State Influences

Since the first junior college enabling legislation was passed in California in 1907, statewide systems of community junior colleges have been established in every state. Each system is different. "Among the most significant causes for these differences are the historical accidents that influenced the development of higher education in the various states. Previous developments in postsecondary education, the position of the state university, the extent of normal school development in the past, the balance between private and public colleges, the legal framework that evolved for establishing community colleges, the level of development of vocational education, the attitudes of the leadership in vocational/technical education, the existing patterns of financial support for public schools—these factors (among others) are unique to each state. The eventual form of community college development that emerged was largely dependent on them." [Wattenbarger 266] The development of these systems is chronicled in the book, *Junior Colleges: 50 States/50 Years*. Although each state's system developed differently, certain factors were consistently present: "cooperation among educators, citizen awareness, careful studies, legislative planning, persistent leadership." [Yarrington xi]

Public two-year colleges are organized around three general patterns. The oldest pattern includes the community-junior colleges, or unified districts, which were created as extensions of secondary education and are nearly obsolete. In these districts, the chief administrative officer is the school superintendent and a specially designated person serves as the dean of the college. The second and most common pattern includes independent community college districts located in local communities, controlled by locally elected or appointed college boards, and supported in part by local tax dollars. These colleges operate within the limits defined by state statutes and under the regulation of a higher state educational authority. The third pattern includes colleges, technical institutes, and area vocational schools which are operated under the direct control of a state agency, such as a state university or state board of higher education. These colleges are financed completely by the state. [Monroe 351–364]

State legislation and agencies provide community colleges directional and operational guidance. Directional guidance is the consequence of master-plans, enabling legislation, determination of priorities, and other indirect influence. Operational guidance is more direct by setting forth specific procedures or restraints through legislation, executive order, or state governing agencies. While state regulations ideally define the nature and intent of the two-year college and its relationship to other segments of higher education, and then give colleges the freedom to plan and implement their educational programs, there is no consistency. Some states regulations are highly detailed and prescriptive and others are more philosophical in nature. Likewise, some states have developed strong regulatory agencies to oversee the community colleges within their states and others permit the local college autonomy. For example, "in a small number of states (Michigan, Missouri, and Oregon), the legislative appropriation of funds to community colleges represents the only act of coordination to which the colleges are subject. In other states (Illinois, Connecticut, Texas, North Carolina, and Maryland), considerable coordination of programmatic and resource decisions in community colleges occurs outside of the legislature through the actions of co-ordinating boards." [Alfred 209–210]

The Illinois Public Community College Act provides an example of directional and operational guidance for independent community college districts. The Act sets forth specific procedures for the creation and organization of individual community college districts within the state and the election of their board members, and outlines their powers and duties. It defines the comprehensive community college program as one which "includes 1) courses in liberal arts and sciences and general education; 2) adult education courses; and 3) courses in occupational, semi-technical or technical fields leading directly to employment." [Illinois 1] The Act also addresses open admissions by stating: "The community college districts shall admit all students qualified to complete any one of their programs including general education, transfer, occupational, technical, and terminal, as long as space for effective instruction is available." [Illinois 13]

In addition, the Act creates a twelve member Illinois Community College Board with the responsibility for providing statewide planning and coordination; organizing new community colleges; cooperating with the colleges in continuing studies of student characteristics, admission standards, grading policies, and other problems of community college education; entering into contracts with other governmental agencies; determining standards for the physical plant, instruction and teaching, library, administration and supervision; and approval of new instructional programs. [Illinois 3–4] Thus, the Act defines the powers and duties granted to both the state board and to the local college.

Following a review of state legislation affecting community colleges, Martorana concluded that 1) state legislators and governors generally treat community colleges relatively well in appropriating funds; 2) the general public policy framework supports the values typically associated and attached to community college education; and 3) state legislative action demonstrates appreciation of the educational services community colleges provide. [Martorana 42]

Community college revenue is generated from federal aid, state revenues, local taxes, tuition, and alternative funding. As shown in Figure 2.1, in 1990, 4.7 percent of two-year college revenue was received from federal appropriations, grants, or contracts, 44.4 percent from state revenues, 16.9 percent from local taxes, and 22.4 percent from tuition. Alternative funding, including private gifts and endowments, sales and services, etc., accounted for 11.7 percent of the total revenues of community colleges. [NCES 18] In

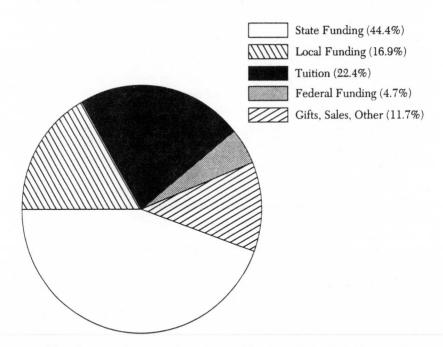

FIGURE 2.1 Sources of Revenue for Public Two-Year Colleges in 1990
Although revenue generation varies among states, the trend has been for federal funding to decline, for state and local revenue to remain constant, and for tuition and alternative funding to increase.   Source: National Center for Education Statistics. *Current Funds Revenues and Expenditures of Institutions of Higher Education: Fiscal Years 1983–1991*. Washington, D.C.: U.S. Department of Education 1993: 17–18.

1989, Cohen charted the shifting proportions of revenue generation over eighty years and cited the trend in which states increased the percentage of community college funding while the local district percentage decreased. [Cohen 128] In addition, the reliance on alternative funding sources is increasing. For example, in 1986, alternative funding provided 2.9 percent of the two-year college revenue. By 1990, alternative funding increased to 11.7 percent. [El-Khawas 32–33, NCES 17–18]

Wattenbarger describes four basic approaches to state plans for financing community colleges. First, the negotiated budget approach permits each college to negotiate an operating budget with the state legislature. Second, the unit rate formula divides the total state appropriation for community colleges among individual colleges based upon their FTE enrollments. Third, the foundation program formula base appropriates funds based upon an established amount of money for each FTE or for each student credit hour. Fourth, cost center basis funding combines the unit rate and the foundation program formulas by calculating costs for specific defined categories and allocating funds to colleges based on the number of students enrolled in each of the cost centers. In conclusion, he outlines the ideal formula for state support as one which "would provide funds for all programs in a format related to the program costs as well as to the number of students served in each program. The data base for these statistics would be the most recent available, with flexibility for accommodating special unanticipated problems." [Wattenbarger 271–272]

Local Influences

The majority of public community colleges are controlled at the local level by a governing board authorized by state legislation and overseen by a state educational authority. The concept of a lay governing board representing the local population is an old idea in education. Public schools have used elected boards for decades. Local community college boards usually consist of five to nine members elected by the voters in the district at large for four year terms. Quoting from *Building Communities*, "As a group, trustees are surrogates for a larger constituency. Their assignment is to keep the institution enlightened and more responsive. Trustees also have an obligation to represent college interests to constituents beyond the campus." [Building 43]

Quoting from the handbook of the Association of Community College Trustees, Cohen lists the responsibilities of trustees as "selecting, evaluating, and dismissing the president; ensuring professional management of the institution; purchasing, constructing, and maintaining facilities; defining the role and mission of the college; engaging in public relations; preserving institutional independence; evaluating institutional performance; creating a climate for change; insisting on being informed; engaging in planning; and assessing board performance." [Cohen 111] The board of trustees should not be involved in the day-to-day operations of the college.

Local funding for community colleges comes from local tax revenue and from tuition and fees. On the average, 16.9 percent of community college revenue is generated through local government funding and 22.4 percent through tuition; however, the variations among the states are wide. [NCES 17–18] For example, Kansas provides 59 percent of community college funding through local revenues while fifteen states provide none. Vermont generates 43 percent of its funding through tuition while California generates only 4 percent. [Building 45]

The community college also is influenced through interactions with its total community. Area business, industrial, and professional organizations aid the development of the vocational programs, help encourage public support, and provide private donations or services. Advisory committees and boards provide feedback as to the effectiveness of the instructional programs and services provided. The public media influences the attitudes of district residents. Interaction with area schools and colleges encourages articulation agreements and cooperative programs. Alumni organizations and college foundations promote the college and help generate funds. As the "people's college," each individual community college has a responsibility to the local community it serves.

Governance and Funding Trends

The power, authority, and influence affecting community college governance and funding is shifting from internal to external constituencies. A variety of national, regional, state, and local influences increasingly are affecting community colleges through public support, legislative regulation and oversight, funding, and program evaluation and accreditation. Community colleges are continuing to face questions about their governance and the costs and benefits of a community college education. They are competing for a portion of limited state funds which must be shared among public schools (K–12) and higher education as well as other state agencies and programs. Their enrollments are challenged by K–12 schools and four-year colleges and universities which are expanding into traditional community college student markets.

Major responsibility for providing the primary support for community college education continues with the state legislatures. Along with this primary funding, the states are requiring more complete and complex reporting systems and are assuming stronger statewide coordination. However, the cost of these reporting systems, inflation, competing political interests, and the goal of the balanced state budget influence the state funding available. Consequently, the universal trend toward increasing fees in continuing.

In response to these influences, community college leaders now are involving selected constituencies in the decision process. They are reviewing recruitment and retention efforts and are eliminating or modifying programs which are weak or not cost effective. They are seeking alternative sources of revenue through auxiliary enterprises, external contracts, and grants. They are developing articulation and cooperative agreements with K–12 and baccalaureate degree-granting institutions resulting in mutual benefits. They are building alliances with appropriate public and private-sector constituencies to lobby for increased funding for education.

"The future shape of governance can best be described as one of organizational dualism, in which multiple systems for decision making will be utilized consisting of four groups of decision makers: faculty, trustees and administrators, agencies of state and federal government, and private-sector organizations." [Alfred 219]

Selected Bibliography

ALFRED, RICHARD L., and DAVID F. SMYDRA. "Reforming Governance: Resolving Challenges to Institutional Authority." In Renewing the American Community College, ed. William L. Deegan and Dale Tillery. San Francisco: Jossey-Bass, 1985.

BRENEMAN, DAVID W., and SUSAN C. NELSON. Financing Community Colleges: An Economic Perspective. Washington, DC: Brookings Institution, 1981.

Building Communities: A Vision for a New Century. Washington, DC: AACJC, 1988.

COHEN, ARTHUR M., and FLORENCE B. BRAWER. The American Community College. Second Edition. San Francisco: Jossey-Bass, 1989.

EL-KHAWAS, ELAINE, DEBORAH J. CARTER, and CECILIA A. OTTINGER. Community College Fact Book. New York: Macmillan, 1988.

FONTE, RICHARD W. "Community College Formula Funding: A Policy Analysis Framework," Community College Review 15 (Fall 1987): 5–13.

FOUNTAIN, BEN E., and TERRENCE A. TOLLEFSON. Community Colleges in the United States: Forty-nine State Systems. Washington, DC: AACJC, 1989.

Illinois Public Community College Act With Additional Acts Affecting Districts. 1985 edition. St. Paul, MN: West Publishing Company, 1986.

MANNING, THURSTON E. "Evaluation and Accreditation of Institutions of Postsecondary Education," North Central Association Quarterly 61 (Fall 1986): 261–267.

MARTORANA, S. V. "Community Colleges in State Legislation: Favored or Threatened and So What?" Community College Review 10 (Spring 1983): 39–46.

MONROE, CHARLES R. Profile of the Community College. Washington, DC: Jossey-Bass, 1972.

National Center for Education Statistics. *Current Funds Revenues and Expenditures of Institutions of Higher Education: Fiscal Years 1983–1991.* Washington, DC: U.S. Department of Education, 1993.

NCA: A Handbook of Accreditation, 1990–92. Chicago: North Central Association of Colleges and Schools, 1990–92.

RICHARDSON, RICHARD C. JR., CLYDE E. BLOCKER, and LOUIS W. BENDER. *Governance for the Two-Year College.* Englewood Cliffs, NJ: Prentice Hall, 1972.

VAUGHAN, GEORGE B. "The Community College Mission," *AACJC Journal* 58 (February/March 1988): 25–27.

WATTENBARGER, JAMES L. "Dealing with New Competition for Public Funds: Guidelines for Financing Community Colleges." In *Renewing The American Community College,* ed. William L. Deegan and Dale Tillery. San Francisco: Jossey-Bass, 1985.

YARRINGTON, ROGER. *Junior Colleges: 50 States/50 Years.* Washington, DC: AAJC, 1969.

3

The Community
College Today

By virtue of their local control and community emphasis, no two community colleges are identical. Each one assumes the flavor of its own local district. Vaughan's five constants continue to provide a general description of the community college today. It is an institution of higher education. It reflects the needs of society. It emphasizes teaching over research. It is committed to open access resulting in a diverse student population. It offers a comprehensive program. [Vaughan 25–26]

Thus, although legally established by state legislation, each individual community college is responsive to its local community. This, in turn, affects its administrative organization, faculty, student population, and comprehensive program. For purpose of this book, community college refers to the independent, public, comprehensive community college.

Administrative Organization

The common administrative organization in a community college follows the bureaucratic model. This "presents the college as a formal structure with defined patterns of activity that are related to the functions spelled out in law and policy decisions. The positions are arranged in the shape of a pyramid, and each series of positions has specified responsibilities, competencies, and privileges. This organization is held together by authority delegated from the top down, with persons at the top receiving greater benefits than those at the bottom; the lowest levels of the triangle are occupied by faculty and students." [Cohen, 1989, 93]

This model is demonstrated through the college's organizational chart which provides a graphic portrayal of the positions and functions within the college as well as their inter-relationships. It charts the way the institution has organized in order to accomplish its mission. Richardson et al note that "the best organizational structure is one which is responsive to the needs of those who belong to the institution while at the same time promoting the objectives for which the institution exists." [Richardson, 1972, 120] Factors affecting the college's administrative structure include the size and complexity of the institution, the formality of communication desired, and the delegation of responsibility and authority.

The most frequent organizational structure consists of the college president at the top of the pyramid, reporting to a board of trustees. The president not only must be an effective day-to-day administrator, but also must take leadership in conveying a larger educational vision to the college community and beyond. Minimally, a staff member responsible for community relations reports directly to the president. Occasionally, staff members responsible for institutional research and economic development also report to the president.

The major "line" administrators, responsible for specific functional areas always include vice presidents for instruction and business, and frequently one for student services. The Vice President for Instructional Services is the chief academic officer responsible for overseeing the instructional divisions, developmental education, continuing/community education, and learning resources. The Vice President for Business Services is responsible for the college budget and purchasing, as well as auxiliary services such as the bookstore, campus police, and physical plant maintenance. The Vice President of Student Services is responsible for services which enhance a student's academic life, such as admissions and registration, student activities, athletics, and financial aid. In response to the increasing emphasis for student assessment and counseling as an integral part of the instructional program, some colleges are merging student services into the instructional program as part of the Vice President for Instructional Services's responsibilities.

Although academic divisions reporting to the Vice President of Instructional Services take many patterns, three patterns most frequently emerge. The first, most prevalent in smaller colleges, creates divisions based upon student objective: adult, continuing, and community education; career education; transfer studies; business and industry assistance; and learning resources. (Figure 3.1) The second, more common in larger colleges, merges both arts and sciences faculty with career faculty into homogenized instructional divisions by related discipline. An example is the Division of Engineering and Technology. Also, student services has been placed under the Vice President for Instructional Services. (Figure 3.2) The third administrative organization, created to foster responsibility for program outcomes, organizes instructional divisions by degree-granting program. Student assessment and academic advising as well as program accountability are program-specific responsibilities within each division. (Figure 3.3) [Richardson, 1989, 34–38]

Learning Resources, also referred to as Instructional Resources, Educational Resources, or Academic Support Services, nearly always is an individual division reporting directly to the Vice President of Instructional Services. The learning resources program (LRP) reflects "the institution's educational goals, curricula, size and complexity, as well as the diversity of resources needed to accommodate different modes of learning." [Standards 757] Consequently, the LRP administrator reports to the chief academic officer and holds the same administrative rank and status as others with similar institution-wide responsibilities. He would hold rank in the institution as

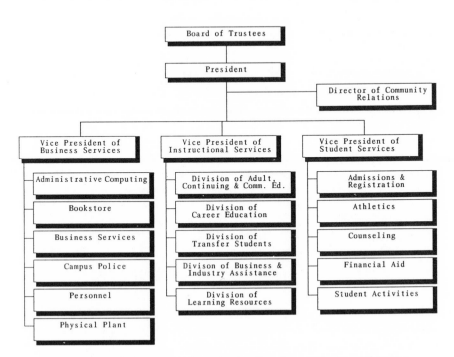

FIGURE 3.1 **Administrative Organization Based upon Student Objectives**

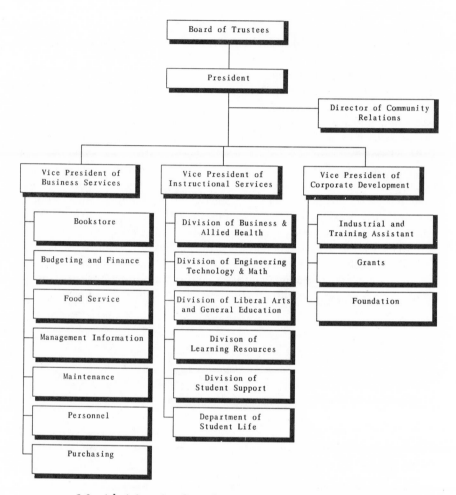

FIGURE 3.2   Administrative Organization Arranging Instructional Divisions by Discipline and Assigning Student Services to Instruction

Dean of Learning Resources. This direct line of report to the chief academic officer and equality with other division deans enhances the integration of the learning resources division into the total instructional program and ensures no conflict of interest with LRP service or resource allocations with any other instructional division.

At the base of this bureaucratic organization are the faculty. Faculty influence the community college organization formally through participation in a faculty senate, on committees, and through collective bargaining units.

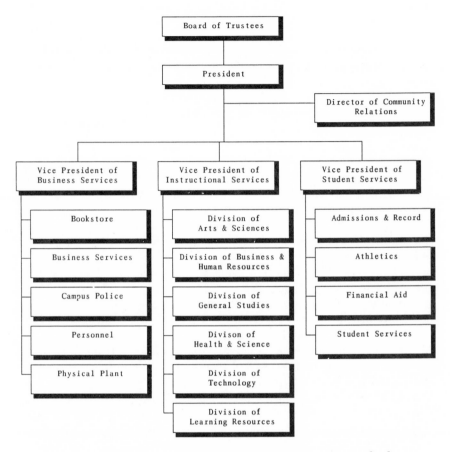

FIGURE 3.3   Administrative Organization Merging Assessment and Advising into Instructional Divisions and Grouping Divisions by Degree Granting Programs

The faculty senate provides a forum to discuss and resolve issues of concern to the academic community. It provides an avenue for faculty to accept, reject, or modify the actions of the committees. It provides a means to improve communication and to promote an understanding of college issues through discussion and debate among each other and with administrators. It provides an avenue of input for policy formulation while the administration reserves the responsibility for policy implementation and interpretation. Topics of discussion may include administrative organization, the academic calendar, attendance policies, student assessment and placement, etc.

Faculty committees are created to investigate, advise, and recommend actions on various administrative issues and services. For example, the curriculum committee reviews and recommends addition, modification, or deletion of courses. The recruitment and retention committee works with admissions, counseling, and marketing personnel to address recruitment and retention issues. The learning resources committee enhances communication regarding the development and evaluation of LRP services and provides a formal link between learning resources administrators and users.

Faculty also exert their influence on the college through collective bargaining agreements. By the mid-1980s, over two-thirds of the full-time faculty in community colleges were working under contracts negotiated collectively. The National Education Association and the American Federation of Teachers were the most prominent agents. [Cohen, 1989, 119] Contract negotiation has included "contract management procedures; rights of bargaining agents; governance items, such as personnel policies and grievance procedures; academic items, such as class size and textbook selection; economic benefits; and working conditions, such as parking facilities and office space." [Cohen, 1989, 120]

Formal student influence on community college administration is channeled through the student government. The student government, in turn, oversees the various student organizations, such as Young Engineers, African-American Student Association, Women's Soccer Team, etc. In addition, some colleges invite a student representative to serve as a non-voting member of their Board of Trustees.

Building Communities encourages "a broad-based governance design, ranging from the most formal to the most informal, to handle the full range of issues to be considered. If a college has collective bargaining, for example, it also needs a faculty senate and short-term committees, as well as conversations in the corridors to handle less formal day-to-day decisions. A community college, more than any other institution in higher education, needs flexibility." [Building 43]

Faculty

"The community college should be the nation's premier teaching institution. Quality instruction should be the hallmark of the movement. Community colleges, above all others, should expect the highest performance in each class and be creative and consistent in the evaluation of results." [Building 25] Thus, the Commission on the Future of Community Colleges reaffirms the teaching emphasis of community college faculty. Student assessment, academic advising, and active teaching take priority over research and publication. The strongest faculty teach the core courses where their interest and expertise are most needed.

Discipline faculty, counselors, and learning resources faculty usually hold the rank and responsibilities of faculty in the community college. Discipline faculty conduct four or five classes per term, thirteen to sixteen hours per week. [Cohen, 1989, 68] They are responsible to "teach, work with students individually and in groups, prepare instructional materials, make decisions on curricular modifications, and judge their clients' progress through the use of periodic measures of student learning." [Cohen, 1987, 70] Each week, the typical counselor spends "18 hours in academic/educational and vocational counseling, four hours in personal counseling, six hours in administration, and 12 hours in all other counselor responsibilities, including teaching, testing, professional development, research, supervision, and miscellaneous other duties." [Keim, 1988, 43] Learning resources faculty most frequently are reference librarians. They typically provide direct reference services sixteen hours per week in addition to providing bibliographic instruction, developing instructional materials, participating in collection development, creating specialized bibliographies, serving as liaisons to other instructional departments, and more.

Full-time faculty, who number less than half the total faculty by head count, teach three-fourths of the classes. [Cohen, 1989, 68] As seen in table 3.1 the majority are male with 67 percent teaching in the transfer curriculum and 61 percent in the occupational/technical curricula. Most are over the age of forty and are experienced teachers. Less than 10 percent are members of ethnic minorities. The highest degree earned by most is the masters degree with doctorates earned by 25 percent of the transfer and 10 percent of the occupational/technical faculty. Most full-time faculty belong to professional associations, but few give presentations or participate in publication activities. [Keim, 1989, 38–39]

New faculty are recruited out of graduate school, from their trade, or from other community colleges or are promoted from the part-time faculty ranks. A masters degree in the appropriate discipline or comparable experience in the occupational/technical field and appropriate certification are required for selection. An understanding of and commitment to the mission of the community college is desired. Keim found that few faculty had completed formal coursework on the community college, that many had been students at community colleges, and that fewer new faculty had public school teaching experience. [Keim, 1989, 38, 40]

A recent study conducted by the Carnegie Foundation for the Advancement of Teaching concluded that "community college faculty have the clearest sense of purpose of any sector of higher education, and feel good about their institutions. . . . We asked faculty from each sector of higher education whether 'their interests lie primarily in research or in teaching.' The com-

TABLE 3.1 Composition of Full-Time Community College Faculty

Characteristics	Transfer (%)	Occupational/ Technical (%)
Distribution by sex		
Male	67	61
Female	33	39
Average age		
40 or older	80	65
Race/Ethnicity		
White	93	90
African American	6	4
Hispanic	1	—
Asian American	—	1
American Indian	—	4
Academic preparation		
Doctorate	25	10
Masters	71	57
Baccalaureate	4	20
Academic experience		
Average no. of yrs.	14.4	10.2

Full-time faculty account for 41 percent of the total community college faculty demonstrating a nationwide trend in the increasing proportion of part-time faculty. Source: Marybelle C. Keim, "Two-Year College Faculty: A Research Update," *Community College Review* 17 (Winter 1989): 34–43.

munity college faculty answered resoundingly 'teaching,' and when asked 'should teaching effectiveness be the primary criterion for promotion of faculty?,' they were nearly unanimous in their agreement." [Carnegie 24] Teaching effectiveness, faculty service, and community service are the evaluative criterion used at most community colleges.

The Commission of the Future of Community Colleges notes that while teaching effectiveness, not publication, is the primary emphasis of the community college faculty member, each should be a "dedicated scholar." The Commission expands the definition of scholarship: "In addition to the scholarship of discovering knowledge, through research, it is also important to recognize the scholarship of integrating knowledge, through curriculum development, the scholarship of applying knowledge, through service, and above all, the scholarship of presenting knowledge, through effective teaching." [Building 26]

The Commission continues this concept by redefining the role of the faculty member as a classroom researcher. Classroom researchers "are primarily interested in gaining insights that will strengthen their base of professional knowledge about teaching. They seek to learn what works, as well as why it works—all in order to become more effective in their role as teachers and facilitators of student learning." [Cross 2]

The learning resources program provides the instructional support facilitating this emphasis on effective classroom teaching. LRP staff are familiar with the college's mission, its curriculum, and its student population. LRP staff are trained in curriculum development. They can provide a spectrum of instructional materials appropriate for different learning styles. They can encourage the use of technology as a tool for teaching and learning. They not only directly participate in instruction themselves but also enhance the instructional process throughout campus.

Student Population

Characteristic of the community college is its diverse student population resulting from the college's commitment to open access. Open access may be defined by accessible physical location within the local community, affordability due to low tuition and financial aid programs, and minimal admissions requirements. In addition, each community college serves the needs of its local population. This community influence results in special programs which attract special populations. Examples include special courses and/or tuition waivers for senior citizens, displaced homemakers programs attracting adult women, evening and weekend course schedules as well as workplace course offerings for employees seeking to upgrade job skills, English as a second language program for immigrants, and more.

The average community college student attends college part-time and is a woman 28 years old. She is from a middle to lower economic background, achieved lower high school grades academically, and is more likely to be a minority than her four-year counterparts. As shown in the table 3.2, in 1988, 4.9 million students, or 43 percent of all undergraduates, attended community colleges. Of these, 68 percent attend part-time taking six credit hours or less. Women comprise 57 percent of the enrollment. More than half the students enrolled are 25 years old or older with the average age 28. Approximately 20 percent of first-time entering freshmen at community colleges come from families with an annual income under $20,000 compared to 14 percent at four-year institutions. Community colleges enrolled 46 percent of high school seniors with a grade average of "B − " or below while its four-year counterpart enrolled only 25 percent. Only 9 percent of high school seniors with an "A" grade average enrolled in community colleges while 71 percent attend four-year institutions. A higher percentage of minorities attend community colleges, with 23 percent attending the community college

TABLE 3.2   Comparison of Two-Year and Four-Year College Student Populations, 1988

Population Characteristics	Two-Year (%)	Four-Year (%)
Undergraduate enrollment	43	57
Enrollment by sex		
Female students	57	54
Male students	43	46
Age of students		
19 and under	22	24
20 to 24	27	40
25 to 34	28	23
35 and over	24	13
Enrollment status		
Part-time students	68	n/a
Full-time students	32	Majority
Minority enrollment		
Students of Color	23	16
High school academic achievement		
"A" average	9	71
"B −" to "C −" average	35	24
"D" average or lower	11	− 1
Family annual income of entering freshmen		
Under $20,000	20	14
Over $50,000	28	41

Source: Deborah J. Carter, "Community and Junior Colleges: A Profile," *Research Briefs* 1 (1990): 2–3.

compared to 16 percent attending four-year institutions. Of this 23 percent, 10 percent are African Americans, 8 percent Hispanics, 4 percent Asian Americans, and 1 percent American Indians. [Carter, 1990, 2–3]

A recent survey conducted by the Carnegie Foundation for the Advancement of Teaching surveyed community college students to determine their primary reason for enrolling in college. "Thirty-six percent said preparation for transfer to a four-year college or university. Half related their enrollment to acquiring skills needed for an occupation. Fifteen percent indicated they wanted to fulfill a personal interest, and less than 5 percent enrolled to improve basic English, reading, or math skills." [Carter, 1989, 65]

In a survey of nontraditional students, Bers and Smith found that most students related their decision to attend college "to some significant personal event or dramatic change at work." [Bers 41] Convenience and affordable costs were the primary reasons these students selected community colleges. When asked about their college experiences, these students listed supportive, yet challenging, instructors, and conveniently available courses as the most important aspects. [Bers 42]

These reasons why students select community colleges reflect the mission of the community college. First, nearly every American has convenient access to a community college campus or extension center or has instructional access via distance learning alternatives. Community colleges or extension/ satellite centers permit direct access to courses for nearly everyone. Telecommunications technologies allow students to participate in classes from remote sites via video, audio, and/or computer interaction. In addition, classes are scheduled to permit access during evenings, weekends, or days to accommodate nearly every student. Some campuses even provide childcare services to increase accessibility.

Second, community colleges provide an affordable education. In 1990–1991, the average cost of tuition and fees at a community college totaled $1,336 compared to $2,273 at a public four-year college. In addition, room, board, and other miscellaneous costs further increase the total college costs for four-year college attendance. [Average A36] Due to this affordability, community colleges provide an avenue to higher education for low-income students.

Third, community colleges select supportive, yet challenging faculty who prefer teaching over research. These faculty prefer student assessment and counseling programs to encourage placement of students into appropriate level courses which in turn improve the student's probability of success. These faculty emphasize the development of lifelong learning skills and employ teaching methods responsive to the abilities and learning styles of their students.

Comprehensive Program

The community college's comprehensive program demonstrates the college's commitment to open access. The program offers something for nearly everyone including the college-parallel and general education courses which can be transferred to other colleges and applied toward a bachelor's degree, career courses which include technical and occupational courses, developmental education providing remedial courses, counseling services providing assessment and placement guidance, and community service opportunities which provide cultural and leisure experiences.

The degree offered by the community college is the associate degree. The associate in arts (A.A.) and associate in science (A.S.) degrees are awarded predominantly in college-parallel programs. The associate in applied science degree (A.A.S.) is typically considered a nontransfer degree. Cohen cites three functions of the associate degree. It offers a terminal degree to students who might not plan to continue their studies. It offers a signal to four-year colleges and universities indicating that the recipients have been prepared academically similar to their freshman and sophomore students. It suggests to prospective employers that the students completed a pattern of formal education making them suitable for entering the workplace. [Cohen, 1987, 16]

The college-parallel program was the original program of the community college originating with the Elitist Movement of the 1850s. College-parallel courses provide the first two years of a bachelor's degree. General education courses became requirements in the community college curriculum with the goal of increasing individual awareness of information and improving ability to participate in society responsibly. Generally, the A.A. or A.S. degrees require approximately thirty units of general education and thirty subject major or related electives. Courses are carefully monitored to assure transfer via articulation agreements. Figure 3.4 shows the variety and proportions of subjects in which associate degrees were awarded in 1990.

Career education, or occupational/technical education, was encouraged first in the community college by the Truman Commission in 1947 and again later by the Carnegie Commission in 1967. By the late 1970s, career enrollments grew to over fifty percent of the student population. [Brindt 116]

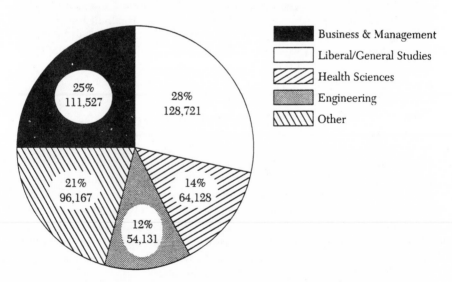

FIGURE 3.4   Associate Degrees Awarded, 1990   Source: National Center for Education Statistics, *Digest of Education Statistics 1992*, Washington, DC: U.S. Government Printing Office, (1992): 243.

Today career education emphasizes preparation for employment or for job upgrade. Course offerings are based upon community needs with a variety of special linkages with area high schools, service agencies, businesses, and industries. Industry surveys, such as *Workforce 2000: Competing in a Seller's Market: Is Corporate America Prepared*, advisory committees, licensure exams, and student interests affect the career offerings. Specialized coursework may be offered on a contractual basis to local companies through the Division of Business and Industry Assistance or Worker Reentry Program.

The Associate of applied science degree or certificate of completion are the terminal degrees for career students. Generally, the A.A.S. degree requires approximately 15 units of general education coursework and 45 units of subject or related electives while the certificate requires 5 units of general education coursework and 35 units in the subject major or related electives. Eaton found that most community college students take a combination of college-parallel and career coursework. Rarely do students take purely college-parallel or career coursework. [Eaton, 1990, 19]

Developmental education, recommended by the Carnegie Commission in 1967, is considered preparation for entrance into career or college-parallel coursework or attainment of personal goals through assisting students to overcome skill deficiencies. These students may be referred to as remedial, developmental, high-risk, low-achieving, or disadvantaged. Coursework nearly always includes English, reading, and mathematics, and occasionally English as a second language, study skills, and GED examination preparation. This is the fastest growing segment of the community college program.

For developmental students to be identified, a systematic assessment and placement system is necessary. The Learning, Assessment, Retention Consortium (LARC) of California Community Colleges designed a model comprehensive assessment and placement system interrelating assessment, advisement, instruction, and follow-up. "Based on an assessment and placement system, students are assessed. Based on guidance and placement systems, students are advised and placed. Based on a program delivery system, students are instructed. Based on a research system, student progress is followed up and evaluated." [Bray 37]

In addition to this model assessment and placement system, McCabe proposes not only using assessment testing for placement into developmental courses but also for restricting the courseloads of students testing deficient. He also recommends orientation in study skills and career planning, providing continual supportive feedback on progress, and organizing the students' curriculum to include a combination of developmental and regular coursework. [McCabe 106–107]

Instruction generally is provided through individualized learning laboratory guidance or in small classes. Parnell notes that approximately fifty hours of intensive one-on-one tutoring is required to raise an adult one grade level in reading or 150 hours of adult basic education classroom time to advance one grade level in reading or math. [Parnell 46] Learning labs frequently use microcomputers, videocassette players, and similar technologies to provide drill and practice exercises for individual students while classroom teachers employ diverse teaching styles to accommodate the individual needs of students.

Counseling services traditionally have been a function of the student services area. However, due to increasing emphasis on assessment and career and academic advising, integrating counseling with instruction and emphasizing mentoring have been proposed. Thus, through an emphasis on academic advising, counselors "will be directly engaged in the learning enterprise. Counselors will see their role as more educational and instructive rather than therapeutic. To develop student knowledge, values, and skills, counselors need to be close to the curriculum." [Eaton 1985, 10] Counseling services staff will coordinate the comprehensive assessment and placement system described earlier.

Community services provides "college activities other than courses applicable to a degree or certificate that are undertaken on behalf of the surrounding community. Continuing education also centers on noncredit classes, but is usually funded in part through self reimbursement, whereas community service tends more to be self-supporting." [Cohen, 1987, 45–46] Topics may be cultural, recreational, or general interest. Specific activities sponsored through community services and continuing education may include short courses, concepts, lectures, seminars, theatrical productions, film series, tours of local historic sites, and more.

Conclusion

Vaughan's five constants continue to provide a general description of the community college; however, no two colleges are identical. In addition to a community college's mission statement, its organizational chart and governance structure, the composition of its faculty, its student demographics, and the comprehensiveness of its programs and services reflect the external influences of the state legislature, the district Board of Trustees, and the local community.

Selected Bibliography

"Average College Costs, 1990–91," *Chronicle of Higher Education* 37 (October 3, 1990): A36.

BERS, TRUDY H., and KERRY SMITH. "College Choice and the Nontraditional Student," *Community College Review* 15 (Summer 1987): 39–45.

BRAY, DOROTHY. "Assessment and Placement of Developmental and High-Risk Students." In *Teaching the Developmental Education Student*, ed. Kenneth M. Ahrendt. San Francisco: Jossey-Bass, 1987.

BRINDT, STEVEN, and J. KARABEL. *The Diverted Dream: Community Colleges and the Promise of Educational Opportunity in America, 1900–1985.* New York: Oxford University Press, 1989.

Building Communities: A Vision for a New Century. Washington, DC: AACJC, 1988.

Carnegie Foundation for the Advancement of Teaching. "Community Colleges: A Sector with a Clear Purpose," *Change* 22 (May/June 1990): 23–26.

CARTER, DEBORAH J. "Community and Junior Colleges: A Recent Profile," *Research Briefs* 1 (1990): 1–8.

———. "Profile: Two-Year Colleges and Their Students," *Educational Record* 70 (Spring 1989): 64–66.

COHEN, ARTHUR M., and FLORENCE B. BRAWER. *The American Community College.* Second Edition. San Francisco: Jossey-Bass, 1989.

———. *The Collegiate Function of Community Colleges: Fostering Higher Learning Through Curriculum and Student Transfer.* San Francisco: Jossey-Bass, 1987.

CROSS, K. PATRICIA. "Leadership for Teaching and Learning," *Leadership Abstracts* 3 (March 1990): 1–2.

EATON, JUDITH. "The Challenge for Change at the Community College," *Educational Record* 66 (Fall 1985): 4–11.

———. "3 Myths of Transfer Education," *AACJC Journal* 60 (June/July 1990): 18–20.

KEIM, MARYBELLE C. "Two-Year College Counselors: Who Are They and What Do They Do?" *Community College Review* 16 (Summer 1988): 39–46.

———. "Two-Year College Faculty: A Research Update," *Community College Review* 17 (Winter 1989): 34–43.

McCABE, ROBERT H. "The Educational Program of the American Community College: A Transition." In *Colleges of Choice: The Enabling Impact of the Community College*, ed. Judith S. Eaton. New York: Macmillan, 1988.

PARNELL, DALE. *The Neglected Majority.* Washington, DC: Community College Press, 1985.

PERRIN, TOWERS. *Workforce 2000: Competing in a Seller's Market: Is Corporate America Prepared?* The Hudson Institute, 1990.

REYES, PETRO, and SUSAN B. TWOMBLY. "Perceptions of Contemporary Governance in Community Colleges: An Empirical Study," *Community College Review* 14 (Winter 1986/87): 4–12.

RICHARDSON, RICHARD C. JR., CLYDE E. BLOCKER, and LOUIS W. BENDER. *Governance for the Two-Year College.* Englewood Cliffs, NJ: Prentice Hall, 1972.

RICHARDSON, RICHARD C. JR., and HOWARD L. SIMMONS. "Is It Time for a New Look at Academic Organization in Community Colleges?" *Community College Review* 17 (Summer 1989): 34–39.

Staffing Information Handbook for Learning Resources Programs. Suisun City: Learning Resources Association of California Community Colleges, 1988.

"Standards for Community, Junior, and Technical College Learning Resources Programs," *College & Research Libraries News* 51 (September 1990): 757–767.

VAUGHAN, GEORGE B. "The Community College Mission," *AACJC Journal* 58 (February/March 1988): 25–27.

4

Current Issues

In his metaphor for mission, Vaughan envisioned the mission of the community college as encapsuled in a balloon. As external and internal forces interact with this mission, the shape of the balloon changes to accommodate the forces. Thus, the successful college "will squeeze, push, and pull on the mission to make it conform to community needs. . . . The healthy college is constantly faced with tensions that influence the mission, which vie for space in the balloon." [Vaughan 26–27]

Reviewing the past twenty years, Vaughan cited "two major tensions that kept the community college movement in something of a constant state of upheaval: growth in enrollments, programs, personnel and building; and the very newness of the community college idea to much of society, to students, and to those of us who were employed in them." [Vaughan 27] Current issues facing community colleges include leadership and governance, finance and politics, faculty issues, program quality, facilities and technology, enrollment issues, and diversity.

Leadership and Governance

The Commission on the Future of Community Colleges cites the need for the creative leadership and new models of governance to address the issues of the future. "Building communities requires creative leaders, and the president is the key. The president must move the college beyond day-to-day

39

operations. He or she must call upon the community of learning to affirm tradition, respond to challenges, and create inspiring visions for the future." [Building 41]

Furthermore, the Commission cautions that the presidents cannot do the job alone and recommends "that community college governance be strengthened and that its fundamental purpose be to renew the community as a whole. Specifically, we urge that a wide range of decision-making arrangements be available on campus." [Building 43] Thus, the Commission proposes that the individuals affected by campus decision-making should be actively involved in the process and that leadership development should be encouraged among faculty and mid-level administration as well.

The pyramid structure of bureaucratic governance would be slightly modified to encourage collegiality and faculty participation in governance. Thus, "presidents and trustees will need to rely more on the faculty to be involved in developing and setting a mission based on recognition of the full value of both community needs and collegiate values. Administrators other than the presidents need to be recognized and involved more fully in decision-making and direction-setting at the policy level. The faculty will also have to accept new roles and responsibilities in generating more shared governance and responsibility schema." [Raisman 21] Collaboration among all members of the college would result in a unified, coherent statement of mission to guide the institution.

For the college to effectively address current issues, a process for systematic review and change is necessary. Richardson identifies five basic techniques for institutional change. They include special task forces, staff development, faculty revitalization, structural change, and strategic planning. The most formal and comprehensive technique is strategic planning which uses a systematic screening of the external environment and the assessment of institutional strengths and weaknesses in relation to opportunities and threats in that environment. Strategic planning makes use of the administrative structure and standing committees minimizing the involvement of special task forces. [Richardson 31–32]

Whichever technique for institutional change is implemented, an adequate database for decision-making is required. Such a database may include demographic trends and their implications, course success/attrition rates, comparative budget expenditures, FTE program costs, transfer student performance and occupational student employment success, etc. This data frequently is compiled by the Director of Institutional Planning in cooperation with Learning Resources staff. The learning resources staff collect and organize needed information, maintain the college archives, scan the environment for trends, research specific topics under consideration, and present the conclusions effectively in both written and graphic form.

Finance and Politics

Adequate finances were cited as the top major challenge facing college administrators in 1990 according to *Campus Trends 1990*. [El-Khawas, 1990, 15] Survey respondents indicated that spending decisions reflected institutional priorities. Greatest demand for increased funding among public two-year colleges were support for computer equipment and software (88%), health insurance costs (77%), faculty compensation (73%), programs serving adult learners (65%), faculty development (64%), and collaboration with high schools (62%). [El-Khawas, 1990, 40]

Greatly affecting institutional priorities and mission are the external influences from national, state, and local funding sources. Breneman and Nelson analyzed community college funding and noted "the growing tension between the evolving educational mission embraced by the colleges and the financing policies endorsed by state officials. This tension between mission and finance goes to the core of what the colleges are, who they serve, and what they will become." [Breneman vii–viii] Specific issues include: Should society or the individual pay for education? How expansive should community college educational services be and how should these activities be financed? How should the competition among the many educational providers be resolved?

A recent survey to determine who was responsible for securing funding for public two-year colleges concluded that "the major responsibility was attributed to the college presidents. Boards of Trustees were ranked second followed by other administrators and then faculty members." [Graham 55] Increasingly, community colleges are employing resource development officers to coordinate fund raising efforts. Others are exploring alternate funding opportunities and assigning responsibilities to appropriate administrative areas. For example, alumni and foundation activities would be assigned to the Institutional Development Officer, contract education assigned to the Division of Business and Industry Assistance in cooperation with the Division of Learning Resources, and grantsmanship support assigned to the Institutional Development Office in cooperation with the Division of Learning Resources.

Faculty Issues

Hiring and retention of faculty was cited as the second major challenge facing college administrators in 1990. "The specific issues primarily involve campus responses to the changing labor market; most often cited were concerns about recruitment, hiring, and retention of faculty, along with concerns about adequate salary and compensation levels for faculty." [El-Khawas, 1990, 16]

"Howard Bowen and Jack Schuster (1986) have estimated that two-thirds or more of today's college faculty will need to be replaced between 1985 and 2009. William Bowen and Julie Ann Sosa (1989) have projected that, starting about 1997, many academic fields—in both the arts and the sciences—will encounter an outright deficit of persons available for vacant faculty positions." [El-Khawas, 1990, 1] Contributing to this anticipated shortage are the retirement of experienced faculty, the addition of new academic programs creating the need for new faculty positions, the competition with industry and government for knowledgeable staff, decreased numbers of students selecting teaching as a career, and existing shortages in high demand fields.

According to *Campus Trends 1990*, 71 percent of the public two–year colleges anticipate an increased pace of faculty hiring for full-time positions during the next five years. Fifty-three percent of the respondents expect to hire six to fourteen percent of their full-time faculty positions within the next two years. [El-Khawas, 1990, 20–22]

In addition to teaching talent, the Commission on the Future of Community Colleges emphasizes "that all prospective community college teachers should communicate effectively, demonstrate the ability to use educational technology, show a commitment to the community college philosophy and the students to be served, and demonstrate qualities of leadership, as well. Beyond excellence, which is central, the recruitment of new faculty must focus on diversity." [Building 12] The majority of full-time faculty are white males while the majority of students are African American or Hispanic females. Community colleges have a responsibility for providing their students role models or mentors.

Proactive recruitment techniques are recommended for locating and hiring these faculty members. Proposed methods include contacting the colleges and universities with strong programs in the disciplines in which there are vacancies and asking for the most promising candidates to be identified. [Roueche 1] "Grow-your-own" programs—in which talented community college students have been identified and assisted through their subsequent college years in exchange for their return to their home community college as teachers—have been proposed especially as an incentive for minority faculty recruitment. [Andrews 26–27] Future teachers could be identified and offered opportunities to serve as peer tutors or teachers aides. Graduate fellowships could be made available to minority students who plan to teach in community colleges. [Building 14]

As the academic labor market becomes more competitive, the financial pressure on the college budget may increase. Competition for faculty recruitment may result in increased salaries and benefits as well as improved working conditions, such as reduced teaching loads or teachers aides.

Increasingly, colleges are looking to part-time faculty to alleviate staffing and financial pressures. According to *Campus Trends 1990*, 66 percent of the public two-year colleges are currently making extensive use of part-time faculty by having them teach more than 25 percent of the courses offered. [El-Khawas, 1990, 20] Nearly 60 percent of all community college faculty teach part-time. The Commission on the Future of Community Colleges notes that part-time faculty can enrich the college through diversity and experience, but cautions that a healthy balance between full-time and part-time faculty must be maintained. [Building 12]

Once quality faculty, full-time and part-time, have been recruited and hired, community colleges have an obligation toward comprehensive professional development. New faculty would be oriented to college procedures, available support services and resources, characteristics of the student body, and the culture of the institution. Ongoing opportunities which emphasize helping faculty teach more effectively and provide faculty "renewal" may include seminars, workshops, presentations, departmental retreats, leaves, and sabbaticals. Professional development topics may include success stories shared by "classroom researchers," community college history and mission presented as a credit course, newer teaching techniques and media advancements introduced by learning resources staff, and more.

Some learning resources programs assume leadership for campuswide staff development. Rationale for this responsibility include the Division of Learning Resources's position, separate from other instructional divisions but reporting directly to the chief academic officer, in the college's formal organizational structure; existing LRP staff liaison and instructional support activities permitting assessment of needs; and the information role of LRP staff who can locate and disseminate announcements of commercial staff development activities or who can coordinate locally created opportunities.

Program Quality

According to a 1988 National Governors' Association report, nearly every state has already attempted to expand assessment activities in public institutions. [Astin 35] The Council of Postsecondary Accreditation's regional associations require colleges to systematically assess their mission-related institutional outcomes. [Altieri 15] Consequently, community college administrators cite program quality as the third most important challenge. [El-Khawas 41] In *Campus Trends 1990*, 87 percent of the public two-year college respondents indicated their institutions were currently participating in student assessment activities with 53 percent responding to state mandates and 48 percent responding to accreditation requirements. [El-Khawas, 1990, 38]

Evaluation of program quality may take many forms. Hammons suggests a periodic and systematic evaluation of individual courses and programs, including general education and community service offerings, to learn ways to improve them and to see if they should be continued. [Hammons 6] Altieri describes a student outcomes grid which charts desired student outcome (knowledge, program achievement, satisfaction, career achievement, and community impact) with measurement sources and urges that the results be used for improvement of teaching, the curriculum, and the college's services. [Altieri 16–17] Astin reviews four state approaches which include value-added assessment for incentive funding, competency testing, mandated assessment with local control, and challenge grants. [Astin 36–40] *Building Communities* recommends that "each community college develop a campus-wide assessment of institutional effectiveness. Such a program should include a periodic reexamination of mission and goals, specific programs, individual student outcomes, retention rates, and the performance of graduates." [Building 47]

Issues affecting program assessment relate directly to the mission of the community college. It is an institution of higher education which mirrors its home community. It provides open-door access to education regardless of race, age, or station in life. It provides a comprehensive instructional program. Thus, the college is serving a heterogeneous population with a majority of nontraditional students. The educational purposes of these students range from obtaining an Associate Degree with intent to transfer to a four-year college to enrolling in one course to improve a skill or interest. Consequently, the Commission on the Future of Community Colleges cautions that "quality must be measured by meeting students where they are, by good teaching, and by providing the support services students need to fulfill their academic, career, and personal objectives." [Building 47]

Whatever the assessment method implemented, the objective is to improve campuswide and program quality reflecting the mission of the college. In *Campus Trends 1990*, when asked how assessment results were used, 99 percent of the public two-year college respondents stated for reports to deans and department chairs, 96 percent for reports to faculty, 85 percent for reports to student affairs, 84 percent for program or curriculum evaluation, and 82 percent for curriculum changes. [El-Khawas, 1990, 38]

Program assessment affects the learning resources program. Lutzker reports that "the Middle States Commission on Higher Education now expects that each accredited institution have a bibliographic instruction program, and that a library's effectiveness within the teaching/learning environment of the institution be clearly demonstrated." [Lutzker 14] In addition, available learning resources materials and services must be documented for focused program accreditation, such as for the National League of Nursing or the Engineering Council for Professional Development. In addition, the Division of Learning Resources must evaluate its resources and services for program planning purposes.

Facilities and Technology

Facilities and technology were listed as the fourth major issue facing community administrators. [El-Khawas, 1990, 41] Primary concerns included renovation and renewal of physical facilities and the addition of the computers and high-tech instrumentation necessary to support and enhance the curriculum. When asked about changes in the allocation of budgeted funding, the administrators noted increases for computer equipment and software (88%), planning new buildings (59%), and maintenance of buildings and facilities (45%). [El-Khawas, 1990, 40]

Since the community college building boom occurred in the 1960s and 1970s, the necessity to renovate and renew existing facilities is to be expected. Roofs and carpets wear out. Both economic and ecological concerns encourage improvement of lighting and HVAC systems. The proliferation of computers and electronic aids requires upgraded electrical service and modified classroom and work areas. The advent of telecommunications necessitates appropriate conduits and cabling for implementation and expansion. The desire to serve students with disabilities, coupled with federal regulations, requires modifications to permit accessibility to all services.

Technology has greatly impacted community college's campuses. Telecommunications networks enhance communication through voice, video, and data transfer. Management information systems transform raw data into trend analysis necessary for strategic planning. Technology permits remote student registration and improves the tracking of student progress. Computer spreadsheets enable budget oversight and analysis. And the benefits increase daily.

Technology is an important tool in the instructional process. Print, radio, and television extend educational opportunities to those who may not be able to attend class on campus. Film and television media bring a variety of experiences and places into the classroom supporting instruction. Interactive computers and other teaching aids respond to individual student learning styles and needs. The information world is more accessible through

electronic tools and resource sharing networks. College laboratories repli-
cate the technology used in industries. With these endless potentials for
technology, the Commission of the Future of Community Colleges cautions
that "televisions, calculators, word processors, and computers cannot make
value judgments. They cannot teach students wisdom. That is the mission
of the faculty, and the classroom must be a place where switches are sometimes turned off." [Building 28]

In addition, *Building Communities* recommends that community colleges
develop campuswide plans for the use of technology to support both administration and instruction, that they use technology to extend the campus,
and that new uses for technology be explored. "Specifically, community colleges should lead the way in creating electronic networks for learning, satellite classrooms, and conferences that connect colleges from coast to coast,
creating a national community of educators." [Building 28]

The Division of Learning Resources is the campus leader for implementing the use of technology. While the classroom faculty member's role is to
structure the learning process by integrating traditional and nontraditional
instructional techniques, learning resources staff provide support for the instructional delivery system. They provide access to hardware and materials,
assist in the development of specialized instructional materials, instruct faculty and students in the effective use of various instructional tools, extend
the campus through teleconferences and distance learning, provide ready
access to information resources through traditional and electronic information tools, oversee the campus learning laboratories, and provide consultation with building construction or renovation to ensure future voice, video,
and data communication.

Enrollment Issues

In *Campus Trends 1990*, 24 percent of the community college respondents
cited enrollment issues as an important challenge to be faced in the next five
years. [El-Khawas, 1990, 41] These issues were characterized by concerns
for recruitment and retention and serving new populations. Historically,
community colleges have focused upon the needs of students as individuals.
New populations responsive to employer-driven need and community advancement efforts will be served. [Lorenzo 42–43]

Of the *Campus Trends 1990* respondents, 82 percent cited headcount enrollment increases between FY89 and FY90 plus increases in each of the
following categories: first-time freshmen (80%), part-time students (71%),
students aged 25 + (52%), transfer students (39%), African Americans (34%),
Hispanics (26%), Asians (25%), and international students (25%). [El-Kha-

was, 1990, 33] When forecasting enrollment trends for the next five years, 61 percent of the respondents expected enrollments to increase between 1– 10 percent and 23 percent expected enrollment increases between 11–20 percent. [El-Khawas, 1990, 34]

Enrollment trends are based upon demographic data and the planned outreach to new nontraditional populations. Between 1990 and 2010, the population over 45 years is projected to increase from 32 percent to 41 percent while younger population groups are expected to decline. Among the younger population groups, only the 18–24 year old group is anticipated to maintain ten percent of the population by the year 2010 and to have increased in numbers. [El-Khawas, 1988, 140–141] Figure 4.1 shows this data in absolute terms.

These projections suggest that the competition, among four-year colleges, proprietary schools, and community colleges, to recruit new students in the traditional 18–24 year age group will increase. Recruitment techniques may include dual enrollment, 2-Plus-2, early identification, and advanced placement programs in collaboration with high schools. In addition, recruitment of nontraditional students will increase through subcontracts with business and industry, through creation of community development partnerships, through special programs reaching out to special populations (such as Women in New Goals, College for Seniors, ESL programs, and more), and

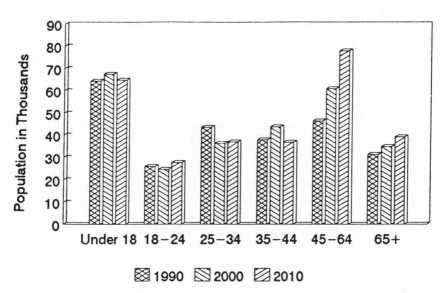

FIGURE 4.1 Population Projections by Age Source: Elaine El-Khawas, Deborah J. Carter, and Cecilia A. Otting. *Community College Fact Book.* New York: Macmillan, (1988).

through ensuring a responsiveness to student needs by remaining accessible financially, physically, and conveniently. More colleges will adopt the "student as consumer" concept.

Another enrollment issue is student retention. Cohen found that personal factors were more important than institutional factors in determining student retention. "Students drop out because of job-hour conflict, change of residence, transfer to another college, and other such personal matters as the difficulty in sustaining study and employment simultaneously or in managing family finances and responsibilities. Many drop out because they have obtained the goal for which they matriculated; they may have needed only a course or two to satisfy their objectives." [Cohen 56] However, *Building Communities* considers retention an institutional concern and proposes "a comprehensive First Year Program with orientation for all full-time, part-time, and evening students. Such a program should include advising, an early warning system to identify at-risk students, plus career counseling and mentoring arrangements." [Building 11]

Learning resources staff participate in student recruitment through the production of radio and television spots and promotional programs to be presented in area high schools, at employment fairs, etc. Librarians build alliances with area high schools through exchange programs, cooperative resource sharing agreements, and encouraging high school students to use college facilities for class projects. Through acquisition of or production of remedial and/or supplementary instructional aids responsive to diverse learning styles, learning resources staff promote retention. Learning resources assistance and instruction responsive to individual needs and abilities promotes student success. Finally, all learning resources staff participate in student and community organizations promoting cooperation and developing a responsive rapport.

Diversity

Diversity was cited as a major challenge facing community colleges in the next five years by 22 percent of the respondents in *Campus Trends 1990*. [El-Khawas, 1990, 41] Community colleges serve student populations with diverse abilities, from a variety of cultural and ethnic backgrounds, and with international backgrounds and visions. The colleges are committed to providing access to higher education regardless of race, age, or station in life.

Nielsen describes four diverse student groups based upon ability. He cites the first group as well-prepared and highly motivated. These students require enrichment programs and extended opportunities to be challenged. The second group lacks preparation but has high expectations. Refresher courses or remediation efforts combined with counseling and student services provide these students with the foundation for a successful college experience. The third group is reasonably prepared but lacks motivation and self-esteem. These students must be convinced of the value of education, require nontraditional approaches to instruction, and need counseling support. The final group lacks both preparation and motivation, but sees the community college as the last chance. Individualized assistance through learning laboratories, peer tutoring programs, and counseling may help these students succeed. [Nielsen 46–47]

Focusing on cultural and ethnic diversity, Kappner cautions, "Demographics dictate that we at the community colleges should be in the forefront of planning for diversity. The students we prepare today will be the workers, students, and teachers of tomorrow, and they must be well-equipped to meet the challenges of the workplace and of society as a whole." [Kappner 21] She notes that 43 percent of all African American students in higher education, 55 percent of all Hispanic students, 41 percent of all Asian students, and 57 percent of all native American students are enrolled in community colleges. [Kappner 17] Activities designed to promote appreciation of diversity include workshops to increase racial/cultural awareness, courses in ethnic/minority studies, special recruitment and retention initiatives which may include mentoring, monitoring progress, counseling, and academic assistance.

The concept of cultural diversity expands even further with the community college's international vision. In 1990, approximately 40,000 foreign students or one-third of all undergraduate students in the United States were enrolled in community colleges. Factors encouraging these increased foreign student enrollments include lower tuitions, more relaxed admission requirements, smaller student populations and class sizes, and more individualized instruction and counseling services. [King 37]

Many colleges are internationalizing their curricula. Some are focusing on separate new international courses and programs while others are merging an international dimension into existing courses across all disciplines and programs. Bailey et al summarize studies of successful internationalization programs in community colleges and concluded that "although many provide instruction in international trade, the majority incorporate courses in foreign arts and culture into their foreign-language programs or they infuse such materials in their study-abroad programs or in such classes as anthropology, geography, history, humanities, political science, sociology, or writing." [Bailey 33]

In addition, some community colleges are establishing two-year college programs in foreign locations to enable foreign students to begin their college work in their home country before transferring to colleges in the United States. [Greene 21] Others participate either independently or through consortia with the goals of providing foreign technical assistance programs, opportunities for international study, and services in the development of international education. Still others become subcontractors to private companies that enter into contracts to provide technical assistance abroad. [King 38–39]

This diverse student population requires the support of the learning resources program. Learning resources staff provide resources and instructional delivery systems which convey information in a variety of formats. They cooperate with classroom faculty in curriculum design and provide hands-on materials production laboratories. They sponsor faculty development activities which help faculty work more effectively with various instructional techniques. They oversee learning laboratories. They attend the annual International Federation of Library Associations and Institutions conference, participate in international exchange opportunities, and travel widely.

Conclusion

"The unparalleled growth of our nation's community colleges stands as a testimony that these institutions have served society's purposes, and their success will assure their existence well into the future." [Lorenzo 42] Indeed, the community college mission has remained constant while responsive to the external and internal forces interacting with it. The continued success of the community college depends upon its responsiveness to the needs of the future as well as it has the past. Similarly, the effective learning resources program reflects the college's mission and responds to the special issues facing the college as a whole. It is an integral part of the entire institution.

Selected Bibliography

ACEBO, SANDRA C., and KAREN WATKINS. "Community College Faculty Development: Designing a Learning Organization." In *Enhancing Staff Development in Diverse Settings*, ed. Victoria J. Marsick. San Francisco: Jossey-Bass, 1988.

ALTIERI, GUY. "A Structural Model for Students Outcomes: Assessment Programs in Community Colleges," *Community College Review* 17 (Spring 1990): 15–21.

ANDREWS, HANS A., and WILLIAM MARZANO. "Meeting the Looming Faculty Shortage: Development from Within," *AACJC Journal* 61 (December/January 1990–91): 26–29.

ASTIN, ALEXANDER. "Can State-Mandated Assessment Work?" *Educational Record* 71 (Fall 1990): 34–41.

BAILEY, LIZ, NANCY E. BUCHANAN, and MARGARET HOLLEMAN. "The LRC's Role in Helping Faculty Internationalize the Community College Curriculum." In *The Role of the Learning Resources Center in Instruction*, ed. Margaret Holleman. San Francisco: Jossey-Bass, 1990.

BOCK, DANIEL E., and W. ROBERT SULLINS. "The Search for Alternative Sources of Funding: Community Colleges and Private Fund-Raising," *Community College Review* 15 (Winter 1987): 13–20.

BRENEMAN, DAVID W., and SUSAN C. NELSON. *Financing Community Colleges: An Economic Perspective*. Washington, DC: Brookings Institution, 1981.

Building Communities: A Vision for a New Century. Washington, DC: AACJC, 1988.

CATANZARO, JAMES L., and ALLEN D. ARNOLD. *Alternative Funding Sources*. San Francisco: Jossey-Bass, 1989.

COHEN, ARTHUR M., and FLORENCE B. BRAWER. *The American Community College*. Second Edition. San Francisco: Jossey-Bass, 1989.

EL-KHAWAS, ELAINE. *Campus Trends 1990*. Washington, DC: American Council on Education, 1990.

EL-KHAWAS, ELAINE, DEBORAH J. CARTER, and CECILIA A. OTTINGER. *Community College Fact Book*. New York: Macmillan, 1988.

FIFIELD, MARY L., ET AL. "Workers for the World: Occupational Programs in a Global Economy," *AACJC Journal* 61 (August/September 1990): 15–19.

GRAHAM, STEVE, and DUANE ANDERSON. "Sources of Financing for Community Colleges," *Community College Review* 13 (Summer 1985): 50–56.

GREENE, WILLIAM E. "Establishing American Colleges Abroad," *AACJC Journal* 61 (August/September 1990): 20–24.

HAMMONS, JIM. "Five Potholes in the Road to Community College Excellence," *Community College Review* 15 (Summer 1987): 5–12.

HOCKADAY, JEFF, and JEROME J. FRIGA. "Assessment of Institutional Effectiveness: A Practical Model for Small Colleges," *Community College Review* 17 (Winter 1989): 28–33.

KAPPNER, AUGUSTA SOUZA. "Creating Something to Celebrate: Planning for Diversity," *AACJC Journal* 61 (December/January 1990–91): 16–21.

KING, MAXWELL C. "The Community College's International Vision," *AACJC Journal* 61 (August/September 1990): 37–40.

LORENZO, ALBERT L. "Anticipating Our Future Purpose," *AACJC Journal* 61 (February/March 1991): 42–45.

LUTZKER, MARILYN. "Bibliographic Instruction and Accreditation in Higher Education," *College & Research Libraries News* 51 (January 1990): 14–18.

NIELSEN, NORM. "Responding to the New Student Diversity," *AACJC Journal* 61 (April/May 1991): 45–48.

RAISMAN, NEAL. "Moving into the Fifth Generation," *Community College Review* 18 (Fall 1990): 15–22.

RICHARDSON, RICHARD C. JR. "Improving Effectiveness Through Strategic Planning," *Community College Review* 15 (Spring 1988): 28-34.

ROSTEK, STEPHEN, and DEBORAH JEAN KLADIVKO. "Staff Development and Training." In *Issues in Personnel Management*, ed. Richard I. Miller and Edward W. Holzapfel, Jr. San Francisco: Jossey-Bass, 1988.

ROUECHE, JOHN E. "Insuring Excellence in Community College Teaching," *Leadership Abstracts* 3 (June 1990): 1–2.

VAUGHAN, GEORGE B. "The Community College Mission," *AACJC Journal* 58 (February/March 1988): 25–27.

PART II

THE LEARNING RESOURCES PROGRAM

5

Learning Resources
Program Overview

All academic libraries and learning resources programs share the common responsibility of providing access to information and learning resources necessary to serve their respective user populations. All hold a responsibility to reflect the mission of their parent institutions. All are responsive to their respective institutional educational goals, curricula, student population, size and complexity, and special issues.

The mission of the community college differs significantly from other academic institutions. All community colleges are institutions of higher education which emphasize teaching rather than research. All provide open access to education resulting in a diverse student population. All offer comprehensive instructional programs, including liberal arts transfer, vocational, developmental studies, and community interest courses, supported by student advising and counseling. All mirror the unique characteristics and needs of their local communities. But no two community colleges are identical.

Similarly, community college learning resources programs share a common mission. The learning resources program (LRP) provides resources and services necessary to serve the informational, learning, and developmental needs of its students, faculty, administrators, and broader college community. Each LRP has a responsibility to "promote learning through the academic program of the institution," by providing "the best possible access to wanted information in printed, media, or electronic format, and have the means for delivering the information to an individual user or distributing it to campus classrooms." [Standards 762] Each LRP is responsive to the unique characteristics of its parent institution. Each is an integral part of its parent institution. Consequently, no two learning resources programs are identical.

This chapter provides an overview of the learning resources program. It reviews the evolution of the program from its initial creation as an extension of the high school library to its current integration of library, media, and telecommunications. It also discusses the scope and organization of the LRP as it reflects the mission and characteristics of its parent institution.

Evolution of the Learning Resources Program

Since the first public junior colleges were created as extensions of high schools, community college learning resources programs evolved from high school libraries. In these first junior colleges, college students shared facilities with high school students. Assigned textbook study, reserve readings, and lectures by the instructor were the primary instructional methods. Resources suitable for junior college students were limited. The high school librarian was the sole staff member serving both high school and college students. "As long as the typical public junior college shared facilities and staff with a high school, the extent of library services provided to junior college students was so limited as to be nearly nonexistent." [Genung 44]

Only after junior college transfer students reported back the disadvantage they faced in their junior and senior years as a result of inadequate library experience did junior college instructors seek improved library services and begin requiring research papers. This apparent need "for the use of bibliographical and reference tools and for stronger library collections to support the instructional programs became apparent to the administrator as well as to the instructor. The long-range effect was the growth of a climate favorable to library development in the junior college." [Genung 45]

As legislation was passed providing state and local support for junior colleges as separate entities, separate campuses were established. Within these campuses, new libraries focusing on the needs of junior college students were created. "Library services expanded to meet the changes in instruction, with definite attention given to vocational programs, classroom instructional resources, and the quality of holdings." [Genung 46]

Professional support for the development of library services in junior colleges became a positive influence. In 1930, the Junior College Libraries Section of the Association of College and Research Libraries approved the first set of standards to encourage library service. These standards recommended "a book collection of 10,000 volumes for the first 500 students, an annual expenditure of $5 per student for materials, and a staff of at least two professional librarians." [Wallace 506]

In 1934, the Carnegie Corporation created the Advisory Group on Junior College Libraries to study the needs of junior colleges through surveys and personal visits. Based on this group's findings, the Carnegie Corporation awarded a series of grants to promote the development of junior college libraries. One grant resulted in the publication of Foster E. Mohrhardt's A List of Books for Junior College Libraries, the first bibliographical tool used for collection development and evaluation in a junior college. Another grant enabled Stephens College to employ B. Lamar Johnson as librarian and dean of instruction for the purpose of integrating the library into the instructional process and sharing in campuswide administrative responsibilities. Johnson's book, Vitalizing a College Library, portraying the librarian as a campuswide curriculum leader, was a forerunner of the learning resources concept. In addition, the Corporation "made direct grants for the purchase of materials to 92 junior colleges in amounts ranging from $1,500 to $6,000." [Genung 46] These grants permitted many of the recipient libraries to double in size and improve in quality by using Mohrhardt's list to create the core collection.

Following World War II, junior college enrollments swelled with returning veterans. The typical junior college student was no longer a recent high school graduate, but instead a mature, traveled man with family responsibilities. Increased emphasis was placed on vocational/technical and general education. The Truman Commission redefined the junior college as a community college. "Librarians began serving on curriculum committees and to be seen as educators rather than a caretakers of books. Libraries began a slow but sure transformation from archives to learning laboratories. Libraries increased their non-book holdings and began to utilize microfilm and audiovisual departments began producing software." [Bock, 1984, 38]

The 1960s brought rapid growth in community colleges. "The number of two-year institutions increased from 600 to 1091 and, in the last half of that decade, 100 library/learning resource centers were built. . . . Individualized instruction was leading to audio labs, programmed instruction centers, and the like. What once had been a service of simply film and projector distribution turned into a giant octopus desperately trying to provide all things, including language laboratories, instant-response classrooms, sound systems for field houses or music laboratories, and equipment for large classroom-auditoriums." [Bock, 1979, 6] Innovative techniques and programs, as described in B. Lamar Johnson's *Islands of Innovation Expanding*, were emphasized. Traditional print-oriented library services transformed into learning resources programs.

The 1960 "Standards for Junior College Libraries" recommended by the Association of College and Research Libraries outraged college presidents by recommending "a minimum of 20,000 volumes, ten times that of 1925 and twice that of 1930." [Bock, 1984, 40] A decade later, the American Association of Community and Junior Colleges, the Association of Educational Communications and Technology, and the American Library Association (ACRL) combined efforts to develop the "Guidelines for Two-Year College Learning Resources Programs" which were adopted in 1972. "The *Guidelines* reflected a change in philosophy for library programs, including provisions for the integration of library and audiovisual services, the inclusion of production in these services, and the involvement of learning resources in instruction." [Hisle 618] Components of the learning resources program included acquisition of materials and related access services, instructional development, production of both print and nonprint materials, user services including reference, circulation, and faculty assistance, and auxiliary services such as computer operations, printing, learning labs, and telecommunications.

The Council on Library Resources reported its findings from a 1975 study of thirty-one outstanding community college learning resources programs. "The strength of these programs was in their integration of traditional library and media services with instructional services, both instructional development for faculty and learning assistance for students. This was shown organizationally, in a total materials approach to public catalogs, in some intershelving of materials, in centralized cataloging and processing, and in LRC assignments of faculty librarians to work with instructional divisions of the colleges." [Bock, 1984, 42–43]

The technological developments of the 1980s, improving information access and retrieval and extending the delivery of instruction, directly impacted the learning resources program. The LRP expanded to serve as an information network as well as instructional support system. Computerized systems provided acquisition, cataloging, circulation, inventory, film rental, and other essential LRP services. Standardization of data bases and access to them expanded information access, networking, and resource sharing opportunities internally through campuswide networks and beyond through external partnerships. Video access expanded to include videocassettes, campus cable systems, educational television stations, interactive video, and distance learning.

Responding to the expanding role of the LRP, a joint committee of the ACRL and AECT cooperated to adopt the 1990 "Standards for Community,

Junior, and Technical College Learning Resources Program." These standards, intended to assist in evaluation and developing learning resources programs, emphasized the importance of the learning resources concept with new emphasis on microcomputer and telecommunications technology. These Standards replaced the term "two-year college" in the title with "community, technical, and junior college," to reflect the changing nature of student enrollment patterns in community colleges. [Hisle 619] These Standards also encouraged LRPs to support the AACJC emphasis upon the building of partnerships within and beyond the campus, as described in *Building Communities.*

The community college learning resources program has evolved from its initial creation as an extension of a high school library to its current integration of library, media, computers, and telecommunications. The LRP has consistently responded to the mission of the community college. The changes in higher education and the technologies will further impact the LRP's future development as it continues to evolve responsively.

Scope and Organization of the Learning Resources Program

The scope and organization of the learning resources program reflects "the college's educational goals, curricula, student population, size and complexity, as well as the diversity of resources needed to accommodate different modes of learning." [Standards 757] Consequently, no two learning resources programs are identical in scope and organization.

As the community college evolved, print and nonprint collections and services were merged into one unit named "Learning Resources Center," "Educational Resources Center," "Instructional Materials Center," or other variation. These names reflected efforts to redefine the function and image of the community college library. The 1972 "Guidelines for Two-Year College Learning Resources Programs" included the term "learning resources" in the title to reflect the learning resources program concept in community colleges. "Since publication of the 1972 Guidelines, it has been less and less appropriate to speak of community college libraries. Most colleges and researchers in the field accept and use the LRS (learning resources services) terminology or some similar variation. Today, in most community colleges the term library has become at the least a misnomer, if not altogether anachronistic." [Hisle 618]

Learning resources terminology was again emphasized in the 1990 Standards with the further objective of standardization of name. "It is hoped that the inclusion of the term learning resources in the title, as was done in 1972, will encourage all community colleges to adopt this designation. Consistent use of the term in all areas of the country is necessary if administrators and others are to understand and accept LRS programs as an integral unit within a college." [Hisle 619]

The 1990 "Standards" defined the term "learning resources" as "an organizational configuration which provides library and media materials and services. In addition, learning resources programs can provide various specialized services and perform other instructional responsibilities." [Standards 757] Thus, learning resources programs provide resources and services necessary to serve the information, learning, and developmental needs of its students, faculty, administration, and broader college community.

No universal learning resources organization model exists. Person identifies four groups of influences which impact the organizational development of the LRP. External influences include state laws, the district/state system, trends in higher education, technological developments, and current management theories. Professional influences include guidelines and standards, trends and developments in the profession, and imitative patterns. College influences include size, age, history, general administrative patterns, leadership styles and philosophies, finances, curriculum, facilities, and defined scope of LRP. Internal LRP influences include staff attitudes toward governance, conditions of work, strength and background of the chief administrator, staff talents and abilities, faculty status/collective bargaining, services offered, and number of subsystems needed. [Person 444]

Community college LRPs generally fit into the college's bureaucratic organization with the LRP chief administrator, or Dean of Learning Resources, "responsible for administering the program and for providing leadership and direction so that mission of the program is fulfilled." [Standards 759] As discussed in Chapter 3, the Dean reports to the college's chief academic officer and holds rank and status in the total college organizational structure equal with others with similar campuswide responsibilities. The Dean is a learning resources generalist, with training and experience in library, media, and information science, as well as a competent administrator.

An advisory committee for learning resources enhances communication between the LRP and its users. The Dean chairs this committee composed of campus representatives interested in LRP services. Committee members are appointed, elected, or selected by the appropriate faculty, staff, or student constituencies. The committee's function is to advise, not to administer the operation of the learning resources program. Through the advisory committee's input, the development and evaluation of the LRP is more responsive to the college community.

The two most common organizational patterns for the learning resources program are the traditional and the integrated LRP patterns. Within the

traditional LRP organization, library services are grouped into one department, media services into another, and telecommunications networking services into still another department within the division (Figure 5.1) In this
organization, library services, responsible for the instruction in and access
to learning materials, includes technical services, reference services, and
circulation. Media services provides equipment distribution and maintenance and materials design and production. Telecommunications networking services, a recent addition to this traditional function organization, is
responsible for telecourse support and teleconferences. Some colleges have
merged telecommunications networking into media services for technical
support and into library services for materials access. Other specialized service departments, such as academic skills services responsible for providing
media-based instruction through the developmental learning lab, microcomputer lab, or nursing and allied health lab, may be incorporated into the
Learning Resources Division.

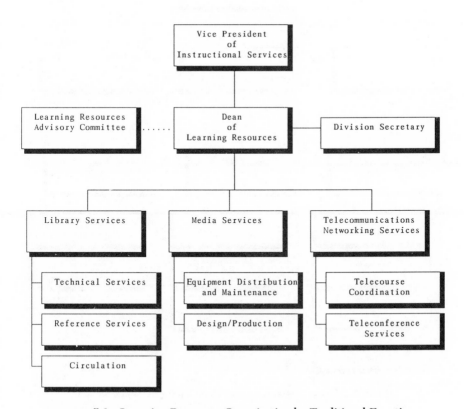

FIGURE 5.1   Learning Resources Organization by Traditional Function

The integrated learning resources organization groups services into departments by a common goal. Within this organization, the traditional library and media components are integrated into a unified learning resources program organized by service goal. Thus, the Learning Resources Division is grouped into three departments: access services, user services, and telecommunications network services. (Figure 5.2) Access services includes acquisition of materials and equipment including purchase, interlibrary loan, and rental; cataloging of materials including database maintenance and materials processing and repair; circulation of both materials and equipment; and equipment maintenance and repair. User services includes information services with reference, collection development, bibliographic instruction, individualized instruction/utilization, and archives; and materials design/

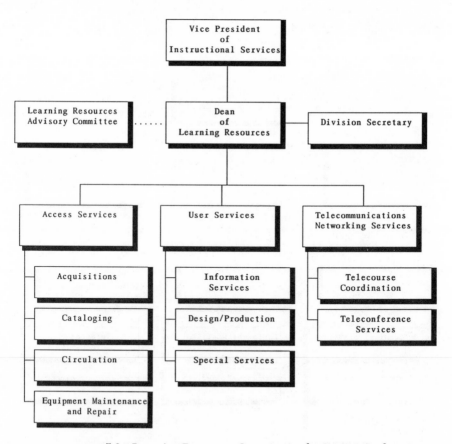

FIGURE 5.2   Learning Resources Organization by Service Goal

production including photography, audio, graphics, and video production. Telecommunications network services includes telecourse support and teleconference services. Some colleges have integrated telecommunications networking services into access services for program access and technical support and into user services for production support. In addition, the division may provide specialized services such as the faculty service center, learning assistance laboratories, staff development, or grantsmanship assistance. The organization of Part II reflects this organization by service goal.

Just as external, professional, college, and internal LRP influences affect the learning resources program's organizational structure, they also affect its staffing patterns and internal governance. External and professional guidelines require or recommend staffing levels in terms of numbers per FTE student and services offered and in terms of professional and classified staff. Institutional size and priorities combined with the internal LRP organization influence the levels of specialization and the responsibilities of professional and classified staff. Faculty status versus academic status for professional staff further influences staffing patterns and governance. The leadership style of the Dean of Learning Resources and of the college also affect LRP staffing patterns and governance.

Conclusion

The role and organization of the community college learning resources program reflect its continuing evolution as it responds to numerous external and internal influences, especially those of its parent institution and of the changing technologies. Person cites three patterns or traditions as community college LRP organizations evolve: "The first is a pattern of accommodating change. The second is the tradition of uniqueness of structure. The third pattern may reflect a possible tension as colleges struggle to integrate library and media services with other parts of the learning resources program and yet not lose focus." [Person 454]

The successful LRP organization is flexible and responsive to the informational, learning, and developmental needs of its students, faculty, administrators, and broader college community, a balance between traditional resources and the newer technologies is maintained to ensure a quality learning resources program serving a diverse population. Its organizational structure encourages communication and cooperation among LRP staff ensuring effective service, responsive to the external as well as internal influences.

Selected Bibliography

BOCK, D. JOLEEN. "From Libraries to Learning Resources: Six Decades of Progress—and Still Changing," *Community & Junior College Libraries* 3 (Winter 1984): 35–46.

————. "From Library to LRC," *Community College Frontiers* 8 (Fall 1979): 4–9.

DEBOER, KEE, and WENDY CULOTTA. "The Academic Librarian and Faculty Status in the 1980s: A Survey of the Literature," *College & Research Libraries* 48 (May 1987): 215–223.

GENUNG, HARRIETT, and JAMES O. WALLACE. "The Emergence of the Community College Library." In *Advances in Librarianship Volume 3*, ed. Melvin J. Voigt. New York: Seminar Press, 1972.

HALSTED, DEBORAH D., and DANA M. NEELEY. "The Importance of the Library Technician," *Library Journal* 115 (March 1, 1990): 62–63.

HISLE, W. LEE. "Learning Resource Services in the Community College: On the Road to the Emerald City," *College & Research Libraries* 50 (November 1989): 613–625.

JOHNSON, PEGGY. "Matrix Management: An Organizational Alternative for Libraries," *Journal of Academic Librarianship* 16 (September 1990): 222–229.

PERSON, RUTH J. "The Organization and Administration of Two-Year College Learning Resources," *Library Trends* 33 (Spring 1985): 441–457.

"Standards for Community, Junior, and Technical College Learning Resources Programs," *College & Research Libraries News* 51 (September 1990): 757–767.

WALLACE, JAMES O. "Newcomer to the Academic Scene: The Two-Year College Library/Learning Center," *College & Research Libraries* 37 (November 1976): 503–513.

WERRELL, EMILY, and LAURA SULLIVAN. "Faculty Status for Academic Librarians: A Review of the Literature," *College & Research Libraries* 48 (March 1987): 95–103.

6

Access Services

The learning resources program provides access to needed information in printed, media, or electronic formats and delivers that information either to an individual user or to a campus classroom. This access is provided through the "institution's own collection of materials, paired with supportive equipment and efficient service delivery systems to ensure that the available physical resources are deployed for the engagement of students with information and ideas." [Standards 762] Since institutional self-sufficiency is not possible, the college's resources and delivery systems are augmented "through such means as cooperative borrowing or renting materials from other institutions, online searching of large databases, and employing the power of electronic transmission." [Standards 762]

Within the Learning Resources Division, Access Services acquires, organizes, and distributes the materials and supportive equipment necessary to convey information in a variety of formats, including various forms of print and nonprint materials, computer software, optical storage technologies, and other formats, suitable for a diverse user population and curricula. "All types of materials conveying intellectual content, artistic and literary works, programmed texts and packaged instruction are considered resources of information that may be used as tools of effective teaching and learning along with books, periodicals, newspapers, government documents, and microform equivalents." [Standards 763]

This chapter introduces LRP collection development and then describes the acquisition, organization, and distribution of materials and supportive equipment through Access Services. Since no two community college LRPs are identical, the examples reflect a composite of sample procedures and forms currently used in community colleges across the country.

Introduction to Collection Development

Collection development is a shared responsibility among all LRP staff and discipline faculty. It is "the process of making certain the informational needs of the people using the collection are met in a timely and economical manner, using information resources produced both inside and outside the organization." [Evans 13] Collection development involves a continuous cycle which includes assessment of information needs and available resources, adoption/revision of a collection development policy, selection of resources, acquisition, weeding, and review of information needs and resources. [Evans 14–16]

Community college collection development is directly related to the college mission. It requires an understanding of the informational and instructional needs of its students, faculty, administrators, and broader college community. The primary purpose of the college's collection development is to support the instructional program. Consequently, appropriate resources are selected to serve diverse student learning styles and abilities; to support transfer, vocational, developmental, and community interest courses; and to use alternative information delivery systems. Faculty research and esoteric requests usually are fulfilled through external sources via resource sharing agreements. Thus, participation in broader cooperative networks is necessary to expand the instructional resources available on campus and to support research needs.

Responsive collection development requires the coordinated effort of every member of the Learning Resources Division as well as discipline faculty with the Dean of Learning Resources or designee ultimately responsible. Information services librarians hold general collection development responsibilities in conjunction with their reference and bibliographic instruction responsibilities. Instruction/utilization staff ensure the collection is responsive to individualized instruction needs. Design/production staff review the collection in response to instructional development requests and contribute locally produced materials to the collection. Circulation staff recommend replacement of missing or damaged materials and additional copies of heavily used titles. Acquisitions staff review the economy of ownership versus rental or interlibrary loan of frequently requested titles. Telecommunications networking staff negotiate supplemental rights to telecourses and suggest teleconference programs appropriate to add to the collection. In addition, every learning resources staff member contributes his personal interests, strengths, and knowledge to collectively develop the college's collection.

Beyond the Learning Resources Division, discipline faculty, administrators, students, and members of the community suggest materials for acquisition. Discipline faculty are especially encouraged to recommend titles for inclusion since they are the subject content specialists who can best ensure the collection reflects the instructional needs of their students. All suggestions are evaluated based upon the following general criteria: 1) purpose, scope, and audience; 2) difficulty; 3) authority, honesty, and credibility of author and publisher; 4) subject matter and curriculum support; 5) comparison with similar works; 6) timeliness; 7) format; 8) price; and 9) demand. [Katz 91–95]

A number of additional considerations affect the selection of print resources. The ownership versus access decision is made with research, out-of-print, and esoteric titles generally obtained through resource sharing agreements. The preservation versus merchandising decision is considered with the realization that students will read new attractive copies of books and not old rebound ones. [Hermenze 2195] The inclusion of textbooks decision is made with the conclusion to include the textbook only if it meets the general criteria for print selection.

Nonprint selection decisions follow the same general criteria with additional consideration given to content, technical quality, format, and format specific criteria. [Evans 197–202] The decision to include only instructional support or both instructional support and recreation resources is influenced by available funding and agreements with area video rental stores. The intended use for instructional support titles, either integrated into classroom lecture or provided as supplemental individualized instruction, determines information format. Generally, only nonprint titles able to "stand alone" as information resources are selected. Intended learner characteristics, instructional purpose and objectives, mode of instruction, and individual characteristics of the various nonprint formats provide additional evaluative criteria. Nonprint materials require preview evaluation to ensure that they meet the desired standards of quality, support the curriculum, and do not duplicate other materials available.

Participation in cooperative collection development and resource sharing agreements expands the information resources available beyond the local campus. Such cooperative agreements range from traditional interlibrary loan cooperation to shared union catalogs and telefacsimile agreements to online resource sharing networks. Simply stated, "resource sharing entails three things: having resources to share, a willingness to share them, and a plan for sharing them." [Gardner 246]

TABLE 6.1   Comparison of LRP Information Materials

		Advantages	Limitations
Print Materials			
No	Motion	• Variety of applications	• May require reading
Yes	Visual	• Requires no equipment	ability
No	Audio	• Easily portable	• Not readily adapted for
		• Best for individual use	group work
Slides			
No	Motion	• Easy to produce	• Can get out of order or
Yes	Visual	• Easy to use	correct position
N/Y	Audio	• Pace controllable	• Mounting not standard
		• May be used with taped	possibly causing jams in
		narration	projector
		• Equipment fairly portable	• Room must be darkened
		• Adaptable for individual	for best use
		or large group use	
Filmstrips			
No	Motion	• Compact; Easy to use	• Easily damaged by torn
Yes	Visual	• Pace controllable	sprocket holes or
N/Y	Audio	• May be used with taped	scratching
		narration	• Difficult to produce
		• Cannot get out of order	locally
		• Equipment fairly portable	• Permanent sequence;
		• Adaptable for individual	Cannot be revised
		or large group use	• Room must be darkened
			for best use
Disc Recordings			
No	Motion	• Simple to operate;	• Easily scratched or
No	Visual	Equipment readily	warped
Yes	Audio	available	• Requires special storage
		• Equipment fairly portable	
		• Adaptable for individual	
		or large group use	
Compact Discs			
No	Motion	• Simple to operate	• Equipment not
No	Visual	• Equipment fairly portable	available in all
Yes	Audio	• Superior audio quality	locations yet
		• Durable; Compact	
		• More compact than	
		records	
		• Adaptable for individual	
		or large group use	

TABLE 6.1 *Continued*

	Advantages	Limitations
Audiocassettes		
No Motion N/Y Visual Yes Audio	• Easy to create and play • Equipment available, easy to operate, and portable • Compact; Requires minimal storage space • Can be combined with slides or filmstrips • Adaptable for individual or large group use	• Occasional problem with poor fidelity, hiss, and noise
16mm Films		
Yes Motion Yes Visual Yes Audio	• Combines visual motion with sound creating realistic image or manipulating time and space • Equipment available and easy to operate • Adaptable for individual use; Best for large groups	• Equipment heavy and bulky • Room must be darkened for best viewing • Fixed sequence and pace • Expensive equipment and materials
Videocassettes		
Yes Motion Yes Visual Yes Audio	• Combines visual motion with sound creating realistic image or manipulating time and space • Equipment available and easy to operate • May be locally produced • Best for individual or small group presentations	• Production quality varies from amateur to professional • Equipment not readily portable • Resolution limited for detail images • Large group viewing requires projection equipment
Computer Software		
N/Y Motion Yes Visual N/Y Audio	• Variety of applications • Some programs include motion and audio • Best for individual use	• May require reading ability • Equipment expensive and not portable • Programming complex

Adapted from Jerrold E. Kemp and Don C. Smellie. *Planning, Producing, and Using Instructional Media*. New York: Harper & Row, 1989.

Robert Heinich et al. *Instructional Media and the New Technologies of Instruction*. New York: John Wiley & Sons, 1982.

Wanda K. Johnston. "Audiovisual Instruction," Lincoln College faculty workshop handout, 1975.

Summarizing the "why," "who," and "how" of developing learning resources collections is the collection development policy. This broad policy statement clearly states the mission of the LRP in relation to the mission of the parent institution; identifies the population and programs which the LRP serves; describes the participants in the collection development process; defines the general criteria regarding selection; includes statements regarding problem areas; outlines methods of collection which do not require financial outlay; acknowledges cooperative agreements and networks; states support of intellectual freedom; and provides for collection renewal. [Gorman 31; Futas xiii]

According to Gorman, the following are reasons to adopt a collection development policy: It "1. Sets standards for procedures to be followed; 2. Reduces the likelihood of bias and personal influence; 3. Provides continuity despite staff changes; 4. Serves as an orientation device for new staff; 5. Provides guidelines for complaint handling; 6. Assists in weeding." [Gorman 196] Thus, collection development policies not only guide the selection process but also communicate the LRPs priorities in light of shrinking budgets, expanding information resources, limited space, and censorship challenge.

Challenging economic times, the information explosion, and changing technologies will increase the importance of the management aspect of collection development. LRP staff will review the cost benefits of adding information resources to the college's core collection versus accessing them through cooperative networks. Legal and financial aspects of copyright compliance and participation in resource sharing agreements will be resolved. Cooperative collection development and group purchase discounts will become a normal activity with interlibrary lending considered a central function of information access. The integration of information technologies will reduce the distinctions among different information formats, will bring the information to the user, and will impact access procedures. In conclusion, quoting Evans, "Whatever the future holds, one thing that is not likely to change is the intellectual challenge of creating the most appropriate resource collection for a community." [Evans 417]

Materials Acquisitions

Acquisitions is defined as the "process concerned with the ordering and receiving of materials through purchase, rental, free loan, gift, or local production; it begins when selection is completed." [Hicks 41] This is a business operation focusing on procuring the largest number of selected materials within the desired period of time. The organization and staffing of acquisitions is determined by the size, priorities, level of automation, and budget of the learning resources program. Specific acquisitions procedures follow guidelines set forth by state regulations, network cooperative purchase agreements, and the parent institution.

The Acquisitions Process

The acquisitions process generally includes three stages: preorder, firm order and recordkeeping, and materials receipt. The stages of this process may be modified to accommodate the variety of materials acquired, including nonprint materials and off-air video licenses, rental and free loan materials, donations, locally produced materials, as well as licensed teleconferences and telecourses with supplemental rights.

Materials requests come in a variety of forms ranging from a scribbled scrap of paper to initialed entries in bibliographies. Thus, the preorder stage involves converting bibliographic verification, source, and price data into a standardized format using a materials request form (Figure 6.1). Bibliographic verification and location of source and price data require searching title, author, or subject in standard print bibliographies, such as *Books In Print, Cumulative Book Index, Audiovisual Marketplace,* or NICEM publications; in CD-ROM acquisition systems, such as Ingram's LaserSearch, Bowker's *Books-In-Print Plus,* or Baker and Taylor's *B&T LINK;* in online databases and utilities, such as *A-V Online* or OCLC and WLN; or in publishers' catalogs. Rarely, if ever, are out-of-print titles searched and purchased. Duplication of ownership or order is checked through the public catalog, the "on order" file, and the "in process" file.

```
MATERIALS REQUEST FORM            | LRC Use ONLY
                                  |
 Title:                           |  __BIP+
                                  |  __CBI
                                  |  __OCLC
 Author:                          |  __NICEM
                                  |  __PubCat
 Publisher/Distributor:           |  __NoFind
                                  |     ------
 Year:     Edition:     Price:    |  __CCat
                                  |  __OnOrder
 Notes:                           |  __InProc
                                  |     ------
 Requested by:                    |
                                  |
 Review Source:                   |
```

FIGURE 6.1 Materials Request Form

The order and recordkeeping stage includes materials purchased, rental, or licensing of materials from appropriate sources by monitoring budget availability, following college requisition guidelines, ensuring copyright compliance, monitoring order status, and maintaining records of all correspondence until the title is received and the account is closed. Seldom do community colleges use blanket orders, approval plans, or exchanges in their acquisition process; instead, materials usually are ordered on a title by title basis, augmented by a continuation plan for selected reference works and subscription plans for periodicals and microforms which are reviewed annually.

Most colleges rely on the services of a jobber, such as Baker & Taylor, Brodart, Blackwell North American, or Ingram, and a few publishers to fill their orders. Through jobbers, acquisitions staff not only obtain a discounted purchase price but also economize on labor and obtain additional beneficial services, such as online ordering which expedites the order process, continuation services, and cataloging/processing services.

Monitoring the budget requires employing accounting techniques to maintain accurate and current balances on all budgeted acquisitions funds, including encumbering or setting aside funds as titles are ordered, reconciling the account as invoices are received or titles are cancelled, and providing a running balance. Effective budget monitoring also requires a knowledge of the annual ordering cycles for periodical and microform subscriptions and continuation orders. Record maintenance includes keeping order and receipt files, accounting records, vendor addresses and terms-of-purchase files, and correspondence files including claiming unfilled orders, cancelling orders, and correcting billing errors.

Receipt of materials involves checking the material received with the original order and ensuring the order is complete and the material undamaged. With nonprint materials, receipt requires checking the components for technical quality (i.e., proper audio in a video program or scratches in a film). Once the receipt of the material is approved, the item is passed on for cataloging while its "on order" status is changed to "in process" and notification of receipt is forwarded to the bookkeeper for payment.

Nonprint Materials Purchase or License

Acquisition of nonprint materials for purchase or license requires a modification to the acquisition process. Acquisitions staff verify the bibliographic data in the request and locate both the purchase and, as applicable, the rental sources and prices. Similar nonprint holdings in the collection are noted. This information, combined with format data, is entered onto the Materials Preview Evaluation (Figure 6.2). A preliminary cost-benefit analysis considering the economics of purchase versus rental, anticipated future

```
┌─────────────────────────────────────────────────────────────────────┐
│                    MATERIALS PREVIEW EVALUATION                        │
│                                                                        │
│  Title_____     │
│                                                                        │
│  Format_____ Length_____ B/W___ Color___         │
│                                                                        │
│  Producer/Distributor_____ Production Date_____        │
│                                                                        │
│  Purchase Price_____ : Rental Fee_____ Availability_____       │
│                                                                        │
│  Current holdings on subject_____       │
│                                                                        │
│  Materials Evaluation:                                                 │
│                                                                        │
│       Authenticity: accurate,                                          │
│          impartial, current    ___Excellent ___Good ___Poor           │
│       Appropriate for purpose:                                         │
│          concepts, data, scope,                                        │
│          vocabulary, treatment  ___Excellent ___Good ___Poor          │
│       Interest: credibility,                                           │
│          stimulation, appeal    ___Excellent ___Good ___Poor          │
│       Organization: logical,                                           │
│          balanced               ___Excellent ___Good ___Poor          │
│       Usefulness: format,                                              │
│          curriculum support,                                           │
│          long term value        ___Excellent ___Good ___Poor          │
│       Technical quality:                                               │
│          audio, visual          ___Excellent ___Good ___Poor          │
│                                                                        │
│  Curricular Support:                                                   │
│                                                                        │
│  Does this material fulfill a curricular need that is not served       │
│  through resources available in the Learning Resources Division?       │
│       ____Yes ____No                                                   │
│                                                                        │
│  If purchased, would use of this material by your students be          │
│       ____Required or ____Optional;                                    │
│       ____Self-instructional or ____Integrated into class lecture      │
│                                                                        │
│  On an annual basis, how many times would you estimate the program     │
│  will be used for your purposes? _____times per year          │
│  for which courses?_____        │
│                                                                        │
│  Recommendation:                                                       │
│                                                                        │
│  I recommend this material for ___Purchase ___Rental ___Neither        │
│                                                                        │
│  Signature_____ Date_____           │
│                                                                        │
└─────────────────────────────────────────────────────────────────────┘
```

FIGURE 6.2   Materials Preview Evaluation Form

use, and available funds determines whether the title should be ordered for preview.

If the program is to be off-air taped for potential licensing, a similar cost-benefit analysis is considered plus the "Guidelines for Off-the-Air Recording of Broadcast Programming for Educational Purposes" [Talab 40] are followed. Generally, a faculty member may request off-air taping of a program which may be shown in the classroom once during the first 10 days and reviewed during the next 35 days. After the 45-day holding period ends, the program must be erased or licensed for retention. Assistance obtaining off-air license information is available through the local educational television station, PBS Video, the Television Licensing Center, and the Great Plains National Instructional Television. [Talab 6–7] When a program is available both through commercial distribution and off-air licensing, the commercial production is commonly purchased.

Once the preorder stage is completed, the materials are previewed for purchase or license consideration. Nonprint previews ensure the materials meet the standards of quality desired, support the curriculum, and do not duplicate other materials available. The Materials Preview Evaluation form is completed and a final cost-benefit analysis reviewed. If the nonprint title is to be purchased, the preview copy is either returned or retained for purchase following the agreement with the distributor and the acquisitions process continues through the order and recordkeeping stage.

Rental and Free Loan Materials

Rental and free loan materials requests also require modification to the acquisitions process. Faculty members commonly request rental and free loan materials using a Materials Rental Request form (Figure 6.3) at least four weeks in advance of desired show date. However, to permit the most cost-effective rental of popular titles, six week or longer advance request is advised with provision of alternate showdates encouraged.

The preorder stage begins with the verification of the nonprint title ensuring the specific production (producer, actors, full or abridged) sought by the faculty member is requested. The rental or free loan source and fee are located using tools such as the *Educational Film & Video Locator*, the *Educators Guide to Free Materials*, university rental catalogs, producers catalogs, and *A-V Online*. Usually, materials rented from college and university media centers are available at a lower rental fee than those obtained from commercial sources. To determine cost-effectiveness, purchase source and price data as well as anticipated rental frequency are compared with the rental fee and availability. Rental need is established through a check of the public catalog and of the rental order file. Once the preorder process is completed and the decision to rent, purchase, or neither is made, the material is ordered through the accepted acquisition process.

Following receipt of the rental request, the distributor sends a written confirmation notice. Acquisitions staff, in turn, notify the faculty member of this confirmation through a Materials Confirmation Notice (Figure 6.4) a multipart form used for confirmation notice, arrival notice, audiovisual equipment request, rental material record, and office copy. [Koenig 50–51]

MATERIALS RENTAL REQUEST

Requestor:_____   Phone:_____Date:_____

Department:_____   Course #_____

To expedite your rental request, please provide complete
information. Provide showdate and alternate minimally one week
apart. We will not substitute date or rentals without your
authorization.

Title	Date		Source & Cat#	Fee		LRC USE ONLY			
	1st	2nd				PPrice	Freq	LH	RNT

FIGURE 6.3   Materials Rental Request

When the rental or free loan material arrives, the faculty member is notified and the material is routed to Circulation for distribution. The return
date is monitored to ensure the material is returned according to the agreement with the distributor. Once the material is returned, the courier or
postal return receipt is forwarded to the bookkeeper so the account can be
closed.

Donations and Other Acquisitions

The college's collection development statement includes a statement regarding its policy toward acceptance of donations or gifts. Generally, donations
are accepted with the understanding that the LRP retains the right to determine disposition. Acquisitions staff acknowledge the donation but cannot
legally appraise donations for tax purposes. Instead, an acknowledgement
letter on college stationery is sent: "XYZ Community College wishes to acknowledge with thanks your recent donation to the Learning Resources

```
                    MATERIALS CONFIRMATION NOTICE
    Title:_____        Instructor:_____

           _____        Department:_____

    Source:_____        Phone:_____ Office:_____

           _____        Confirmed Showdate:_____

           _____

    Order Code #_____    |   Date Received_____

    Rental Fee:_____    |   Date Due_____

    Format:  ___16mm ___Video      |   Date Returned_____

             ___Other_____   |   Date Invoiced_____

    Length:  _____minutes        |

    ___Confirmation ___Arrival ___AV Request ___Film Copy ___Office
```

FIGURE 6.4   Materials Confirmation Notice

Center." Some colleges also acknowledge receipt of donations through the College Foundation.

The materials donated are reviewed for retention based upon accepted selection criteria. Those selected for retention are checked for duplication in the collection and physical condition compared. The retained titles are routed to Cataloging while the remainder are set aside for booksales or disposed of appropriately.

Other acquisitions include locally produced materials from the Materials Design and Production Services, videotaped teleconferences from Teleconference Services, and telecourses with supplemental rights negotiated through Telecourse Support Services. These acquisitions are routed directly to the receipt stage of acquisitions where they are reviewed according to accepted selection criteria and checked for duplication in the collection. The retained titles are routed on to cataloging.

Interlibrary Loan

Resource sharing through interlibrary loan (ILL) services range from cooperation with other libraries to establish a print or CD-ROM union catalog, access to a national online bibliographic utility such as OCLC for holdings data, or participation in a regional online resource sharing network. Common to each resource sharing agreement is the compilation of holdings information, establishment of protocols for sharing these holdings, and creation of a delivery mechanism for both requests and materials. The information explosion, changing technologies, and increasing user demands are causing a steady increase in resource sharing. Use of the internet and document delivery systems will also affect ILL procedures.

Existing automation levels, staffing patterns, and interlibrary loan volume determine the placement of interlibrary loan services in the LRP. Common placement for ILL is in acquisitions with its verification and location sources and order procedures; however, some LRPs place ILL in reference where librarians can screen requests or in circulation where materials access is emphasized.

The preorder stage of ILL begins with bibliographic verification and location of the owner library. Due to their instructional support purpose, nonprint materials are rarely shared through ILL. For photocopy ILL requests, the guidelines developed by the National Commission on the New Technological Uses of Copyrighted Works (CONTU) must be followed. These guidelines place limitations on copying from periodicals and books and require libraries to maintain records proving adherence. Specifically, no more than five photocopies per year may be copied of articles published within the current five years of a periodical title or as long as the copyright is in force for a book. In addition, the requesting library must verify compliance with Section 108(g)(2) of the copyright guidelines on the ILL request form. [Miller 74–76, 127–128] In addition, acquisitions staff monitor ILL requests for collection development purposes. If a book or periodical title or specific subject is requested frequently, the title or subject area is reviewed for acquisition.

Following the preorder stage, the ILL request follows the accepted protocols of the resource sharing network and progresses through the order and recordkeeping and receipt stages of acquisitions. Most interlibrary loans are free; however, occasionally a fee is charged requiring additional accounting. Once the photocopy is received or the book is received and returned, the account is closed.

Cataloging

The purpose of the public catalog is to enable the user to easily identify and locate all the learning resources materials which may be useful in a given situation. Thus, the goal of Cataloging is to describe learning resources materials, to create access points from a controlled vocabulary, to assign call numbers grouping materials by subject, and to physically prepare them for circulation. Since community colleges serve a diverse student population and a broad curriculum, the desire to create a user-friendly public catalog and an accessible collection of materials affects cataloging decisions.

In most colleges, the decision to use either the Library of Congress or the Dewey Decimal Classification System has been made with no plan to undertake a cumbersome reclassification process. The Library of Congress system is used predominately in four-year colleges and universities with very large collections due to the system's growth potential and frequent revision and updating. The Dewey Decimal system is most frequently used in school and public libraries as well as many college libraries. Thus, the majority of community college students are familiar with the Dewey Decimal system. It arranges subjects from general to the specific in a logical order supporting standard research strategies. Consequently, the Dewey Decimal system is more appropriate for community college students.

The dictionary versus divided catalog decision is another decision. In the dictionary catalog, main, added, and subject entries are combined word by word into one alphabet. Divided catalogs separate main and added entries into one alphabet and subject entries into another. The dictionary catalog is more appropriate in a community college since it does not require the user to determine whether an author or title or subject entry is wanted, it interfiles works by and about an author, and it provides ample "see" and "see also" references. As CD-ROM and online public catalogs become more sophisticated, available access points will expand to include keyword, automatic switching (synonym operation), Boolean operations, and more eliminating this decision.

The all inclusive versus separate by format catalog decision is resolved through the philosophy and organization of the LRP. However, supportive of diverse student learning styles and abilities and of nonprint materials used in many vocational programs, most community colleges integrate all information resources, print and nonprint, into one public catalog. Thus, information on any subject and in any available format is consolidated in one location.

Use of the standard card catalog, the CD-ROM catalog, or an online catalog is the final decision. If the learning resources center is to remain the college's information center and is to assume responsibility of preparing users for accessing information throughout their lives, the necessity of moving from the manual card catalog toward a computer-based system exists. Other considerations include the high maintenance costs for the traditional card catalog, the improved ease and accuracy of file maintenance in a computer-based system, the initial hardware and retroconversion costs, and the potential to distribute holdings information via terminals to sites in and beyond the LRC.

In addition to the resolution of these decisions, Cataloging staffing and processes very based upon the size, level of automation, priorities, and budget of the learning resources program. The standards, protocols, and agreements of network memberships also affect staffing and processes.

The Cataloging Process

The cataloging process begins as materials are received from Acquisitions and ends when they are sent on to Circulation. The process generally includes cataloging and classification, file maintenance, and physical processing. Every title arriving in Cataloging is given a Cataloging Checklist to record its progress.

Cataloging and classification involves establishing the title's unique identity through a physical description, describing its contents through subject headings, and assigning a call number which groups materials by subject and permits location identification. Cataloging and classification date is obtained through commercial sources, copy cataloging, or through original cat-

```
Cataloging Checklist


____  Title received
       from Acquisitions

____  Cat and Class Check
       ____  Copy cat search
       ____  Edit or orig
              cat & class
       ____  Data entry

____  Physical process ck
       ____  Property stamp
       ____  Location labels
       ____  Package for use

____  File Maintenance ck
       ____  Activate record
       ____  Notif Requestor
       ____  Pull "In Proc"

____  Pass to Circulation

Please initial and date
  all of the above items.
```

FIGURE 6.5   Cataloging Checklist

aloging. Commercial cataloging involves the purchase of a catalog card set, the machine readable cataloging (MARC) record, and possibly full processing for each item. Sources include vendors such as Baker & Taylor, Brodart, and Gaylord. Colleges without the adequate staffing or which cannot afford to be members of a network use commercial cataloging services.

Copy cataloging involves using a cataloging record created elsewhere and modifying it to meet the college's unique requirements. Sources of copy cataloging are the Library of Congress's cataloging-in-publication (CIP) data, found on the verso of the title page; CD-ROM systems such as the Library Corporation's BiblioFile, General Research Corporation's LaserQuest, and Library of Congress's CDMARC Bibliographic; and online utilities such as OCLC Incorporated and WLN (Washington Library Network).

Most community college's rely on copy cataloging when available and complete original cataloging, creating a new record for the title, only when necessary. Thus, cataloging and classification requires a search for an existing cataloging record followed by the editing of the record as necessary. If the record is not available, original cataloging is completed. Some cataloging staff prefer to edit records at the computer keyboard while others prefer completing a Cataloging Workform (Figure 6.6), a preprinted template listing the standard categories of information required, prior to data entry and any requests for offline products.

Since the purpose of cataloging and classification is to help the user locate necessary information materials efficiently, Cataloging staff follow the *Anglo-American Cataloging Rules,* Second Edition (AACR2) guidelines for all book and nonbook formats. Figure 6.7 gives an example of nonprint cataloging using AACR2. For nonprint formats, special attention is given to the general material designation (GMD) following the title; the physical description describing components and program length; and the summary. Subject headings are selected with sensitivity to the varied vocabulary abilities among the community college population. Cross references are abundant. As feasible, colleges which have not yet shifted to a computer-based system are establishing a database of MARC records in preparation for the transition.

Physical processing includes property stamping or applying other ownership identification, affixing a call number and any unique location information, and physical packaging. Ownership identification and the call number are placed as uniformly as feasible on each item. To promote ease of access for multimedia materials, all components of a title are packaged in one container. The title and call number are placed on the container side in a visible manner. The main entry card or OPAC screen print is attached to the container cover to assist browsers.

Nonprint materials require additional special processing. For example, 16mm films require ample green leader and red trailer and the call number written on the leader. Phonograph records are usually stored in protective

```
                    CATALOGING WORKFORM


    Type:_____  Bib lvl:_____  Source:_____  Lang:_____

    Repr:_____  Enc lvl:_____  Conf pub:____  Ctry:_____

    Indx:_____  Mod rec:_____  Govt pub:____  Cont:_____

    Desc:_____  Int lvl:_____  Festschr:____  Illus:____
```

010	043
LCCN_____	Area Code_____
020	045
ISBN_____	Chron. Code_____
040	090::
Cat. Source_____	

```
1_ _ _ _  Main entry
_____

24_  _ _  Uniform title
_____

245   _ _  Title


          $h [                    ]
_____

250 Edition

260 Imprint
_____

300 Collation
_____

440 Series
_____

5_ _  Notes

520 Summary
_____


6_ _  _ _  Subject
_____

6_ _  _ _  Subject
_____

6_ _  _ _  Subject
_____

7_ _  _ _  Added entry
_____

7_ _  _ _  Added entry
_____

8_ _  _ _  Series
_____
```

FIGURE 6.6   OCLC Cataloging Workform

```
721.09   The Grain in the stone   [videorecording]
G75          / BBC-TV and Time-Life Films. --
            New York: Time-Life Multimedia, 1973.
            1 cassette (VHS)(52 min.) : sd.,
         col. ; 1/2 in. + discussion guide. --
         (Ascent of Man, no. 3.)
            SUMMARY:  Focuses on the architectural
         expressions of man throughout history.

            1. Architecture--History.
         2. Anthropology.  I. Bronowski, Jacob.
         II. Series.
```

FIGURE 6.7   Example of Nonprint Cataloging Using AACR2.   The format may vary with automation; however, browsers appreciate the complete data.

plastic jackets. Slides are loaded into a carousel tray with the ring locked. Audiocassettes and videocassettes have the record-protection tab removed. Computer software is packaged in its original container if sturdy or in a protective diskette holder with its documentation inside a binder, backup copies are copied as permitted by the license, and a copyright warning is affixed to the package of all circulating copies. [New 16]

Community college LRPs rarely bind periodicals. Instead, individual issues are circulated which increases accessibility. Most periodicals are retained only five years with longer runs of selected titles available in microfiche. Thus, periodical processing includes affixing a date label in the upper left corner of the cover, properly stamping the issue, and reinforcing the spine.

In addition, processing staff oversee the repair or replacement of damaged materials. Rarely, are books rebound; instead, they are mended as feasible or replaced with the same title or a similar more current one since community college collections are contemporary working collections, not research collections. Broken sprocket holes, weak splices, and damaged leader are repaired in 16mm films and filmstrips. Films and filmstrips are cleaned and lubricated periodically. Slides are remounted as necessary. Audio- and videocassettes are rewound periodically to prevent magnetic print-through of the message from one layer to the next.

File maintenance includes terminating the "in process" status of the title, activating its computer-based record or creating and filing its catalog cards, notifying the requestor or interested faculty of its receipt, and passing it on to Circulation. In addition, file maintenance involves maintaining the authority file, correcting errors found in the database, reclassifying titles for better access, and removing cataloging records for withdrawn titles.

Circulation

The objective of Circulation is to maximize the availability of information materials and to implement their use in an efficient and effective manner. Thus, materials from the learning resources center and those rented or borrowed from external sources are paired with supportive equipment and delivery systems for the benefit of the user. Community college LRCs provide materials in multiple formats to a variety of user groups through different delivery methods. Some materials are loaned for individual use outside the LRC. Some are restricted to use in the LRC or on LRC audiovisual equipment. Some materials are scheduled for classroom use or for distance learning.

User groups, such as student, faculty, staff, and special borrowers, are identified and a registration system is developed. This system is driven primarily by the college's student registration and faculty/staff payroll systems. Student and staff borrowers hold general college IDs which are additionally validated in the LRC if required. Special borrowers, such as alumni, faculty emeriti, and community residents, are registered individually with more restrictive borrowing privileges acknowledged and IDs issued.

Open stack versus closed stack and format separate versus format integrated shelving decisions affect collection access and control. Open stacks encourage browsing and encourage the LRC user's self-reliance in locating materials. Closed stacks lessen chances that the material will be mishandled, misplaced, or stolen and require the user to depend on the public catalog and circulation staff to obtain desired materials. Format separate shelving conserves space by grouping like formats together. Integrated shelving makes all materials retrievable to everyone and enhances browsing. As feasible, open stack, format integrated shelving is encouraged for community college LRCs. This arrangement encourages browsing, may lead a reluctant reader to a book, and treats all formats equally in accessibility and importance. Only reserve materials require closed shelving. Phonograph records, 16mm films, periodicals, and microforms require open stack, format separate shelving.

Charging overdue fines is a public relations issue affected by the size of the collection, the philosophy of the college, and the potential usefulness of a fine procedure in encouraging prompt return of materials. Another consideration is the cost-benefit of fines as related to the time developed to fine records and accounting and the lost good will. Alternatives include sending only reminders and billing the material as lost after thirty days overdue or sending only reminders and withholding semester grades until overdue obligations have been met.

Summarizing the "who," "what," and "how" of circulation is the circulation policy. This policy sets the framework for controlling the access, use, abuse, or theft of LRC materials and equipment. It identifies who may use which materials by describing privileges extended to students, faculty, staff, and special borrowers. It identifies available audiovisual equipment and material resources and notes any restrictions in access and loan period. It outlines procedures for renewals, recalls, overdue fines, and replacement fees for lost or damaged materials. Once established, this policy is widely publicized through signage, brochures and flyers, and student and faculty handbooks.

In addition to resolution of these decisions and the establishment of the circulation policy, circulation staffing and processes vary based upon size, level of automation, priorities, and budget of the learning resources program. Network membership agreements also affect circulation processes.

The Circulation Process

The circulation process generally includes obtaining the material and/or equipment, charging it to a user, checking and discharging it, recordkeeping, and reshelving. Most circulation transactions involve charging a print or nonprint material to an individual for use either outside the LRC or in the public access computer/audiovisual area. Unless the material is on reserve, the user will bring it from the open stacks and will present it with his LRC identification to circulation staff. If the material is on reserve, the user will present his LRC identification and request the title from circulation staff who will retrieve it from the closed reserve shelving.

Circulation staff then charge the loan of the material to the user. Charging records the loan transaction by matching the user's identification and the material borrowed with the due date. A variety of circulation systems exist ranging from manual card systems to computer-based systems, such as NOTIS and Innovative Interfaces. Whatever the system used, accuracy in detail, ease of use, and privacy for the user are essential.

Once the material is returned, it is checked for damage, missing components, and overdue status. If all is well, the material is discharged cancelling the loan record. If damage or missing components exist or if the material was overdue, appropriate billing or overdue fines are assessed following the established circulation policy. Damaged items are passed to Cataloging for repair and those with missing components are sent to Acquisitions for review and possible replacement.

Recordkeeping responsibilities include sending overdue reminders, handling billing and fine procedures, and maintaining statistical circulation data regarding collection use patterns. Circulation staff also participate in collection development by suggesting missing titles which need replacement and by monitoring user requests for holds and recalls suggesting the need for multiple copies.

Shelving requires the rapid return of the discharged material to the shelves for further use. Shelvers are also responsible for shelf-reading or monitoring the order and condition of the materials in the collection. Materials in need of repair are sent to Cataloging for repair.

Other general responsibilities of circulation staff include scheduling conference rooms, unjamming and filling photocopiers, shifting the collections as necessary, participating in collection inventories, and other miscellaneous responsibilities.

Audiovisual Equipment/ Materials Distribution

Audiovisual equipment and materials distribution is the circulation service which provides instructional support to the classroom or special events. This service may be provided through equipment pools centralized in the LRC, through equipment stored in each academic department or building, through media equipped classrooms, through special use classrooms in the LRC, and through campus cable systems. The audiovisual equipment and materials distribution process begins when the requestor completes an AV Equipment/Materials Request form (Figure 6.8). Circulation staff then schedule the equipment and material as requested and confirm its availability.

On the show date, the equipment and material is charged to the requestor and prepared for pick-up or delivered and set-up as requested. Once the scheduled use is complete, the equipment and material are returned or retrieved as agreed. Following use, the material is checked for completeness, repaired and cleaned as necessary, discharged, and reshelved. The equipment piece is checked for return of all accessories and for operation of all functions, is given basic preventative maintenance care (e.g., brushing the film path or cleaning the projection lens), and is discharged and reshelved for the next use or passed to Equipment Maintenance and Repair with an Equipment Malfunction Report (Figure 6.9), if necessary. Usage statistics are maintained.

AUDIOVISUAL EQUIPMENT/MATERIALS REQUEST

Name:_____   Class or Event:_____

Phone:_____   Address:_____

Use Date:_____   Time:_____ Until:_____

Location:_____

_____Deliver   _____Will Pick Up   _____Will Return_____

_____Operator   _____Set-Up   _____AV Pick-up_____

AV HARDWARE	AV MATERIALS
Projection Equipment:	Source/Material:
___16mm Projector	
___Carousel Slide Projector	___LRC Owned
___Overhead Projector	
___Opaque Projector	___Requestor Provides
___Sound/Slide Projector	
___Sound/Filmstrip Projector	___Rental/Free Loan/Preview
___Accessories_____	Title:_____
Audio Equipment:	Call #:_____
Playback Only	Format:_____
___Audiocassette	
___Reel-to-Reel Tape	Special Instructions:
___Record Player	
___Compact Disc Player	
___Portable PA	
___Accessories_____	
Record/Prod. Length_____	
___Audiocassette	
___Reel-to-Reel Tape	
___Accessories_____	
Video Equipment:	
Playback Only	
___1/2" VHS w/TV	
___3/4" UMatic w/TV	
___19" TV Receiver Only	Rcd by_____ Date____ Time____
___Accessories_____	Dlvd by_____ Date____ Time____
Record/Prod. Length_____	Rtd by_____ Date____ Time____
___Camcorder	Ckd by_____ Date____ Time____
___Accessories_____	Note:

FIGURE 6.8   AV Equipment/Materials Request Form

```
                    EQUIPMENT MALFUNCTION REPORT

     Please use this form for reporting equipment malfunctions.  The
     more specific you can be describing the problem, the quicker we
     can locate and remedy it.  Return this report to the LRC as soon
     as possible so repair action can be taken.  Thank you.

     Reported by:_____    Date:_____   Time:_____

     Type of Equipment:_____   ID Number:_____

     Location:_____

     Malfunction:    ___Lamp Doesn't Work      ___Film/Tape Jams

                     ___Rewind Doesn't Work    ___Film Won't Load

                     ___Sound Problem          ___No Power

                     ___Other_____

                     _____

                     _____
```

FIGURE 6.9   Equipment Malfunction Report

Reserve Materials

Materials may be placed in closed stack reserve by either discipline faculty or LRC staff. The purpose of reserve is to limit the loan period for a material permitting access to an increased number of users or to restrict its access, thereby increasing its security. Print and nonprint materials owned by the LRC or by the requesting faculty member may be placed on reserve by completing a Reserve Request form (Figure 6.10).

Since library reserve is considered an extension of the classroom, photocopied materials placed on reserve must comply with the copyright guidelines for classroom use. Generally, the guidelines permit single copies of research or preparation for teaching (e.g., an entire chapter from a book or a whole article, story, or poem), but are more restrictive for multiple copying for classroom use by requiring compliance with the tests of brevity, spontaneity, and cumulative effect. They further prohibit using either single or multiple copies of works to create or substitute for anthologies; to duplicate "consumable" work such as workbooks, standardized tests, exercises; to substitute for purchase of books or periodicals; or to be repeated from term to term. [Miller 116–118] In addition, the photocopied material must cite the source and carry the statement, "Notice: This material may be protected by copyright law (Title 17 U.S. Code)."

RESERVE REQUEST

Reserve materials must comply with copyright regulations.

Course and Number_____   Instructor_____

_____   Department_____

Check Loan Period: Phone_____ Office_____

____ 90 min. Library Use Only   Date of Assignment_____

____ 1 day loan   Number of Students_____

____ 3 day loan   Comments_____

____ 7 day loan   _____

Removal Date_____   _____

CALL NO.	TITLE	AUTHOR	SOURCE

FIGURE 6.10   Reserve Request Form

If the guidelines are not met or if the requestor plans to use the photocopied material another semester, copyright permission is required. To obtain permission, a request is sent, together with a self-addressed return envelope, to the permissions department of the publisher. The request includes the title, copyright date, author, material to be duplicated, number of copies, type of reprint, and purpose (Figure 6.11 is an example of a per-

COPYRIGHT PERMISSION REQUEST FOR LIBRARY RESERVE

To: _____ From: _____

_____ Date: _____

_____

We hereby request permission to make copies of the following information in order to place it on reserve in the Learning Resources Center at Broome Community College.

Author or Editor: _____

Article or Chapter Title: _____

Periodical or Book Title: _____

For Periodical - Volume # _____ Issue date _____ Pages _____ ISSN _____

For Book - Copyright date _____ Pages _____ ISBN _____

Number of copies to be placed on reserve: _____

Time item will remain on reserve: _____

These copies will be used exclusively for educational purposes, with no direct or indirect commercial advantage, and will include notice of copyright.

Please indicate your permission below and return this form within two weeks from the above date. A return envelope is enclosed for your convenience.

☐ Permission granted.

☐ Permission granted with the following restrictions: _____

_____

☐ Permission denied. (If so, is there another means by which we can make this material available to a large number of students?)
     ☐ Alternate Source: _____

Name *(Typed)* _____ Position _____

Signature _____ Date _____

FIGURE 6.11 Permission Letter for Reserve Photocopies (Courtesy of Broome Community College)

mission request letter.) If permission is denied, alternatives include not using the material, purchasing reprints if available, or licensing the materials through the Copyright Clearance Center, 21 Congress Street, Salem, MA 01970.

Equipment Maintenance and Repair

The purpose of Equipment Maintenance and Repair is to ensure the availability of reliable, well-maintained computer and audiovisual equipment campuswide permitting the effective use of information materials. Thus, the primary responsibility of the equipment technician is to maintain and repair computer and audiovisual equipment, to recommend purchase or rental of equipment, to prepare it for distribution, and to assist with special related projects.

The centralized versus decentralized equipment purchasing issue requires resolution with all orders for equipment purchases processed through the LRC. Centralized purchasing permits standardization of brands and models ensuring cost-effective stocking of replacement parts and lamps, encouraging ease of operation for users, and permitting exchanges from the college equipment pool during repair. [Vlcek 116]

The commercial versus institutional maintenance issue requires a cost-benefit analysis comparing the volume, cost, proximity, and turnaround time for commercial repair with the development of a repair facility including space, staffing, test equipment, and parts inventory. A smaller college may find it most cost-effective to hire a repair generalist to perform basic preventative maintenance and repairs and to send complex repairs to a commercial repair service.

The size, the organizational structure, level of computer use campuswide, service priorities, and budget of the learning resources program affect Equipment Maintenance and Repair staffing, responsibilities, and procedures. Some colleges assign this area responsibility to design special media facilities and to provide large scale audio support for special events. Some colleges merge responsibility for telecommunications into this area. Some colleges separate maintenance and repair of audiovisual and computer equipment into separate service areas. All these decisions affect Equipment Maintenance and Repair staffing and procedures.

Equipment Services

The equipment maintenance program includes preventative maintenance, breakdown maintenance, and recordkeeping. The preventative maintenance program services equipment and makes repairs before a breakdown occurs. Following maintenance instruction included in equipment service manuals, equipment is cleaned and lubricated, parts are inspected and tested, and worn parts are replaced prior to breakdown. Many colleges focus on summer as the peak time for preventative maintenance and review heavily used equipment more frequently based upon experience, the manufacturer's recommendation, and staff availability.

Breakdown maintenance occurs when the equipment fails and repairs are necessary. Notification of needed equipment repair comes either through the written Equipment Malfunction Report or through a telephone call for help. Malfunctioning equipment first is checked for operator error, such as unit unplugged, incorrect threading, etc. If it does need repair, the equipment history is checked for warranty coverage either due to recent purchase or due to recent repair and for past repair history and cost-effectiveness of repair. The equipment is then either repaired through a commercial service or in the college's repair area or it is withdrawn from the inventory.

Equipment history records like Figure 6.12 are maintained for each piece of equipment. These records bring together purchase cost and date; special lamp, stylus, or battery requirements; and maintenance and repair history including cause and frequency of repair, and resulting repair costs. These records help the technician identify consistent breakdowns resulting from a misalignment or other cause and help identify pieces of equipment which should be replaced rather than repaired.

Equipment Selection and Purchase

The equipment selection and purchase process includes determining need, selecting the appropriate equipment, purchasing it, and preparing it for distribution. Equipment is purchased to resolve replacement or additional equipment needs. The need to replace equipment is based upon its reliability and the cost-effectiveness of its repair. The need to purchase additional equipment is determined by user demand for larger quantities, for upgraded models with desired features, and for use of new information formats. An analysis of equipment age, use patterns, and advances in technology results in a long-range equipment replacement plan. Table 6.2 lists the life-spans of various types of information access equipment. *The Equipment Directory of Video, Computer, and Audio-Visual Products,* trade show participation, and publications such as *Tech Trends, Educational and Industrial Television,* and *InfoWorld* introduce new equipment and provide price data for planning purposes.

General criteria for selecting equipment includes usefulness, performance, compatibility, portability, ease of operation, reliability, safety, cost-benefit, repairability and service, and reputation and warranty. [Vlcek 119] Additional criteria specific to the equipment's intended use is considered. Most colleges standardize equipment makes and models whenever possible

```
                    EQUIPMENT HISTORY RECORD

Description:_____

      Make:_____  Model:_____  Serial #:_____

      College ID#:_____  Other:_____
Supplier:_____

      P.O.#:_____  Date:_____  Price:_____

Remarks:  Lamp:_____  Stylus:_____  Battery:_____

      _____


Maintenance Record:

Date | Repairs                          | Parts | Labor | Total
```

FIGURE 6.12 Equipment History Record

to simplify use of equipment and to reduce maintenance problems. Equipment selection techniques include competitive testing or demonstration, equipment evaluation forms, and review of specifications.

College and state purchasing regulations guide the equipment purchase process; however, the process generally requires a request for bid or quotation. This request for bid or quotation may be a short form listing only the brand name and model number with additional requirements, such as provision of a maintenance manual and parts list and one year warranty, or a long form listing exact equipment requirements in detail, such as lamp size and aperture, length of power cord, weight, warranty, etc., as well as any

TABLE 6.2 Longevity and/or Obsolescence of Information Access Equipment

Equipment Type	Years
16mm projector	10
Slide projector	11
Sound slide projector	8
Sound filmstrip projector	9
Overhead projector	11
Opaque projector	14
Audiocassette recorder	9
Record player	9
Portable PA system	7
Videocassette recorder	7
Television monitor/receiver	9
Video camera/camcorder	5
Microcomputer system	5
LCD panel	4
Video projector	5
CD-ROM player	5
Microform reader/printer	6
Telefacsimile equipment	3

Rapid changes in technology affect equipment life spans
as obsolescence becomes as great a factor as longevity.

unique specifications. Some colleges include a "service what you sell" phrase or require the vendor to be a franchised dealer for the equipment being bid to ensure warranty coverage and efficient repair service. Some include as statement "If dealer suggests alternate, all technical data must be provided and a unit made available for evaluation." [Schmid 135–138] Following the bid process and selection of vendor, standard purchase procedures are followed.

Once the equipment arrives, all functions are tested and accessories noted. The equipment piece is placed on the inventory and marked with appropriate identification logos and numbers. An Equipment History Record is created and the equipment is placed into service. Spare lamps, batteries, etc. are ordered as necessary.

Summary

The learning resources program provides access to desired information through the college's own collection of materials or through those borrowed or rented from external sources paired with appropriate supportive equipment permitting their effective use. Access Services acquires, organizes, and distributes these materials and supportive equipment necessary to convey the desired information. The college's collection development policy provides a framework for the selection and acquisition of these materials. Access Services includes materials acquisitions through purchase, rental or free loan, donation, or interlibrary loan; cataloging; circulation of materials and related equipment; and equipment maintenance and repair.

Selected Bibliography

BLEIL, LESLIE A., and CHARLENE RENNER. "Copy Cataloging and the Bibliographic Networks." In *Technical Services Today and Tomorrow*, ed. Michael Gorman. Englewood, CO: Libraries Unlimited, 1990.

BLOOMBERG, MARTY, and G. EDWARD EVANS. *Introduction for Technical Services for Library Technicians*. 5th ed. Littleton, CO: Libraries Unlimited, 1985.

BREIVIK, PATRICIA SENN, and E. GORDON GEE. *Information Literacy: Revolution in the Library*. New York: American Council on Education, 1989.

———. "Librarians Prepare for an Information Age," *Educational Record* 70 (Winter 1989): 13–19.

DESMARAIS, NORMAN. *The Librarian's CD-ROM Handbook*. Westport, CT: Meckler, 1989.

EVANS, G. EDWARD. *Developing Library and Information Center Collections*. Second Edition. Littleton, CO: Libraries Unlimited, 1987.

FLEISCHER, EUGENE, and HELEN GOODMAN. *Cataloging Audiovisual Materials: A Manual Based on the Anglo-American Cataloguing Rules II*. New York: Neal-Schuman, 1980.

FUTAS, ELIZABETH. *Library Acquisition Policies and Procedures*. Phoenix: Oryx Press, 1977.

GARDNER, RICHARD K. *Library Collections: Their Origin, Selection, and Development*. New York: McGraw-Hill, 1981.

GORMAN, G.E., and B.R. HOWES. *Collection Development for Libraries*. London: Bowker-Saur, 1989.

"Guidelines for Audiovisual Services in Academic Libraries," *College & Research Libraries News* 48 (October 1987): 533–536.

HEINICH, ROBERT, ET AL. *Instructional Media and the New Technologies of Instruction*. New York: John Wiley & Sons, 1982.

HERMENZE, JENNIE. "The Classics Will Circulate!" *Library Journal* 107 (November 15, 1981): 2191–2195.

HICKS, WARREN B., and ALMA M. TILLIN. *Developing Multi-Media Libraries*. New York: R.R. Bowker, 1970.

HUBBARD, WILLIAM J. *Stack Management: A Practical Guide to Shelving and Maintaining Library Collections*. Chicago: American Library Association, 1981.

KATZ, WILLIAM A. *Collection Development: The Selection of Materials for Libraries*. New York: Holt, Rinehart and Winston, 1980.

KEMP, JERROLD E., and DON C. SMELLIE. *Planning, Producing, and Using Instructional Media.* New York: Harper & Row, 1989.

KOENIG, DAN. "Streamline Your Handling of Free-Loan Films," *Audiovisual Instruction* 22 (November 1977): 50–51.

MILLER, JEROME K. *Applying the New Copyright Law: A Guide for Educators and Librarians.* Chicago: American Library Association, 1979.

"New Regulations for Computer Software Lending," *Library Journal* 116 (May 15, 1991): 16.

NIEMEYER, DANIEL, and BARBARA A. BLACK. "Deliver Media Services . . ." *Tech Trends* 34 (November/December 1989): 34–39.

OLSON, NANCY B. *Cataloging of Audiovisual Materials.* 3rd Edition. DeKalb, IL: Media Marketing Group, 1991.

POST, RICHARD. "Longevity and Depreciation of Audiovisual Equipment," *Tech Trends* 32 (November 1987): 12-14.

SCHMID, WILLIAM T. *Media Center Management: A Practical Guide.* New York: Hastings House, 1980.

SCHMIDT, KAREN A. "Acquisitions: The Ordering, Claiming, and Receipt of Materials." In *Technical Services Today and Tomorrow,* ed. Michael Gorman. Englewood, CO: Libraries Unlimited, 1990.

"Standards for Community, Junior, and Technical College Learning Resources Programs," *College & Research Libraries News* 51 (September 1990): 757–767.

TALAB, R.S. *Copyright and Instructional Technologies: A Guide to Fair Use and Permissions Procedures.* 2nd Ed. Washington, DC: Association for Educational Communications and Technology, 1989.

VEIHMAN, ROBERT A. "Some Thoughts on Intershelving," *Audiovisual Instruction* 18 (March 1973): 87–88.

VLCEK, CHARLES W., and RAYMOND V. WIMAN. *Managing Media Services: Theory and Practice.* Englewood, CO: Libraries Unlimited, 1989.

WEIL, BEN H., and BARBARA F. POLANSKY, ed. Modern Copyright Fundamentals: Key Writings on Technological and Other Issues. NY: ASIS, 1989.

WYNAR, BOHDAN S. *Introduction to Cataloging and Classification.* 7th Ed. by Arlene G. Taylor. Littleton, CO: Libraries Unlimited, 1985.

7

User Services

In addition to providing access to and delivery of information, the learning resources program provides assistance in locating or creating and using information resources to serve the instructional and informational needs of the college's students, faculty, administration, and broader college community. Learning resources staff are actively involved in the total educational program through "participation in curriculum development and approval because the identification and acquisition of resources to support any curricular changes requires time for planning services that may be needed, reading lists that could be provided, bibliographical instruction that must be given, and priorities on use of resources that should be given." [Standards 758] Thus, learning resources staff facilitate learning indirectly by supporting and expanding classroom instruction and directly by teaching students the information-seeking skills necessary for their immediate academic success and lifelong learning.

In addition, learning resources staff support the informational needs of the college through providing location and interpretation assistance with the information desired for students' class assignments, for faculty's preparation of class presentations, for individual research, and for campuswide strategic planning purposes. In many institutions, learning resources staff also maintain the college archives, lead the staff development program, facilitate grantsmanship efforts, oversee the teaching resources center, coordinate learning assistance laboratories, and more.

Within the Learning Resources Division, User Services provides the services which help students, faculty, administrators, and, on some campuses, community residents use the resources available through direct information assistance and bibliographic instruction; through instructional design assistance and materials production; and through other specialized services. At some colleges, User Services assume responsibility for direct instruction of communications classes. Others include telecommunications support as part of User Services.

This chapter summarizes the provision of information services, instructional design/production services, and other specialized services available through User Services. The examples reflect a composite of successful procedures and forms from community colleges nationwide.

Information Services

The purpose of Information Services is to provide direct assistance to the LRC user in locating and using the information resources available in the LRC and beyond. Thus, information specialists help access and interpret available resources in relation to the requestor's purpose and ability. All possible resources—print, nonprint, and electronic formats, in the reference and general collections, on site and beyond—are used.

Technology has expanded the role of information specialists from only assisting with the LRC's on site resources to also accessing a global network of knowledge containing all types of information in all types of formats. Information specialists use and provide guidance with on site resources in print, nonprint, and electronic formats as well as with remotely accessible databases. They are equally comfortable using print resources, CD-ROM tools, online databases, or audiovisual resources as information sources. They evaluate information needs and resolve them via the most appropriate method.

The size, organizational structure, level of computer use campuswide, service priorities, and budget of the learning resources program affect Information Services staffing, responsibilities, and procedures. Most colleges follow the integrated model of academic librarianship in which the information specialists provide direct information assistance in addition to fulfilling responsibilities for bibliographic instruction, collection development, and other specialized services. These specialized services include maintenance of the college archives, coordination of displays and other promotional activities, creation of special subject bibliographies, development of area resource files, etc.

In addition, many college learning resources programs promote liaison activities in which each information specialist is assigned to one or more instructional programs on campus. The specialist participates in formal department meetings, informal conversations, and other activities to determine ways the LRC can augment the educational process.

Information Assistance

The diversity of the college community served separates community college information services from those at other academic institutions. The purpose for the information sought may be to help transfer, vocational, or developmental students fulfill class assignments, to assist faculty members in updating their instruction content or research student learning styles, to monitor demographic and employment trends for administrative strategic planning, or to gather information supporting a community resident's personal interests. The ability of LRC users range from the holder of a Ph.D. to the developmental student, from the information-seeker who is a skilled researcher to the one paralyzed with library anxiety, from the person who gathers information conceptually through reading to the one who requires concrete visual or aural information, and more.

This diversity in population served affects the acquisition and organization of available information resources. Since the majority of the student population are part-time students juggling family, work, and college responsibilities, should the reference collection be lean with more resources available for circulation? Should duplicate titles be acquired with one copy placed in reference and one in the circulating collection? Should information resources be made available in a variety of formats and readily accessible to the user? These questions are resolved with a sensitivity and responsiveness to the needs of the diverse population served. Lean reference collections, duplicate titles as feasible, and varied information resources are the community college norm. Electronic tools, such as Wilson's *Readers Guide Abstracts*, Microsoft's *American Heritage Dictionary*, or Grolier's *Academic American Encyclopedia*, attract developmental students to try information resources as well as assist the more sophisticated LRC user.

If the information sought is not available on site, should online search services, leading to full text or bibliographic citation for interlibrary loan access, be provided as part of information assistance? Funding availability and philosophy generally affect the answer to this question; however, community colleges tend to provide free online services to faculty, administration, staff, and students more frequently than other academic institutions. [Johnston 377] In addition, they actively participate in cooperative resource sharing networks resulting in either interlibrary loan services or in direct access to cooperating libraries.

As an institution of higher education, the community college's primary mission is instruction. Information specialists share this responsibility by helping LRC users develop information-seeking skills both serving their immediate needs as well as developing their lifelong information literacy skills. Should the information-seeker be expected to locate his own information with the guidance of the information specialist or should he expect the provision of complete information without participating in the search? The decision of how much one-on-one LRC instruction to include while providing information assistance is determined on a case by case basis in accordance with institutional LRP guidelines.

The information assistance process begins with the information interview in which the request for information and its purpose are clarified. The information specialist actively listens to the information-seeker and clarifies the information need by seeking content background, checking perceptions, and using verbal and nonverbal communication skills. Once the information need is determined, the specialist determines the print, nonprint, or electronic resources to consult and conducts the information search accessing both on site and external resources. As appropriate, the information-seeker participates in the search learning lifelong information gathering skills in the process. When the information is found, the information specialist and information-seeker evaluate the usefulness of the answer and continue or modify the search as necessary until the information need has been satisfied.

At the conclusion of providing information assistance, the specialist marks the Information Assistance Tally (Figure 7.1) form located at the reference desk. This tally form records the quantity of questions and patterns of use for purposes of ensuring adequate staffing, noting needed point-of-use instructional aids and signage, and sharing comments regarding unusual questions and assignments, etc.

Information services specialists also promote and provide LRP services through compilation of special subject reading lists, creation of displays promoting special interests or services, encouraging "assignment alerts" through which they ensure appropriate supportive resources are available, and more.

Bibliographic Instruction

The goal of academic bibliographic instruction is to teach LRC users how to use the LRC in particular and libraries in general—the who, what, when, where, why, and how of library use. Its role "is not only to provide students with the specific skills needed to complete assignments, but to prepare individuals to make effective life-long use of information, information sources, and information systems." [Model 257] Bibliographic instruction is a facet of the broader concept of information literacy.

The Middle States Association of Colleges and Schools has taken a lead among regional accrediting agencies by including information literacy in its outcomes assessment. "Of particular interest to Middle States is the extent

```
INFORMATION ASSISTANCE TALLY

Date_____
```

| TIME | LOCATION | | QUESTIONS | | |
	Desk	Phone	Reference	TYPE Direction	Equipment
7:30 – 10:00					
10:00 – 12:30					
12:30 – 2:30					
2:30 – 4:30					
4:30 – 10:00					

```
SPECIAL NOTES/QUESTIONS/ASSIGNMENTS:

_____

_____

_____

_____

_____
```

FIGURE 7.1   Information Assistance Tally

to which students have mastered the ability to retrieve and use information. Most often, learning in this area begins with the courses offered in the general education program, and is refined as students move into more specialized curricula." [Framework 18] This increased emphasis on information literacy and course-integrated instruction will impact bibliographic instruction throughout the nation. In addition, community colleges are actively exploring articulation programs which bridge the gap between high schools and community colleges expanding the LRC user population.

Given the community college's mission, its varied curricula, and diverse population served, information services specialists develop instructional programs which offer various approaches to bibliographic instruction. "Ideally, the program would incorporate the following key elements of adult education: 1. several starting levels, 2. several profitable points of termination, 3. several rates of advancement." [Janney 16] In addition, Breivik cites six elements "that must be part of any good learning experience: it imitates reality; is active, not passive; is individualized; makes provision for a variety of learning styles; is up-to-date; and finally, is essential to lifelong learning." [Ford 33]

Consequently, community college bibliographic instruction commonly follows three modes: group instruction including either general orientation or specific course-integrated lessons; point-of-use instruction including pathfinders, signage, computer help screens, audiocassettes, etc.; and individualized instruction by information specialists. Instructional content consists of three levels of complexity: general procedural and location orientation; introduction to basic library tools including the card catalog, indexes, and general reference books; and instruction in the use of advanced and/or specialized reference tools. Electronic resources are included in the instruction program as additional tools for locating relevant information. The bibliographic instruction program is integrated into the student's broader educational goals and permits him to select from a variety of instructional alternatives.

Bibliographic instruction is an integral part of the curriculum for many courses, such as developmental reading, English composition, career English, technical writing, and introductory courses in most vocational programs. For group instruction, information specialists create goals and instructional plans for each course to ensure consistency in inclusiveness and presentation. For example, the goals for Developmental Reading 020 may be that students should feel comfortable in the learning resources center, be aware of the variety of resources available, be able to use the catalog and find desired resources, view the learning resources center as a source of information and recreational resources, and know that LRP staff are available to help. In contrast, goals for English Composition II emphasize that students should reinforce research skills already acquired, develop advanced research and critical evaluation skills, understand how these skills will transfer to other libraries and throughout life, and know that LRP staff are available to help. Special subject instruction for vocational students introduces the learning resources center including its resources and their use, explains how this information will transfer to other libraries and throughout life, and focuses on the professional literature in their field.

Although group instruction follows standard instructional goals and plans, instructional pace and techniques are varied to accommodate the students participating. For example, honors sections receive the same information at a more rapid pace; summer classes include more students from other colleges and require greater emphasis on local procedures and transferability of skills; evening students are frequently older and more motivated and require more pragmatic examples. The method of instruction may include lecture, visual, audiovisual, and print resources.

Not all LRC users are enrolled in classes which include bibliographic instruction. Some are uncomfortable asking a librarian for help. Others just want to use the resources immediately. For these LRC users, point-of-use instructional aids such as Figure 7.2 are necessary. Brochures, signage, and self-guided walking tours introduce the LRC by providing LRC hours, floorplans, resources, and services are commonly used. Near the catalog is instructional signage explaining its use plus if an online public access catalog (OPAC) is used, introductory and help screens as well as command prompts are provided. Specialized aids for paper and electronic indexes, including a statement of purpose for the index and a sample entry with explanatory labels, are posted near each index. Search strategy hints may be provided.

Additional individualized instruction resources include special subject pathfinders responding to course-related group instruction and assignments as well as frequent library user requests. Such pathfinders may include "How to Find Book Reviews," "Dietetic Technology," or "Researching an Employer." Each pathfinder includes a selective bibliography of reference resources, suggested subject headings for the catalog and indexes, a list of related periodicals which contain pertinent information, and encouragement to ask an information specialist for further assistance. LRC users are invited to take desired pathfinders for their use.

Increased use of the newer technologies has impacted the scope and content of bibliographic instruction. Instruction content has been expanded to include a conceptual foundation of information generation, organization, and retrieval followed by "the critical evaluation of any information: how it was gathered, its currency, the principles by which it was selected, its intended audience, its implicit or explicit biases. Students would be encouraged to work in an orderly way, first considering the various aspects of a topic, then honing in on a single one for research, and next identifying key issues, terms, and tools for accomplishing their research." [Dunn 220] In addition to conceptual instruction in information storage and retrieval and critical thinking, procedural instruction to introduce each system's unique file structure, command language, and other idiosyncrasies, as well as techniques for subject searching, multi-database access, and more are added.

PERIODICAL ABSTRACTS ONDISC
SEARCH STRATEGIES

COMBINING SEARCH TERMS

AND   Both terms must be present. Use to narrow a search.

 abuse *and* elderly

OR   Either the first or the second term may be present.
                 Use to expand a search by including synonyms.

 elderly *or* aged

AND NOT   The first term but not the second term must be present.

 abuse *and not* child

COMBINE SETS   Type set numbers within square brackets.
                   For example, to combine set(1) abuse and set(2) elderly or aged, type [1] and [2]

PARENTHESES   Expressions within parentheses are processed first.
                   abuse and (elderly or aged)

TRUNCATION   Use a ? at the end of a word to find variant forms or variant spellings.
                   advertis? retrieves advertisements, advertising, advertisers

SEARCHING BY FIELD   A search can be restricted to a specified field rather than the entire record.
                         Use the code followed by the search term in parentheses.

Field	Search Form	Example
subject	su(subject term)	su(older people)
author	au(last, first)	au(safire, william)
date	da(date)	da(1990)
journal title	jo(title of journal)	jo(rolling stone)
company	co(name of company)	co(boeing)
type	ty(type of article-editorial, review, interview, speech, etc.)	ty(review)
special feature	sf(graph, map, photograph, etc.)	sf(illustration)

For additional field codes, see a reference librarian.

FIGURE 7.2   Point-of-Use Instructional Aid

Selection of Materials

Collection development is a responsibility shared among discipline faculty and all LRP staff. However, due to their direct interaction with learning resources users as well as their liaison activities and participation on the college curriculum committee, information services specialists hold major responsibility for the overall quality and balance of available information re-sources. Thus, they select materials in all subject areas and in a variety of formats with the goal of ensuring a balanced, quality collection responsive to the mission of the institution.

Selection is usually a title-by-title process following the general guidelines of the LRP's collection development policy, as discussed in Chapter 6. The selection process begins with a knowledge of the population served, of the existing campus resources, and of the realm of resources available. With this basic awareness, general evaluative criteria judging the quality of the re-source in terms of its content and presentation are used. Since the LRP serves a heterogeneous user population, information resources are selected representing all ability levels and standard formats. Therefore, more specific criteria include authority of creators, scope of coverage, treatment and level, arrangement, format, and special features. [Gorman 194–195]

Information services specialists rely on current and retrospective selection aids. Forthcoming and current reviews are available in library-oriented re-view journals including *Choice, Library Journal, Booklist,* and *New Technical Books.* Popular current reviews are available in sources such as the *New York Times Book Review, Newsweek,* and *Time.* Special subject reviews are published in publications such as *Nursing Outlook, RQ, Selected U.S. Government Publications,* and *PC Magazine.* In addition, *Library Journal* frequently devotes special issues to "best" titles in selected subject areas. Commercial sources, such as publishers catalogs and jobbers selection plans, promote current titles. These commercial sources can be useful due to their timeliness and scope, but must be approached with caution since they are not selective.

Retrospective lists include core and award lists as well as special subject bibliographies and are used for focused collection development projects. Utilization of any retrospective list requires cautious analysis of the purpose and intended audience of the list. For example, *Books for College Libraries,* 3rd ed., represents a basic collection supporting the curriculum of four-year institutions. There are no up-to-date resources on core collections for com-munity colleges. As an attempt to fill this need, *Choice* is planning to publish several specialized bibliographies per year of interest to community college librarians, with the first published June 1991 on welding. [Annotated 1590] In addition, the American Library Association distributes pamphlets listing the "Outstanding Books for the College Bound" in various subject areas as well as "Contemporary Classics 1944–1980." Special subject bibliographies include titles such as *Information Sources in Science and Technology, Core Collection in Nursing and the Allied Health Sciences: Books, Journals, Me-dia, Business Information: How to Find It, How to Use It,* and *High/Low Handbook: Encouraging Literacy in the 1990s.*

Just as materials selection is a necessary aspect of collection development, so is weeding. Weeding is defined as "the process of removing material from the open shelves of a library and reassessing its value in terms of current needs." [Gorman 323] Thus, weeding complements the selection process in collection development.

Unlike the research library whose goal is to provide an archive for all knowledge, the community college learning resources center provides a working collection of materials intended to serve specific uses, then after that period of usefulness is over and/or specific titles are superseded, the materials no longer justifying their retention are withdrawn. Weeding increases convenient access to a quality collection by removing unwanted titles which hinder ease of use. Collection quality is not determined by the quantity of titles owned; instead, it is measured by how successfully the needs of the students, faculty, administrators, and the broader college community are served.

The LRP's collection development policy commonly addresses the process and general criteria for weeding. Weeding is a continuing responsibility of the information systems librarians. Librarians often divide weeding responsibilities by subject to correlate with the departments to which they serve as liaisons. The criteria for retention parallel those of selection while consideration for withdrawal may include age or obsolescence, physical condition, number of copies in the collection, coverage of the subject by other materials, use, and value to the collection.

The weeding process involves a title-by-title review of the collection noting especially the condition of the item and its content. The information specialist makes a list of subjects as well as specific titles needing updating or replacement and selects for purchase appropriate titles. The information specialist also pulls titles recommended for weeding and inserts into each a withdrawal slip with Figure 7.3 indicating reason for discarding. These titles are then made available for review by other LRP staff as well as by discipline faculty. Once the review period expires, cataloging staff adjust the records of ownership, statistically record the withdrawal, stamp the item "DISCARDED," and dispose of it according to institution guidelines.

Instructional Development and Production Services

The purpose of instructional development and production services is to assist with the selection or creation of a systematic instructional program re-

```
┌─────────────────────────────────────────┐
│          WITHDRAWAL SLIP                 │
│                                          │
│  Reason Withdrawn                        │
│                                          │
│     ___Condition of Item                 │
│           ___Replace?                    │
│                                          │
│     ___Content                           │
│           ___Outdated Information        │
│           ___New Edition on Shelf        │
│           ___More Current Titles         │
│                  on Subject on Shelf     │
│           ___Other_____         │
│                                          │
│     ___Use                               │
│        Not Circulated Since              │
│                                          │
│        _____          │
│                                          │
│     ___Reclassify for Improved           │
│        Access                            │
│                                          │
│                                          │
│  Faculty Review                          │
│                                          │
│  ___Discard                              │
│                                          │
│  ___Withdraw and reassign to             │
│                                          │
│     _____             │
│                                          │
│  ___Retain in Collection                 │
│                                          │
│        Signed:_____          │
│                                          │
└─────────────────────────────────────────┘
```

FIGURE 7.3   Withdrawal Slip

sulting in desired behavioral or learning outcomes. Kemp identified three hierarchical levels of subsequent production services. Most basic is mechanical preparation which includes the preparation of materials using routine techniques, such as mounting illustrations, photographic copy work, video dubbing, etc. Next is the creative production level which involves more inventive production of materials requiring decisions concerning subject matter, content, and format of the product, such as production of slide/tape presentations, video programs, etc. Most complex is the conceptual design level which involves the development of materials supporting the systematic process of instructional development. [Dayton 21]

As the content faculty member's role is shifting from primarily dispensing information in a classroom to creating a learning culture with students responsible for their own learning, the role of the instructional development

(ID) specialist also is shifting toward the higher conceptual design level of service. Nearly every community college offers mechanical production services and most provide higher level creative and conceptual design services. Increasingly, the ID specialist not only is preparing, providing, and assisting with the use of media, but also is "offering guidance and participating in actions that affected curriculum decisions, including writing objectives, organizing content, selecting activities, assigning media functions, formulating evaluations, and interpreting results." [Kemp, 1991, 14] He is helping the faculty member use instructional technology more effectively to create optimal learning experiences suitable for a diverse student population.

In addition to helping faculty members develop instructional programs, instructional development and production services also assist students with course projects, support LRP staff needs for faculty development workshops or in service training, and develop presentations for administrators and public relations staff. The college size, service priorities, and budget affect its staffing, responsibilities, and procedures. The college LRP production policy summarizes services provided, charges for services if any, service priorities and advance preparation time, copyright and proprietary rights agreements, technology and resources available on campus, research and publication support, and personal projects.

The Production Process

The production process includes the information, design, production, and evaluation stages. [Vlcek 143] The information stage involves the initial request for assistance. When the request is made, a Production Request form (Figure 7.4) is completed documenting who requested what within what timeline. Routine requests which do not require any special assistance, such as slide duplication, transparencies from an existing master, or audio duplication, are forwarded directly to the production stage for completion. More complex requests, such as graphic design or video production, are forwarded to the design stage for instructional development consultation.

All production activities must comply with U.S. copyright law. The fair use criteria provide general guidelines for determining the legality for reproducing or adapting copyrighted works. The fair use criteria note 1) the purpose and character of the use, including whether such use is of a commercial nature or is for nonprofit educational purposes, 2) the nature of the copyrighted work, 3) the amount and substantiality of the portion used in relation to the copyrighted work as a whole, and 4) the effect of the use upon the potential market for or value of the copyrighted work. In addition to fair use, tests of spontaneity, brevity, and cumulative effect must be met. [Talab 2–4] If the proposed use of the copyrighted work does not meet the fair use criteria or the three tests, permission for use must be obtained from the

```
┌─────────────────────────────────────────────────────────────────┐
│ PRODUCTION REQUEST                          |Request #:          │
│                                             |                    │
│                                             |Assigned to:        │
│ Date Submitted:_____  Date Needed:_____                │
│                                             |Date Complete:      │
│ Name_____   |                    │
│                                             |Production $$       │
│ Department_____  Phone_____  | Labor:             │
│                                             |  Supply:           │
│─────────────────────────────────────────────|_____│
│ Graphics:                        | Special Instructions:         │
│                                  |   Please include sketch of any │
│ ___Posters/Signs                 |   artwork and related notes.  │
│ ___Original Art                  |                               │
│ ___Design/Layout/Paste Up        |                               │
│ ___Dry Mounting                  |                               │
│ ___Laminating                    |                               │
│ ___Other_____          |                               │
│                                  |                               │
│ Overhead Transparency:           |                               │
│                                  |                               │
│ ___Design Master                 |                               │
│ ___Run Prepared Master           |                               │
│                                  |                               │
│ Photography:                     |                               │
│                                  |                               │
│ ___Original/Field                |                               │
│ ___Copystand                     |                               │
│ ___Slide Duplication             |                               │
│ ___Other_____          |                               │
│                                  |                               │
│ Audio:                           |                               │
│                                  |                               │
│ ___Record Master                 |                               │
│ ___Duplication                   |                               │
│ ___Edit                          |                               │
│ ___Other_____          |                               │
│                                  |                               │
│ Video:                           |                               │
│                                  |                               │
│ ___Portable                      |                               │
│ ___Studio                        |                               │
│ ___Duplication                   |                               │
│ ___Edit                          |                               │
│ ___Other_____          |                               │
│ _____         |_____│
│──────────────────────────────────────────────────────────────────│
│ Supplies Consumed:              Time Spent:                      │
└─────────────────────────────────────────────────────────────────┘
```

FIGURE 7.4   Production Request Form

copyright owner who may be identified through notice of copyright on the work itself or through publications such as the *Audiovisual Marketplace*. Once the copyright holder has been identified, a letter, such as Figure 7.5, requesting permission for reproduction or adaptation of the copyrighted work is sent.

During the design or preplanning stage, the requestor and the ID specialist discuss the project's content, audience, desired outcomes, target com-

---

COPYRIGHT PERMISSION REQUEST FOR DUPLICATION OR ADAPTATION

To:_____ From:_____

_____ Date: _____

_____

We hereby request permission to duplicate, adapt, or use copyrighted materials for the project described below. This project will be used exclusively for educational purposes, with no direct or indirect commercial advantage, and will include credit for your work.

Title of Copyrighted Material: _____

Author: _____

Publisher:_____ Copyright Date: _____

Material to be duplicated or adapted: _____

Type of reproduction or adaptation: _____

Number of copies: _____

Use to be made of material: _____

_____

_____

Distribution of copies: _____

Please indicate your permission below and return this form within two weeks from the above date. A return envelope is enclosed for your convenience.

    ☐ Permission granted.

    ☐ Permission granted with the following restrictions:_____

    _____

    ☐ Permission denied. (If so, is there another means by which we can obtain this material for our project?)

       ☐ Alternate Source: _____

Name (Printed) _____ Title _____

Signature _____ Date _____

FIGURE 7.5 Permission Letter for Use of Copyrighted Work   (Courtesy of Broome Community College)

pletion time, and available resources such as availability of commercially produced material and estimated materials and staffing costs. During this stage, they agree upon the appropriate media, a general content outline, and treatment for the topic. The script and related storyboard are then developed. Before forwarding the production request to the production stage, the specialist estimates timelines for completion of various phases of the project, such as graphics, photography, video, and audio.

During the production stage, the artist, photographer, video and audio technicians work individually on their project components as well as in a team with the specialist and requestor as necessary. Time and materials required for the project are recorded on the Production Request Form.

Once the project is completed, the specialist reviews it to ensure its adherence to LRP quality standards and to the requestor's objectives. Evaluation criteria parallels that used for selection of nonprint materials described in Chapter 6. Once the specialist is satisfied with the completed project, the requestor is invited to evaluate it as well. The project is modified if necessary until final approval and dissemination.

Self-Service Production

In addition to providing direct production support, instructional development and production services also offers facilities for self-service production. This facility may be staffed with a production assistant or may be totally self-service with only point-of-use production aids available. Typical resources available include a photocopier with transparency production capabilities, graphics supplies and equipment, mounting supplies, a camera and photographic copystand, basic audio production equipment, and a microcomputer with graphics capabilities. In addition, the area may provide demonstration equipment introducing and encouraging experimentation with newer technologies, such as interactive video and hypermedia. Some colleges limit access to the self-service production facility to faculty and staff, while others encourage students to use it to enhance their oral presentations and written reports.

Specialized Services

Learning resources programs share the common mission of providing the resources and services necessary to serve the informational, learning, and developmental needs of their students, faculty, administrators, and broader college communities. However, each is responsive to its parent institution's educational goals, curricula, student population, size and complexity, and special issues. Consequently, no two are identical.

Thus, in addition to the components of User Services already discussed in this chapter a variety of specialized services, which help learning resources users to locate or create and use information resources more effectively, may also be integrated into the program. Their inclusion or composition are not identical, but instead reflect the needs of the individual institution. These specialized services may include providing individual use equipment, maintaining the college archives, coordinating the learning achievement center, staffing the faculty support center, and providing grantsmanship assistance.

Individual Use Equipment

Nearly every learning resources program provides individual use equipment encouraging individual LRC users to view, listen to, or use the nonprint and electronic resources available. This equipment minimally includes videocassette, audiocassette, phonograph, sound slide, sound filmstrip, and 16mm film listening and viewing stations. Within recent years, this individual use equipment has expanded to also include microcomputer, CD-ROM, and interactive video stations.

The individual needs of the college determine the organization and scope of the individual use equipment area. If its primary purpose is only to permit individuals necessary access to appropriate equipment, the area may be a circulation responsibility. If its primary purpose is to help individuals gain or use information resources more effectively, the area may be an information services responsibility. Or if its purpose fills multiple roles, it may be a separate unit within User Services. On many campuses, the area is a component of information services with an information specialist responsible for maintaining usage records, recommending operational procedures, developing point-of-use equipment aids, and coordinating the area's staffing.

Who are the primary users of the area? Will they be faculty, administrators, students, and/or community residents? What is their level of expertise with equipment operation? Will students be given assignments to complete in the area? Will classes be scheduled into the area? Answers to these questions determine the number of stations, type of equipment, and staffing levels for the area. In most colleges, the area is open to anyone who can benefit from its use. Since even experienced equipment users will encounter problems or have questions regarding equipment or materials, staffing the area at all times with someone who has been trained in the use and maintenance of the equipment is common. The equipment, especially microcomputers, is compatible with that used elsewhere on campus. Usage determines the need for time restrictions or reservations. Selection of computer software frequently is limited to instructional software which includes tutorials, simulations, or drills and to productivity software such as word processing and spreadsheet programs.

Another consideration with microcomputers is the economy of circulating software, loading programs into hard drives, or using local area networks.

Related issues are the copyright and licensing of computer software and security from computer viruses, vandals, and pirates. Another challenge is the level of instructional support which may range from point-of-use equipment aids, to self-instructional tutorials, to individualized instruction from staff.

The answers to these procedural questions are publicized in an informational flyer which provides individual use equipment users with a description of the available equipment and software, hours the area is open, orientation requirements, explanation of applicable copyright laws and the concept of software piracy, general rules governing the use of the area including prohibition of food and drink, scheduling, and penalties for violation of area rules. [Lane 103]

College Archives

At most community colleges, an information specialist holds responsibility for maintaining the college archives. Preserved in the college archives are not only "official college records, such as all published minutes, reports, catalogs, newspapers, brochures, and non-confidential documents, but also materials containing evidence and information about the development, activities, and achievements of its officers, employees, and students. These materials provide written, pictorial, and audiovisual evidence of the history and on-going development of the college.

The information specialist holding archivist responsibility collects and screens materials considered for retention. Some colleges require all college offices, committees, and departments to send a file copy of all publications, distributions, and reports for the archivist to review. On other campuses, the archivist works closely with the college's public information officer and institutional researcher to actively acquire materials deemed appropriate. The extent of the archives varies with some colleges retaining personal files of college officials in addition to the retention of all public documents and materials.

The archivist then organizes the materials into meaningful units and describes them for ease of retrieval. The materials are organized following established guidelines set forth by the Society of American Archivists in *Archives, Personal Papers, and Manuscripts* or by a locally established record group classification scheme which follows the structure of the college. The archivist also creates a guide and index to the archive.

Finally, the archivist packs the materials in containers for preservation, identifies the contents of the containers on labels, numbers the stack rows and compartments within them, notes the contents of stack rows on labels, and prepares location registers for ease of retrieval.

Access to the college archive is usually restricted. Generally, following the information interview, the information specialist retrieves the material or information requested and notes the material used. On occasion, a researcher is allowed to search a specific file under the supervision of information specialists. Rarely do materials circulate beyond the LRC.

Faculty Support Center

Since the Division of Learning Resources is separate from other instructional divisions and reports directly to the chief academic officer and since LRP staff actively participate in liaison and instructional support activities campuswide, User Services frequently assumes responsibility for the faculty support center either as an individual component or as part of the instructional development and production area. The center offers a variety of services responsive to the unique resources and service requirements of the campus faculty as determined through surveys, interviews, or general observation. These services may include secretarial support, a resources area, and a formal staff development program.

Secretarial support includes assistance with creating class related materials such as syllabi, tests, and handouts and related multicopy services. The secretary compiles a record of all faculty office hours, takes messages, and maintains a current syllabus file. She also supervises students taking telecourse exams or making up missed exams.

The resources area is a user oriented, drop-in center which provides opportunities for all faculty who seek to enhance their teaching effectiveness. This area accommodates the interests and needs of new as well as mid-career faculty in all disciplines by providing materials on learning styles and teaching techniques; the college including the catalog, curriculum committee minutes, student demographics, etc.; specific curriculum disciplines and related teaching methods; announcements of forthcoming professional meetings and faculty development seminars and workshops; and career and retirement possibilities. This area also provides a meeting area for mentoring programs which match senior faculty with new or adjunct faculty members or for consulting activities in which model teachers share their techniques with their peers.

In addition to the informal drop-in area, the faculty support center coordinates formal staff development activities by creating a forum for campus "experts" to share their expertise, inviting external specialists to present relevant workshops and seminars on campus, and coordinating peer visits with colleagues at other colleges. LRP staff conduct workshops in the effective use of instructional tools as well as promote and provide training in the use of the newer technologies.

Learning Achievement Center

The learning achievement center developed through a merging of self-paced learning laboratories, developmental studies, and the use of technology in instruction. It also is known as the academic skills laboratory, learning enrichment center, or reading, writing, and study skills lab. Organizationally, the center may be a unit within the Division of Learning Resources, a separate unit reporting to the chief academic officer, or integrated into subject discipline.

The goal of the center is to help students to achieve their goals, regardless of prior academic preparation. The specific services offered are responsive to student needs, campus priorities, and economics. Services may be offered on a walk-in basis to anyone enrolled at the college or may be restricted to those who enroll in the center's credit courses. Self-instruction developmental or enrichment programs employing computer-assisted instruction, interactive video, or other technologies may be combined with staff or peer tutoring or with small group instruction. Special workshops on topics such as math anxiety, how to take an essay exam, surviving the sciences, or reading a textbook may be offered.

The center's program may extend beyond the college curriculum to coordinate the literacy program for the district. Volunteer literacy tutors are recruited, trained, and paired with participants. Adult basic education (ABE), English as a second language (ESL), and general education development (GED) programs may be coordinated through the center.

Grantsmanship Assistance

With expanding demands for services, increasing costs for technology, and limited revenues, the need to seek external sources of funding is increasing on all campuses. Information specialists are in a key position to provide grantsmanship assistance. Through their role on campus, they are aware of the mission of the college, the specific interests and projects of faculty and staff, and the needs of the institution. They can discuss initial project ideas with the content specialists, assist with the background research, and locate potential funding sources. They can coach the grantwriter about proposal writing techniques, refer him to appropriate support people on campus, review the final grant proposal, and assist with the campus approvals for its submission.

Summary

The variety of services offered by the Division of Learning Resources reflect the variety of conditions under which each operates and the diversity of students and communities they serve. While Access Services provides access to and delivery of information, User Services provides assistance in locating or creating and using information resources to serve the instructional and informational needs of the college community.

User Services includes information services including information assistance, bibliographic instruction, and selection of materials; instructional development and production services; and specialized services including individual use equipment, college archives, faculty support center, learning achievement center, and grantsmanship assistance.

Selected Bibliography

"Annotated Bibliographies for Community College Libraries," *Choice* 28 (June 1991): 1590.

BESSLER, JOANNE. "Do Library Patrons Know What's Good for Them?" *Journal of Academic Librarianship* 16 (May 1990): 76–85.

BRADY, MARY LOUISE, ET AL. "Software for Patron Use in Libraries: Physical Access," *Library Trends* 40 (Summer 1991): 63–84.

DAYTON, DEANE K. "How to Set Limits for a Production Facility," *Instructional Innovator* 27 (October 1982): 20–22.

DESMARAIS, NORMAN. *The Librarian's CD-ROM Handbook.* Westport, CT: Meckler, 1989.

DUCOTE, RICHARD L., ET AL. "Active Learning and the LRC." In *Role of the Learning Resources Center in Instruction,* ed. Margaret Holleman. San Francisco: Jossey-Bass, 1990.

DUNN, ELIZABETH BRAMM. "The Challenges of Automation and the Library Instruction Program: Content, Management, Budget," *North Carolina Libraries* 46 (Winter 1988): 219–222.

EVANS, G. EDWARD. *Developing Library and Information Center Collections.* Littleton, CO: Libraries Unlimited, 1987.

FISCHER, KAREN. "Welding: A Core List for Community College Libraries," *Choice* 28 (June 1991): 1599–1608.

FORD, ROBERT B. JR. "Bibliographic Instruction for the Nontraditional College Student: The Medgar Evers Experience," *The Bookmark* 46 (Fall 1987): 31–35.

"Framework for Outcomes Assessment." Philadelphia: Middle States Association of Colleges and Schools, 1991.

GORMAN, G.E., and B.R. HOWES. *Collection Development for Libraries.* London: Bowker-Saur, 1989.

HALLMAN, CLARK N. "Technology: Trigger for Change in Reference Librarianship," *Journal of Academic Librarianship* 16 (September 1990): 204–208.

JANNEY, SUSAN. "Bibliographic Instruction at Learning Resources Centers in North Carolina," *North Carolina Libraries* 44 (Spring 1986): 16–22.

JOHNSTON, WANDA K. "Online Search Services in the Community College," *College & Research Libraries News* 50 (May 1989): 375–377.

JOHNSTON, WANDA K., and JOAN S. CLARKE. "Bibliographic Instruction and Information Technologies." In *Community College Reference Services*, ed. William Katz. Metuchen, NJ: Scarecrow Press, 1992.

KATZ, WILLIAM A. *Introduction to Reference Work.* 5th ed. New York: McGraw-Hill, 1987.

KAZLAUSKAS, EDWARD JOHN, and WILLIAM MAXWELL. "Faculty Development and the Community College LRC," *Community & Junior College Libraries* 7 (1990): 81–87.

KEMP, JERROLD E. "A Perspective on the Changing Role of the Educational Technologist," *Educational Technology* 31 (June 1991): 13–18.

———. *The Instructional Design Process.* New York: Harper & Row, 1985.

LANE, ELIZABETH S. *Microcomputer Management & Maintenance for Libraries.* Westport, CT: Meckler, 1990.

LUTZKER, MARILYN. "Bibliographic Instruction and Accreditation in Higher Education," *College & Research Libraries News* 51 (January 1990): 14–18.

MELLON, CONSTANCE A. "Attitudes: The Forgotten Dimension in Library Instruction," *Library Journal* 113 (September 1, 1988): 137–139.

"Model Statement of Objectives for Academic Bibliographic Instruction: Draft Revision," *College & Research Libraries News* 48 (May 1987): 256–261.

NOLAN, CHRISTOPHER W. "The Lean Reference Collection: Improving Functionality through Selection and Weeding," *College & Research Libraries* 52 (January 1991): 80–91.

ROBERTS, ANNE F., and SUSAN G. BLANDY. *Library Instruction for Librarians.* Englewood, CO: Libraries Unlimited, 1989.

SCHELLENBERG, T.R. *The Management of Archives.* Washington, DC: National Archives and Records Administration, 1988.

SCHMID, WILLIAM T. *Media Center Management: A Practical Guide.* New York: Hastings House, 1980.

SEIDEN, PEGGY. "Selection of Software for Patron Use in Libraries," *Library Trends* 40 (Summer 1991): 6–41.

"Standards for Community, Junior and Technical College Learning Resources Programs," *College & Research Libraries News* 51 (September 1990): 757–767.

TALAB, R.S. *Copyright and Instructional Technologies: A Guide to Fair Use and Permissions Procedures.* 2nd ed. Washington, DC: Association for Educational Communications and Technology, 1989.

VLCEK, CHARLES W., and RAYMOND V. WIMAN. *Managing Media Services: Theory and Practice.* Englewood, CO: Libraries Unlimited, 1989.

8

Telecommunications
Networking Services

The learning resources program is responsible for providing "a variety of services to support and expand the instructional capabilities of the institution." [Standards 761] Thus, the LRP provides the best possible access to desired information or instructional materials and delivers it to the individual user or through campus classrooms. Within the community college, the concept of "campus classroom" has many facets. It may include the traditional campus classroom. It may include an individualized study course with the student at any locale. It may extend to extension sites in area businesses, prisons, military bases, public libraries, etc. It may extend into the student's home.

The LRP also has responsibility "to integrate new resources of information and new instructional technologies into the ever-changing curriculum, access, and delivery systems." [Standards 762] The development of the silicon chip and of optical disk storage enhanced computer processing capabilities. Digital signals, packet-switching, fiber optics, and satellites impacted the development of telecommunications by improving high-speed, error-free transmission at lower costs. The subsequent convergence of technology and telecommunications has made possible the integration of voice, video, and data transmission as tools for teaching and learning. [Johnston 187–188] Community college learning resources programs are testing and implementing instructional delivery systems to create telelearning opportunities.

Providing access to higher education regardless of race, age, or station in life is one of the constants in the community college mission. Reports, such as *Workforce 2000* and *The Learning Industry*, emphasize the importance of access to quality education for all Americans. Only through improved productivity which is directly linked to a literate and educated workforce can the American economy grow steadily over the next decade. "Missing persons" or those who continue to be disenfranchised by the current system of education must be served. Existing workers and administrators need instructional assistance to adapt to the rapidly changing work world. The delivery of instruction via telecommunications creates a convenient and flexible option for those who cannot afford the time and expense of traveling to class.

Within the Division of Learning Resources, Telecommunications Networking Services coordinates telelearning opportunities through non-credit workshops, seminars, and staff development opportunities offered via video teleconferencing and through credit courses offered via telecourses, interactive teleclasses, and interactive computer conferencing. In addition to telelearning, Telecommunications Networking Services may be responsible for academic computing, the institutional local area network, and the campus television or radio stations. Institutional size, priorities, staffing, and budget affect the scope and organization of Telecommunications Networking Services. On some campuses, the Dean for Non-Traditional Education or Alternative Education oversees telelearning activities and the Division of Learning Resources is responsible only for access to programming and instructional delivery. In such a scenario, Telecommunications Networking Services would be a unit of Access Services or integrated into its existing units.

Telelearning Background

An understanding of telelearning opportunities begins with a review of telecommunications delivery systems and of selected consortia and networks.

Delivery Systems

The delivery of telelearning opportunities in most community colleges is through broadcast television, narrowcast television, computers and modems, and nonbroadcast videocassette distribution. Broadcast television provides nonformal educational programming, such as documentaries, cultural specials, public affairs programming. In cooperation with local colleges and universities, the public television stations broadcasts credit classes in the form of telecourses.

Narrowcast television includes local cable television, Instructional Television Fixed Service, and satellite transmission. Local cable systems use coaxial and fiber optic cable to distribute programming to local subscribers. Programming is received from many types of signals, such as satellite or microwave transmission, and then retransmitted over the normal cable system. Most cable systems currently installed are multichannel with one or more channels reserved for one-way educational delivery. Telelearning opportunities are delivered with one-way transmission via these educational channels.

Instructional Television Fixed Service (ITFS) is a low-powered, limited range, broadcast system with omnidirectional microwave signals commonly traveling approximately twenty miles, although their range can be increased by using signal repeaters, increasing the height of the antennas, increasing receiver sensitivity, or increasing transmitter power. In addition to the main video channel, two subchannels per main channel carry audio, data, and still pictures. Special equipment is required to receive the signal and change its frequency for viewing on a regular television set. The systems are capable of two-way communication, including audio feedback and computer interactivity, encouraging student-instructor interaction; however, one-way video with telephone connections for two-way audio are most common. ITFS systems allow delivery of instruction to area businesses, prisons, hospitals, and other sites as extensions of the campus classroom. ITFS licenses are issued by the FCC to educational organizations for transmission of instructional, cultural, and other educational programs.

Satellite technology provides transmission of television signals from virtually any part of the world and eliminates the need for terrestrial microwave systems. The satellite functions as a relay station in the sky. The program is "uplinked" to the satellite from a ground station and then retransmitted back to earth where it is received by a satellite receiver (downlink). When the combination of a satellite, television, and a telephone link are used together, individuals scattered over a wide geographical area can see and talk with each other at the same time resulting in an interactive video teleconference. Most community colleges currently have or will soon acquire satellite "downlink" capabilities. Video teleconferencing is most often used for staff development activities or special events.

Access to a computer with a model permits interactive computer conferencing. In such a conference, participants communicate by means of computers linked through modems and telephone lines. Through courses taught in the "virtual classroom," an electronically based workspace, students and instructors communicate through computer-mediated systems.

The direct circulation of instructional videocassettes is a heavily used delivery system used for telecourse lessons. Students sign the videocassettes out from the learning resources center, public library, or alternate circulation point and use them at home on their own videocassette players.

Consortia and Networks

Both to reduce program acquisition and licensing costs and to share telecommunications information, issues, and successes, community colleges participate in telecommunications consortia and networks. A commercial network dedicated to college programming is the College Satellite Network (CSN) which distributes approximately one event per month at no charge to colleges. The Public Broadcasting Service—Adult Learning Satellite Service (PBS/ALSS) licenses telecourses, audiovisual resource programming, and interactive video conferences. Satellite Communications for Learning (SCOLA) provides live native language television news coverage via satellite from most countries in the world for use in foreign language classes.

College and university consortia include the National University Teleconference Network and the Community College Satellite Network. The National University Teleconference Network (NUTN), a nonprofit college and university consortia shares programs that are produced by member institutions. The Community College Satellite Network (COSN) is a coalition of community colleges dedicated to the cooperative use of satellite technology.

In addition, community colleges participate in regional and local networks for the purpose of group purchases of equipment and programming as well as for both formal and informal staff development purposes. For example, the Northern Illinois Learning Resources Cooperative (NILRC) draws together forty-four colleges into a cooperative focusing on the goals of resource and information sharing, staff development, and the economy of group purchases of equipment, supplies, and resources.

Primary sources of telecommunications information are the Instructional Telecommunications Consortia and the National Distance Learning Center. The Instructional Telecommunications Consortia (ITC), an affiliate of the American Association of Community and Junior Colleges, disseminates information concerning technology-enhanced instruction and encourages collaboration among institutions regarding project development and telecommunications-based curricular planning.

Through support from the U.S. Federal Government, the National Distance Learning Center (NDLC) operates as a free public service to all users and producers of distance learning programming. It operates a centralized online database containing detailed program listings for credit and noncredit courses, teleconferences, seminars, and in-service training series.

Satellite ORBIT, a monthly publication published to serve as the "guide to complete satellite TV entertainment," provides quick reference to the movies, sports, and specials available through the satellite television channels. It is published through Commtek Communications, Box 607, Vienna, VA 22183. The addresses of most of the other networks and consortia described above are listed in table 8.1.

Telelearning Courses

The primary format for telelearning courses include video telecourses, interactive teleclasses, and interactive computer conferencing. Video telecourses combine videotaped lessons, related reading, and assignments with discussions and examinations. Telecourse lessons are delivered via PBS or local cable television or direct circulation of instructional videocassette. Students attend an introductory orientation session at which they meet their campus faculty member and receive their syllabus and related materials. They then independently follow the prescribed instructional plan set forth in the syllabus with faculty assistance available on request.

Through interactive teleclasses, live instruction is linked among several sites through narrowcast television (local cable, ITFS, or satellite) technology. Interactive teleclasses are most frequently taught with one-way video and two-way audio. Thus, students can see the instructor in the electronic classroom and can respond via microphones from their remote classroom or telephones from their own homes. Interactive teleclasses allow students to participate in regularly scheduled courses from distant locations.

Through interactive computer conferencing, courses are delivered via a computer and modem combined with supplemental instructional materials. Initially, the students and faculty meet through an orientation session during which the course syllabi and procedures are explained and related materials are distributed. Following the initial orientation, students and faculty communicate using electrode mail and bulletin board systems.

The telelearning coordinator is responsible for determining instructional need, locating potential courses and suitable delivery systems, and comparing the feasibility and cost-effectiveness of each course to determine the most appropriate system. Needs assessment includes answering questions such as: What courses should be taught which have too few students to justify? What courses should be taught but no qualified faculty member is available? What student populations could benefit from courses, but cannot attend courses on site? What courses have been suggested by administrators, faculty, and students in the district? What courses have been successful

TABLE 8.1   Selected Telecommunications Networks and Consortia

Commercial Networks Serving Instruction
College Satellite Network (CSN)
5547 North Ravenswood Avenue
Chicago, IL 60640
(312) 878-7300

Public Broadcasting Service—Adult Learning Satellite Service (PBS/ALSS)
1329 Braddock Place
Alexandria, VA 22314
(800) 257-2578

Satellite Communications for Learning (SCOLA)
2500 California Street
Omaha, NB 68178
(402) 280-4063

College and University Consortia
National University Teleconference Network (NUTN)
330 Student Union
Oklahoma State University
Stillwater, OK 74078
(405) 624-5191

Community College Satellite Network (CCSN)
Suite 410
One Dupont Circle
Washington, DC 20036
(202) 728-0212

Resource Information
Instructional Telecommunications Consortia (ITC)
Suite 410
One Dupont Circle
Washington, DC 20036
(202) 728-0222

National Distance Learning Center (NDLC)
Owensboro Community College
4800 Hartford Road
Owensboro, KY 42303
(502) 686-4556

in other community college districts? Participation in the college curriculum committee, Dean's Council meetings, and telecommunications consortia and networks, review of demographic and survey data from Institutional Research, and reading of telecommunications publications provide answers to these questions.

Once instructional need has been identified, potential courses are located and delivery systems identified using questions such as: What courses are available for purchase or license? What courses already taught on campus can be adapted to telelearning delivery systems? Do these courses meet the instructional quality and accreditation standards set forth by the institution and state? If no course is readily available, can it be produced on campus? How cost-effective is the course using the selected delivery system? Consortia participation and newsletters as well as distributor advertising suggest courses available for purchase or license. Evaluative criteria for telelearning courses includes availability and usefulness of the supplemental materials, technical quality, scope and balance of the lessons, accessibility for students, appropriateness for the curriculum, and overall academic quality. The Worksheet for Calculating Telelearning Costs (Figure 8.1) provides an outline for determining cost-effectiveness for the course.

The telelearning coordinator also is responsible for facilitating resolution of issues including course approval and revisions, faculty selection, training, and incentives, copyright and contract or license compliance, and support services for students and faculty. In addition, the coordinator oversees telelearning publicity, student registration, course implementation, and subsequent evaluation.

Interactive Video Teleconferencing

Interactive video teleconferencing allows remote sites using electronic communication to interact via one-way or two-way video or audio. This system provides pictorial quality similar to broadcast television and encourages viewers to be actively involved through asking questions, paraphrasing for clarification, or debating with the presenters. It may be used with large or small groups for special events or regular meetings. Most frequently it is, in essence, a conversation between one or more panelists and a moderator which is carefully paced to allow for call-in periods or supplemental high-interest video segments. The teleconference originates in a television studio, classroom, or conference room where television cameras relay the program to remote sites using satellite transmission. Each receiving site is connected by telephone to the original studio so questions can be asked live on air.

```
        WORKSHEET FOR CALCULATING TELELEARNING COSTS


Course:_____     Course #:_____

Delivery Format:_____


Direct Costs:

        _____    Rent/lease/purchase telelessons
        _____    Telelearning delivery fees
                     (Air time/Telecommunications fees)
        _____    Off-air rights
        _____    Videocassette and supplementary materials
                     for LRC and extension center sites
                     (Materials, duplication, and distribution)
        _____    Faculty compensation
        _____    Non-teaching staff compensation
                     (Clerical support/Classroom facilitator/
                     Site Coordinator pro-rated)
        _____    Misc. supplies and expenses
                     (Telephone/Photocopying/Postage)
        _____    Recruiting and Promotion


In-Direct Costs:
    (Pro-rated)

        _____    Consortia and network memberships
        _____    Overhead


        _____
                   Total    *Divide total direct and in-direct costs
                            by estimated student enrollment to obtain
                            estimated cost per student.


Income:

        _____    Tuition per student
        _____    State reimbursement per student


        _____
                   Total    *Divide total expenses for course by
                            income per student to determine enrollment
                            break-even point.
                            *Income per student should equal or exceed
                            estimated cost per student.
```

FIGURE 8.1   Worksheet for Calculating Telelearning Costs

The teleconference coordinator is responsible for conducting the needs assessment, locating and selecting the programming, and arranging its licensing, receipt, and local arrangements. Teleconference needs assessment is conducted with suggestions encouraged from college and community leaders, reviews of available programming, and consideration of current issues. Teleconferencing is best used for reaching many people with material that is timely and up-to-date in the field. The content is generally delivered through individual presentation, panel discussion, or demonstrations by leading authorities in the field.

The coordinator locates and selects which of many available video teleconferences to offer. In addition to calculating cost-effectiveness, he follows the college's plan defining its purpose for offering video teleconferences. "Most colleges tend to include one or more of the following goals: to help fulfill the college mission; to provide instructor and staff development; to provide opportunities for curriculum enrichment; to offer business and industry new training and information opportunities; or to provide public service through special video teleconference offerings." [Pirkl 26]

Once the teleconference has been selected, the coordinator ensures available downlink capabilities and licenses the program. The producer then provides a printed agenda which identifies the moderator and key presenters and breaks the discussion topic into discrete segments allocating time for telephone participation. He also provides necessary technical information including time and date of program, satellite name, transponder number, audio subcarrier, polarity (either horizontal or vertical), test signal information, and 800 telephone number to call in case of difficulty.

The coordinator is responsible for local arrangements using the Teleconference Project Planning form (Figure 8.2) as a guide. In addition to coordinating advance publicity and registration, he also selects a local moderator to introduce the program, to assist with local telephone participation, and to develop local activities to supplement and present a local perspective on the national presentation. The coordinator also arranges for a comfortable viewing space. This space includes television receivers (calculated at one diagonal inch per viewer), audio amplification for ease in hearing, the participants telephone located in an adjacent room to avoid feedback, and a video recorder to record the teleconference if authorized by the agreement. He creates packets of supplemental materials for all participants. These packets may contain introductory description and objectives of the teleconference, brief biographies of the key presenters, the teleconference agenda, supportive written readings, and an evaluation form. Finally, the coordinator ensures that all downlink equipment works and that a qualified operator will be present. After the teleconference, the coordinator sends "thank yous" to all who helped make the program a success, settles financial accounts, and forwards the teleconference tape to LRC Acquisitions as permitted by the agreement.

Program: _____

Date: _____   Planning Start: _____

Time: _____   Cost: _____

MCC Fee: _____   Paid Participant: _____

                                      Guests: _____

Contact/Source: _____

Persons Involved: _____

Panel: _____

  or

Presenters: _____

Date Completed   **Sequence of Action**

_____ Registration to Downlink or _____

_____ Room Reservations _____

_____ Room Set-Up _____

_____ Refreshments _____

_____ Handouts

_____ Agenda/Program

_____ Folders

_____ Brochure _____

                                  _____

_____ Coordinates _____

_____ News/PR _____

_____ Mailing _____

                                  Summary:

                                  Costs: _____

                                  Revenue: _____

Follow-Up: _____

FIGURE 8.2   **Teleconference Project Planning Form**   Courtesy of McHenry County College, Illinois.

Summary

Responding to the responsibility for providing access to and delivery of desired information for both the traditional and nontraditional student, community college learning resources programs continually review alternative information resources and instructional delivery systems. Recent developments with telecommunications technologies have enabled community colleges to extend the classroom into the community to better serve the nontraditional student. Telecommunications Networking Services coordinates the telelearning opportunities for instruction through telelearning courses and interactive teleconferencing.

Selected Bibliography

DeHart, A. Robert. "There is a Satellite in Your Future." In *Cutting Edge Technologies in Community Colleges*, ed. Ervin L. Harlacher. Washington, DC: AACJC, 1988.

Eurich, Nell P. *The Learning Industry: Education for Adult Workers.* Princeton, NJ: The Carnegie Foundation for the Advancement of Teaching, 1990.

Feder, Eric. "Tips for Teleconference Coordinators," *Tech Trends* 36 (1991): 10–12.

Hisle, W. Lee. "LRC Support of Off-Campus Education." In *Role of the Learning Resources Center in Instruction*, ed. Margaret Holleman. San Francisco: Jossey-Bass, 1990.

Johnston, Wanda K. "Future Directions of Information Technologies as Projected in the Literature," *Illinois Libraries* 73 (February 1991): 187–190.

Kooi, Jana B. "Media Technology Begets Revenue." In *Alternative Funding Sources*, ed. J.I. Catanzaro and A.D. Arnold. San Francisco: Jossey-Bass, 1989.

Munshi, Kiki Skagen, and David P. Stone. *Working with Telecourses.* Washington, DC: Corporation for Public Broadcasting, 1980.

Nugent, Gwen C. "Innovations in Telecommunications." In *Instructional Technology: Foundations* ed. Robert M. Gagne. Hillside, NJ: Lawrence Erlbaum, 1987.

Ostendorf, Virginia A. "Shopping for a Satellite Curriculum," *Access* 3 (November/December 1990): 3–4.

Perrin, Towers. *Workforce 2000: Competing in a Seller's Market: Is Corporate America Prepared.* New York: The Hudson Institute, 1990.

Pirkl, Ray. "Video Teleconferencing: Tapping an Emerging Resource," *AACJC Journal* 61 (October/November 1990): 24–27.

Pohrte, Theodore W. "Telecourses: Instructional Design for Nontraditional Students." In *Role of the Learning Resources Center in Instruction* ed. Margaret Holleman. San Francisco: Jossey-Bass, 1990.

"Standards for Community, Junior and Technical College Learning Resources Programs," *College & Research Libraries News* 51 (September 1990): 757–767.

Talab, Rosemary, and Gerry Bailey. "Copyright, Licensing and Contractual Issues in Distance Education Courses Delivery," *Tech Trends* 36 (1991): 63–65.

U.S. Congress, Office of Technology Assessment. *Critical Connections: Communication for the Future.* Washington, DC: U.S. Government Printing Office, 1990.

———. *Linking for Learning: A New Course for Education.* Washington, DC: U.S. Government Printing Office, 1989.

PART III

LEARNING RESOURCES PROGRAM ADMINISTRATION

9

Introduction to Administration

Today's chief learning resources administrator is "responsible for administering the program and for providing leadership and direction so that mission of the program is fulfilled." [Standards 758–759] Consequently, to be successful, he is committed to the mission of the community college and to the priorities of his own college. He realizes that the community college is an institution of higher education which emphasizes teaching rather than research, provides open access to education resulting in a diverse student population, offers a comprehensive instructional program supported by student advising and counseling, and mirrors the unique characteristics and needs of its local community.

The LRP administrator is a team player actively involved in campuswide leadership. He is cognizant of the trends and issues which will impact the college and participates in the college's planning process. He has vision and introduces new ideas. His interpersonal style builds cooperative working relationships throughout the college. As a representative of the college, he works effectively with external agencies and consortia.

The LRP administrator believes the mission of the learning resources program is to provide the resources and services necessary to serve the informational, learning, and developmental needs of its students, faculty, administrators, and broader college community. He is responsible for developing a learning resources program responsive to his college's educational

131

goals, curricula, student population, size and complexity, and special issues. He promotes LRP services campuswide. He seeks feedback from LRP users and responsively extends or modifies services as appropriate.

The LRP administrator is a generalist, knowledgeable about and equally committed to all aspects of library, audiovisual, and telecommunications resources and services. He believes in the value of his staff and empowers them to effectively serve. He communicates the college mission and priorities, shares his vision, and encourages staff ideas and questions, creates staff development opportunities, and, as feasible, enables job ownership and pride. He does not always set the agenda but instead encourages creative thinking and risk-taking. He is a facilitator and troubleshooter. He strikes a balance between organizational results and the needs of his staff.

The LRP administrator orchestrates college priorities, service needs, LRP staff productivity, and resources into a successful program. He has vision of the future and the ability to anticipate and lead the LRC through change. Problem-solving, short- and long-range planning, budgetary and alternative funding, and facilities management are necessary administrative skills. He realizes the learning resources program cannot stand alone as an isolated unit. Instead, with his leadership, the learning resources program is an integral part of the college.

This chapter describes the current roles of learning resources administrators, reviews the theoretical foundations of management, and introduces relevant trends. Subsequent chapters will focus on program planning and evaluation, public relations and outreach, human resources management, budget and alternative funding, and facilities management.

Roles of Learning Resources Administrators

The traditional view of management, or administration, includes the functions of planning, organizing, staffing, directing, and controlling. However, in 1989, when Mintzberg studied chief executives seeking a realistic description of managerial work, he identified ten "roles" or organized sets of behaviors. Intepersonal roles, which include figurehead, liaison, and leader, arise directly from formal authority and involve basic interpersonal relationships. Informational roles, which include monitor disseminator, and spokesperson, develop through internal and external interpersonal contacts and result in his function as the "nerve center" of the unit. Decisional roles, which include entrepreneur, disturbance handler, resource allocator, and negotiator, involves his formal authority to commit the unit to new action and the information to enable decision making. [Mintzberg 15–21] He further distinguished between internal and external roles with the internal roles ensuring the organization's smooth operation as a single unit and the external roles affecting the organization's relationship with its environment.

Moskowitz redefines these ten roles in terms relevant to the practicing academic library/learning resources administrator:

Internal Roles

1. Leader—supervising subordinates work, including placement, training, motivation, and evaluation of employees
2. Disseminator—sharing and distributing information within the library through staff meetings and personal contacts
3. Entrepreneur—introducing change within the library by developing and implementing new systems and programs
4. Disturbance handler—handling conflicts and crises within the library and taking corrective actions when unexpected disturbances occur
5. Resource Allocator—allocating funds, time, staff, materials, and equipment to specific tasks within the library." [Moskowitz 454]

External Roles

1. Figurehead—carrying out the duties of a ceremonial nature, such as presenting and explaining the library to others
2. Liaison—maintaining contacts outside the library with college administrators and faculty
3. Monitor—receiving information outside the library through professional associations and activities and through verbal communication with colleagues
4. Spokesperson—distributing information to people outside the library and informing outsiders of progress within the system
5. Negotiator—negotiating with organizations or individuals outside the library to secure funding and safeguard interests." [Moskowitz 454]

Results of a recent study, which used Mintzberg's model to examine the managerial/administrative profile of 354 academic library/learning resources directors, found that while all directors shared many administrative commonalities, there were some significant differences. All were clearly more involved with their internal administrative roles rather than the external. However, "because of similarities in their smaller size and more focused institutional missions, baccalaureate and community college directors share more in common as managers than doctoral and comprehensive directors. Less externally oriented than comprehensive directors, baccalaureate and community college directors spend more time with faculty and students, spend less time as negotiators and decision makers, and see technical skills more important to their jobs than do their directors." [Mech 425]

This study reflects the existing roles of library/learning resources administrators responsive of their individual personalities, library/learning resource centers, academic institutions, and broader external environments. However in this era of accountability, limited resources, and automation, the roles of the effective community college learning resources administrator are changing. He maintains a balanced proactive stance. He not only ensures the smooth internal operation of his learning resources program but also actively develops positive external relationships. He develops a leadership strategy and style resulting in the fulfillment of the learning resources program mission and goals.

Theoretical Foundations

A common definition of management is the ability to accomplish group goals by working with and through people. The LRP administrator is responsible not only for managing the LRP but also for providing leadership to LRP staff transforming LRP program potential into reality, resulting in the provision of efficient and effective learning resources services. Understanding of traditional management theory, leadership studies, and communication theory provide foundations for this leadership.

Management Theory

Management theory is derived predominantly from research based in the behavioral sciences, including psychology, sociology, anthropology, and political science. While there is no one universal theory to resolve all management issues, this behavioral science research provides theories focusing on the "behavior of the individual and his or her needs, aspirations, and motivations, as well as the group and the organization. The major assumption is that if management can make employees happy, maximum performance will result." [Stueart 11]

The "Hawthorne Experiment" is the earliest significant behavioral science research. Between 1924 and 1932, Mayo and a group of industrial psychologists conducted a series of studies at the Western Electric Hawthorne Plant in Chicago. These studies, known as the "Hawthorne Experiment," measured the impact of physical working conditions and their impact on employee productivity. They demonstrated "1) that workers are more motivated by social rewards and sanctions than by economic incentives; 2) that workers in their acts are influenced by the group; and 3) that whenever formal organizations exist, both formal and informal norms exist." [Stueart 11] The overriding conclusion of the studies was that any change implying concern for staff resulted in increased productivity.

Maslow's 1954 work, *Motivation and Personality*, suggests that human beings possess five basic needs: physiological, safety and security, social and belonging, esteem and the opinion of others, and self-actualization or growth-to-potential needs. These needs are arranged in a hierarchy of importance based upon the order in which individuals strive to satisfy them. Thus, Maslow's Hierarchy of Needs, Figure 9.1, proposes that motivation

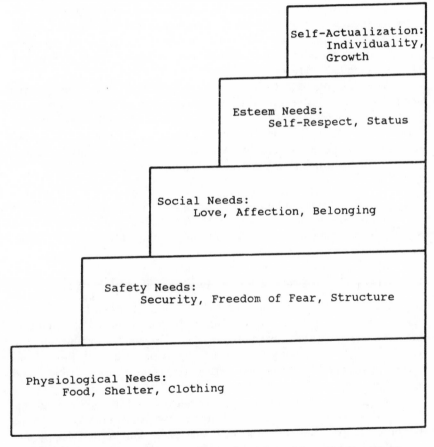

FIGURE 9.1 **Maslow's Hierarchy of Needs**   Adapted from Abraham H. Maslow, *Motivation and Personality*. 2nd ed. New York: Harper & Row, 1970: 35–47.

proceeds up a ladder of human need in which a satisfied need is no longer a motivator. By identifying an individual's current location in the hierarchy, the administrator has assistance in determining the most effective motivational strategy to promote optimal performance.

McGregor introduced his Theory X and Theory Y in his 1960 work, *The Human Side of Enterprise.* This theory describes two sets of contrasting assumptions about man and his relationship to work. "Theory X" describes the negative assumptions for direction and control that McGregor believes managers often use as a basis for human interactions. Thus, Theory X employees are seen as willful, lazy, capricious, and in need of constant supervision. In contrast, "Theory Y" represents the positive assumptions founded in the integration of individual and organizational goals which managers should strive toward. Thus, Theory Y employees are seen as workers who enjoy working, seek responsibility, and are capable of self-control. Administrators who accept Theory Y try not to impose external control and direction over employees but instead allow them more self-direction and control. Table 9.1 details McGregor's theory.

Argyris's Immaturity-Maturity Continuum, described in his *Interpersonal Competence and Organizational Effectiveness* (1962) and *Integrating the Individual and the Organization* (1964), is based upon the effects of organization life on the individual and advocates efforts to build consistency between individual and organizational goals. Argyris sees human maturation as a continuum through which people normally develop in seven ways:

Passive	→	Active
Dependent	→	Independent
Limited behavior modes	→	Many behavior Modes
Shallow, eratic interests	→	Deep, strong interests
Short time perspective	→	Present, past, and future time
Subordinate to everyone	→	Equal or superior role
Lack awareness of self	→	Aware of self and in control

Argyris believes these developmental channels are blocked in many organizations resulting in frustrations manifested through apathy, absenteeism, and other counter-productive behaviors. He encourages organizations to give employees opportunity to mature as individuals at work through increasing responsibility, encouraging participation in decision making, and job enrichment.

Herzberg's Motivation-Hygiene Theory, introduced in 1966 through his *Work and the Nature of Man,* builds upon Maslow's Hierarchy of Needs. Herzberg identifies sets of variables which make workers feel happy and satisfied about their work or which make them feel unhappy and dissatisfied through their environment. The first set, called motivators, are directly re-

TABLE 9.1 McGregor's Theory X and Theory Y

Theory X	*Theory Y*
Traditional View of Direction and Control	Integration of Individual and Organizational Goals
Assumptions:	
1. The average human being has an inherent dislike of work and will avoid it if he can.	1. The expenditure of physical and mental effort in work is as natural as play or rest.
2. Because of this human characteristic of dislike of work, most people must be coerced, controlled, directed, threatened with punishment to get them to put forth adequate effort toward the achievement of organizational objectives.	2. External control and the threat of punishment are not the only means for bringing about effort toward organizational objectives. Man will exercise self-direction and self-control in the service of objectives to which he is committed.
3. The average human being prefers to be directed, wishes to avoid responsibility, has relatively little ambition, wants security above all.	3. Commitment to objectives is a function of the rewards associated with achievement.
	4. The average human being learns, under proper conditions, not only to accept but to seek responsibility.
	5. The capacity to exercise a relatively high degree of imagination, ingenuity, and creativity in the solution of organizational problems is widely, not narrowly, distributed in the population.
	6. Under the conditions of modern industrial life, the intellectual potentials of the average human being are only partially utilized.

Adapted from: Douglas McGregor. *The Human Side of Enterprise*. New York: McGraw Hill, 1960: 33–34, 47–48.

lated to work content, positively influence the degree of work satisfaction, and result in improved performance. Motivators include challenging work, achievement, recognition, increasing responsibility, advancement, and personal growth. Hygiene or maintenance factors relate to the work environment. They neither lead to work satisfaction nor motivation; however, if not present, they lead to employee dissatisfaction. Hygiene factors include quality of supervision, company policy and administration, working conditions, interpersonal relationships, job security, status, and salary. This theory suggests that ensuring hygiene factors alone will not result in improved productivity. Instead, both hygiene factors as well as motivators are required.

Skinner's Principles of Behavior Modification, described in *Contingencies of Reinforcement* (1969), focuses on encouraging appropriate behavior as a result of the consequences of that behavior. Skinner identifies four methods of modifying behavior, including positive reinforcement resulting in continued behavior, negative reinforcement changing the behavior, no reinforcement extinguishing the behavior, and punishment decreasing the frequency of the behavior. Reinforcement may be tangible, such as money or food, or intangible, such as praise and attention. Effective feedback aimed at keeping employees informed to the relationship between various behaviors and their consequences are essential for successful behavior modification. "Other ingredients that successful behavior modification programs include are (1) giving different levels of rewards to different workers depending on the quality of their performance, (2) telling workers what they are doing wrong, (3) punishing workers privately so as not to embarrass them in front of others, and (4) always giving rewards and punishments when earned to emphasize that management is serious about behavior modification efforts." [Certo 392]

The Pygmalian effect is derived from McGregor's Theory X and Theory Y and Skinner's Principles of Behavior Modification. The Pygmalian effect assumes that one person can transform another by believing in him and treating him with new respect, much as Professor Higgins and Eliza Doolittle in Shaw's play, *Pygmalian*. Specifically, "what administrators expect of their subordinates and the way they treat them directly determines the subordinates' performance and career progress; if administrators set feasible high-performance expectations for their staff, the staff generally fulfills them; people work better, harder and more effectively if they are treated with respect, concern, and interest." [Hayes 20]

Leadership Studies

No one definition exists of leadership. "Regardless of how leadership is defined, the successful organization is almost always set apart from less successful ones by the fact that it is headed by a dynamic and effective leader. This leader has the ability to influence others in a desired direction and thus is able to determine the extent to which both individual employees and the organization as a whole reach their goals. Leadership transforms organizational potential into reality." [Stueart 168] The study of leadership takes three forms. The first is to review the behavior and traits of effective leaders, the second is to review leadership styles and their impact on productivity, and the third is to match the situation to the appropriate leadership style.

Behavior and trait studies of effective executives and leaders refute the concept that "leaders are born and not made" and conclude that the skills, abilities, and personalities of successful leaders vary greatly. Drucker's 1966 work, *The Effective Executive*, concludes that while the individual leaders he studied are quite different, they share common practices or habits of the mind. Effective executives know where their time goes; focus their vision on outward contribution; make strengths productive (their own, those of superiors, colleagues, and subordinates, and of the situation); concentrate on the major areas where superior performance can bring outstanding results; and make effective decisions. [Drucker 23–24] Other more recent studies, including Bennis and Nanus's *Leaders: The Strategies for Taking Charge*, Helgesen's *The Female Advantage*, and Peters and Austin's *A Passion for Excellence: The Leadership Difference*, search for the characteristics of the most effective leaders with no one description emerging.

Two prominent theories relating leadership style to production include the Likert Theory of Management and Blake and Mouton's Theory of the Managerial Grid® (Figure 9.2). The Likert Theory of Management, presented in *New Patterns of Management* (1961) and *The Human Organization* (1967), views the organization as a complex system in which leadership, motivation, decision making, communication, and control interact. His Theory of Management categorizes the management of these organizations on a continuum ranging from System 1 to System 4.

"System 1" is an exploitative-authoritative system in which managers hold Theory X assumptions, information flows primarily downward, and nearly all decision making is made at the top of the organization.

"System 2" is a benevolent-authoritative system in which managers demonstrate "master to servant" confidence and trust, information flows primarily downward with occasional upward communication; and policies are made at the top while decisions within a prescribed framework may be made at lower levels.

"System 3" is a consultative system in which managers make most of the decisions but invite input from subordinates, information flows both upward and downward, and broad policy decisions are made at the top while more specific ones are made at lower levels.

"System 4" is a participative system in which managers believe in Theory Y and encourage group participation, communication flows upward, downward, and horizontally throughout the organization, and decision making is spread widely throughout the organization and is well coordinated.

Likert suggests that as the management system moves from System 1 toward System 4, the human needs of employees tend to be more effectively satisfied enabling the organization to become more productive.

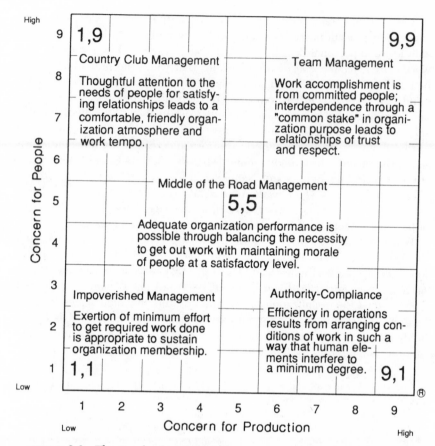

FIGURE 9.2 The Leadership Grid Figure   Source: The Leadership Grid Figure from *Leadership Dilemmas—Grid Solutions*, by Robert R. Blake and Anne Adams McCanse. Houston: Gulf Publishing Company, p. 29. Copyright © 1991, by Scientific Methods, Inc. Reproduced by permission of the owners.

In 1964, Blake and Mouton first introduced *The Managerial Grid* to demonstrate the interrelationship among concern for production, concern for people, and hierarchy or the "boss" aspect. The most recent formulation is entitled "The Leadership Grid" (Blake & McCanse, 1991). "To increase managerial competence and productivity in people, a leader must know of alternative leadership styles and be prepared to select the soundest." [Blake & Mouton, 13] To demonstrate the range of alternative styles, they developed "The Managerial Grid" in which they charted concern for production on the horizontal axis and concern for people on the vertical axis. Based on this Grid, Blake and Mouton described five leadership styles:

- 1,1 Orientation indicates an impoverished manager who has abdicated his responsibility toward productivity as well as his employees by demonstrating minimal concern for both production and people.
- 1,9 Orientation indicates the country club manager with high concern for satisfying human relationships and developing a comfortable, friendly organization even at the expense of productivity.
- 9,1 Orientation indicates an authorative manager who focuses on high production by exercising power and authority at the expense of his staff.
- 5,5 Orientation indicates the middle-of-the-road or compromise manager who seeks to achieve acceptable productivity without unduly distributing people.
- 9,9 Orientation indicates a style which is a goal-centered, team approach seeking results through participation, involvement, commitment, and conflict solving by everyone who can contribute.

Blake and Mouton's Theory of the Managerial Grid provides a framework for understanding organizational behavior as it reflects management style.

Situational Leadership is based on the assumption that the successful leader cannot function in isolation but is affected by a number of interdependent variables. In order to determine which leadership style to follow, the leader must evaluate the forces in the manager, in the follower, and in the situation, and their interaction. Forces in the manager include values, confidence in followers, leadership strengths, tolerance for ambiguity, and security. Forces in the follower include motivations, stage of development, identity with organizational objectives, problem-related expertise, level of skills, and interest in the problem. Forces in the situation include the type of organization, nature of the problem, time constraints, and group effectiveness.

Two leading models of "situational" leadership include Tannenbaum and Schmidt's Continuum of Leadership (Figure 9.3) and Hersey and Blanchard's Situational Leadership Model (Figure 9.4). In 1958, Tannenbaum and Schmidt introduced their Continuum of Leadership Behavior which models leadership decision making style on a continuum extending from autocrat to abdicrat. The model presents "the continuum or range of possible leadership behavior available to a manager. Each type of action is related to the degree of authority used by the boss and to the amount of freedom available to his subordinates in reaching decisions. The actions seen on the extreme left characterize the manager who maintains a high degree of control while those seen on the extreme right characterize the manager who releases

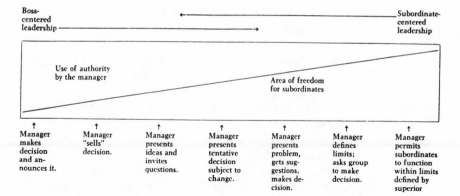

Boss-
centered
leadership

Subordinate-
centered
leadership

Use of authority
by the manager

Area of freedom
for subordinates

↑	↑	↑	↑	↑	↑	↑
Manager makes decision and announces it.	Manager "sells" decision.	Manager presents ideas and invites questions.	Manager presents tentative decision subject to change.	Manager presents problem, gets suggestions, makes decision.	Manager defines limits; asks group to make decision.	Manager permits subordinates to function within limits defined by superior

FIGURE 9.3   Continuum of Leadership Behavior   Reprinted by permission of *Harvard Business Review*. An exhibit from "How to Choose a Leadership Pattern" by Robert Tannenbaum and Warren H. Schmidt, (May/June 1973): 164. Copyright © 1973 by the President and Fellows of Harvard College; all rights reserved.

a high degree of control. Neither extreme is absolute; authority and freedom are never without their limitations." [Tannenbaum 96] When the continuum is extended to its extreme, the result is either autocracy or abdication. The autocrat violates employee values and self-image while the abdicrat is irresponsible and violates concepts of leadership. The effective leader develops the ability to determine what kind of leadership is required in a given situation and has the resources to use that style.

Hersey and Blanchard's Situational Leadership Model adds the dimension of follower readiness to a grid illustrating the interrelationships of task or directive behavior and relationships or supportive behavior. "According to the Situational Leadership Model, as the level of readiness of one's followers continues to increase, appropriate leader behavior not only requires less and less structure (task) but also less and less socio-emotional support (relationships)." [Hersey, 1969, 29] In the model, task behavior is noted along the horizontal axis and the relationship behavior on the vertical axis. The readiness curve runs from right to left denoting the direction the leader needs to move his followers. Readiness is defined as the ability of followers to perform tasks independently, their ability to assume additional responsibility, and their desire to achieve success. The leader's starting point for any given task is determined by the followers' abilities, knowledge, and willingness. For example, leadership style would shift from 1) "telling" or high task/low relationships behavior to 2) "selling" or high task/high relationships behavior to 3) "participating" or high relationships/low task behavior to 4) "delegating" or low relationship/low task behavior. The successful leader assesses the

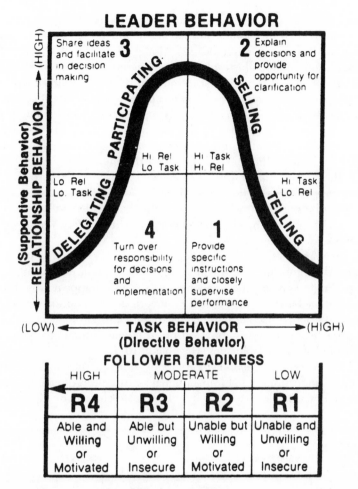

FIGURE 9.4 **The Situational Leadership Model** Source: Paul Hersey and
Kenneth Blanchard. *Management of Organizational Behavior.* Fifth Edition.
Prentice Hall, 1988: Englewood Cliffs, NJ: 287. Copyrighted material from
Leadership Studies, Inc. Used by permission. All rights reserved.

readiness of the follower for each of the tasks in which they are involved and
adapts the leadership style appropriately.

Communication Theory

A significant amount of the administrator's time is devoted to communication; consequently, communication theory is another of the theoretical foun-

dations of management. Communication is the process of sharing a message from one individual to another and having it understood by both parties. The Shannon-Weaver Communication Model (Figure 9.5) and the Berlo Communication Model illustrate the components of the communications process. Shannon and Weaver first introduced their Communication Model for the purpose of illustrating electronic communications in *The Mathematical Theory of Communication* (1949). "As applied to human communication, this model shows in linear fashion that communication consists of an information source (a person sending a message), a transmitter (the voice, for example), a channel (the method by which the method is carried—sound waves in the case of spoken words, or the printed page in the case of written words), a receiver (any of the senses used to pick up the message), and the destination (the person to whom the message was sent). It also introduces the concept of "noise" (any phenomenon that might interfere with the clarity of the message)." [Haggblade 6–7]

Noise, or barriers to communication, comes from external sources, such as unrelated stimuli, unwise selection of communication media, differences in status, limitations of time or money, and physical appearance. Internal communication barriers are caused by inaccurate perception based upon previous experience, lack of basic knowledge, confusion of facts with inferences, poor listening ability, physical or emotional limitations, conflicting nonverbal behavior, or language. [Haggblade 10–13]

In *The Process of Communication* (1960), Berlo emphasizes the importance of the understanding of human behavior as a prerequisite to communication analysis. Berlo's model is based upon psychology or the search for

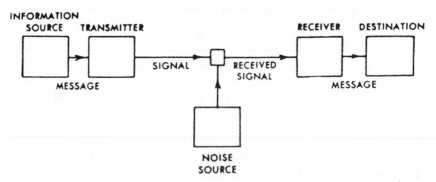

FIGURE 9.5   The Shannon-Weaver Communication Model   Source: Claude E. Shannon and Warren Weaver. *The Mathematical Theory of Communication.* Urbana, IL: The University of Illinois Press, 1949: 34. Copyright 1949 by The Board of Trustees of the University of Illinois. Reprinted with permission.

individual characteristics, sociology or group approach to behavior, and social psychology or the relationship of both personal and social factors which affect communication. Berlo identifies the ingredients in communication as the Source, Message, Channel, and Receiver. If effective communication is to occur, both the source and receiver must have compatible communication skills, attitudes, knowledge, social system, and culture. [Berlo 72–74] Since the purpose of communication is to seek a response from the receiver, the source keeps the receiver in mind as he develops his message by selecting a code or "language" the receiver can understand and will receive favorably, by including content which is convincing and pertinent to his needs, and by treating the message in a manner to achieve his purpose. The channel is the vehicle of communication which includes sight, sound, touch, smell, and taste. An understanding of the interrelationship between the source, message, channel, and receiver and the process of communication results in more effective communication.

In order to ensure that communication has occurred, feedback or some response to the sender's message must result. When used effectively, feedback enables the individuals involved in the communication process to profit from the responses of each other. Feedback is the key element in the completion of the communication process. Three major principles of effective feedback include: 1) Communicators desire feedback. 2) Immediate feedback is the most effective. 3) Feedback must be interpreted accurately. [Haggblade 9–10]

Koontz and O'Donnell cite communication as a manager's most vital management tool. Like Berlo, they emphasize that communication occurs not only with words but also through apparent attitudes and actions. They developed the following ten commandments to help managers improve their communication skills:

1. Seek to clarify your ideas before communicating.
2. Examine the true purpose of each communication and adapt your language, tone, and approach to serve that objective.
3. Consider the total physical and human setting whenever you communicate.
4. Consult with others, where appropriate, in planning communications.
5. Be mindful, while you communicate, of the overtones (tone, expression, receptiveness) as well as the basic content of your message.
6. Take the opportunity, when it arises, to convey something of help or value to the receiver.
7. Follow up your communication by providing feedback so complete understanding and appropriate action can result.
8. Communicate for tomorrow as well as today so they are consistent with long-range interests and goals.

9. Be sure your actions support your verbal communications.
10. Seek not only to be understood but to understand—be a good listener.
    [Koontz 495–496]

Trends in LRP Administration

Community college learning resources programs are going through times of change. Budgets are shrinking and greater accountability is demanded. Rapid technological advances are impacting the complexity and quantity of service requests, staffing patterns, facilities needs, and external cooperative agreements, such as resource sharing and cooperative collection development. New staff members are bringing varied educational and cultural backgrounds, expectations, and attitudes. National management trends are continually changing with new styles championed.

The effective learning resources administrator is a leader who has a vision of the future, but is pragmatic; believes in the value of the LRP and can articulate it; encourages cooperation both within and beyond the LRP; understands resistance to change, but can build the trust and understanding to carry the program forward. He orchestrates college priorities, service needs, LRP staff productivity, and resources into an effective, service-oriented program. He is an assertive leader who accepts responsibility for his actions and the demands of his position. He ensures that staff members know exactly what is expected of them as individuals and as members of a team. [Hulbert 159] He is results-oriented marrying long-term objectives with ambitious short-term improvement projects which cumulate into significant forward progress over time. [Schaffer 89]

The LRP administrator is a change agent and team builder responding to the division's changing organizational structure with the advent of automation. He helps staff modify past assumptions about the storage and delivery of information and about organizational structure. He realizes that the dual organizational structures of faculty collegiality and support staff hierarchy will change as previously separate functional units become interdependent resulting in new communication patterns, as specialized knowledge and expertise for certain tasks are required, and as authority, influence, and information no longer are arranged by organizational level or personnel classification.

The LRP administrator realizes no one simple formula for leadership exists. Instead, his leadership style is based on the principles derived from behavioral research, on the policies of institution, and on his own philosophy of human needs. He adopts a situational leadership style which emphasizes matching a leadership style with a particular environment or work situation.

Thus, he adapts his style of leadership behavior to the needs of his followers and the situation.

Selected Bibliography

BENNIS, WARREN, and BURT NANUS. *Leaders: The Strategies for Taking Charge.* New York: Harper & Row, 1985.

BERLO, DAVID K. *The Process of Communication.* New York: Holt, Rinehart, & Winston, 1960.

BLAKE, ROBERT R., and ANNE ADAMS MCCANSE. *Leadership Dilemmas—Grid Solutions.* Houston: Gulf Publishing, 1991.

BLAKE, ROBERT R., and JANE S. MOUTON. *The Managerial Grid, III.* Houston: Gulf Publishing, 1985.

CERTO, SAMUEL C. *Principles of Modern Management.* Fourth Edition. Boston: Allyn and Bacon, 1989.

DRUCKER, PETER F. *The Effective Executive.* New York: Harper & Row, 1966.

HAGGBLADE, BERLE. *Business Communication.* St. Paul, MN: West Publishing, 1982.

HAWKINS, KATHERINE W. "Implementing Team Management in the Modern Library," *Library Administration and Management* 3 (Winter 1989): 11–15.

HAYES, JAMES L. "The Pygmalian Effect—Helping People Be What You Want Them to Be," *American School & University* 51 (August 1979): 20+.

HERSEY, PAUL, and KENNETH BLANCHARD. "Life Cycle Theory of Leadership," *Training and Development Journal* (May 1969): 26–34.

———. *Management of Organizational Behavior: Utilizing Human Resources.* Fifth Edition. Englewood Cliffs, NJ: Prentice Hall, 1988.

HULBERT, DORIS. "Assertive Management in Libraries," *Journal of Academic Librarianship* 16 (July 1990): 158–162.

JOHNSON, PEGGY. *Automation and Organizations: Change in Libraries.* New York: G.K. Hall, 1991.

LIVINGSTONE, STERLING. "Pygmalion in Management," *Harvard Business Review* 47 (July/August 1969): 81–89.

MASLOW, ABRAHAM H. *Motivation and Personality.* Second Edition. New York: Harper & Row, 1970.

MCGREGOR, DOUGLAS. *The Human Side of Enterprise.* New York: McGraw Hill, 1960.

MECH, TERRENCE F. "Academic Library Directors: A Managerial Role Profile," *College & Research Libraries* 51 (September 1990): 415–428.

MINTZBERG, HENRY. *Mintzberg on Management: Inside Our Strange World of Organizations.* New York: Free Press, 1989.

MOSKOWITZ, MICHAEL ANN. "The Managerial Roles of Academic Library Directors: The Mintzberg Model," *College & Research Libraries* 47 (September 1986): 452–459.

SCHAFFER, ROBERT H., and HARVEY A. THOMSON. "Successful Change Programs Begin with Results," *Harvard Business Review* 70 (January-February 1992): 80–89.

SHANNON, CLAUDE E., and WARREN WEAVER. *The Mathematical Theory of Communication*. Urbana, IL: The University of Illinois Press, 1949.

SHELDON, BROOKE E. "Library Leaders: Attributes Compared to Corporate Leaders," *Library Trends* 40 (Winter 1992): 391–401.

"Standards for Community, Junior, and Technical College Learning Resources Programs," *College & Research Libraries News* 51 (September 1990): 757–767.

STUEART, ROBERT D., and BARBARA B. MORAN. *Library Management*. Third Edition. Littleton, CO: Libraries Unlimited, 1987.

TANNENBAUM, ROBERT, and WARREN SCHMIDT. "How to Choose a Leadership Style," *Harvard Business Review* 36 (March–April 1958): 95–101.

"Ten Commandments of Good Communication." In *Management: A Book of Readings*, Second Edition, ed. Harold Koontz and Cyril O'Donnell. New York: McGraw Hill, 1968.

10

Learning Resources Program Review and Planning

Learning resources program review and planning is "the process of getting an organization from where it is to where it wants to be in a given period of time by setting it on a predetermined course of action." [Stueart 21] It involves a cycle which assumes the learning resources program is dynamic and undergoing continual change responsive to internal and external influences. Internal influences include changes in staffing patterns and abilities, inflation and budgetary constraints, patterns of use, modified facilities, etc. External influences involve changes in college administration and priorities, requests for additional services, membership and accreditation requirements from external agencies, the information explosion and emerging technologies, professional standards and trends, etc.

The chief learning resources administrator is "responsible for administering the program and for providing leadership and direction so that mission of the program is fulfilled." [Standards 758–759] Consequently, he is responsible for leading the program review and planning cycle which includes gathering relevant information, reviewing the learning resources mission and goals, developing an action plan, and implementing the plan. He does not complete the program review and planning process alone; instead, he enlists the participation of everyone who will be involved in the implementation of

149

the action plan. Thus, all learning resources staff, the Learning Resources Advisory Committee, the college administration, and the broader college community participate in the program review and planning cycle.

The program review and planning cycle repeats itself on a regular basis, minimally with a full program review every three to five years and with a more abbreviated review annually in conjunction with setting annual objectives and justifying the budget. Additional focused reviews are scheduled in conjunction with regional and specialized accreditation visits.

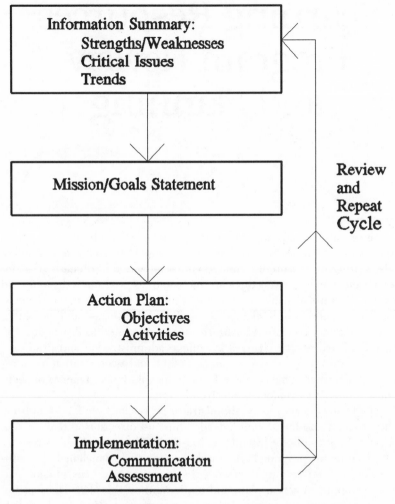

FIGURE 10.1   Program Review and Planning Cycle

The successful program review and planning process results in the development of a highly respected, learning resources program with staff and fiscal resources focused on common program goals and priorities. The process encourages a vision of the future with consideration of internal and external influences. It ensures a coordinated program with staff working toward achievement of common goals related to the improvement of learning. This chapter describes the program review and planning cycle which includes gathering relevant information, clarifying the mission, developing an action plan, and implementing the plan.

Gathering Relevant Information

The first stage of the program review and planning cycle involves the gathering of objective information about the learning resources program, determining its strengths and weaknesses, plus identifying environmental factors which affect both the LRP and its parent college. The gathering information stage asks, "What is our current situation? What are our strengths and weaknesses? What are trends which will affect the LRP and the college?" Answers to these questions can be categorized according to source of information or evaluation criteria. These categories include professional, external college, collegewide, and internal learning resources program information.

Professional Information

Although useful to LRP staff, professional information rarely is accepted by college administrators as a relevant justification for increased budget or staff through the program planning process. However, professional standards, such as the "Standards for Community, Junior, and Technical College Learning Resources Programs," provide guidelines or goals to strive toward in program development. The Standards enable LRP staff to compare the college's resources and program with accepted national standards in terms of staffing, collections, services, etc.

Another source of professional information is the comparison of the college's learning resources program with that of other comparably sized community colleges. This technique compares colleges with similar demographic and economic environments providing LRP staff current program comparison data. Data compared includes LRC budget, percent of the college instructional budget, hours open, staff size, collection size, and service statistics. An example of this comparison technique is the collection of data elements by the Northern Illinois Learning Resource Cooperative each year. General information such as district size, population, assessed valuation, annualized head count, LRC staff FTE, and hours open per week provides the base information for comparing circulation and distribution, collection size, services provided (interlibrary loan, database searches, presentations, reference transactions, telecourses offered, etc.), and equipment data. Members compare their individual LRP programs either with the total membership or with members sharing similar demographics.

Other professional considerations include trends in the library/media profession and in higher education. Examples include the national focus on information literacy, the emphasis on accountability and outcomes measures, the impact of telecommunications technology enabling improved connectivity resulting in cooperative collection development and resource sharing networks, the shifting instructional emphasis from teaching to learning, and emerging instructional technologies, such as CD-ROM networking, interactive video, and hypermedia. Information regarding these trends is gathered through active participation in professional organizations, including the American Library Association (ALA), the Association of Educational Communications and Technology (AECT), the American Association of Community and Junior Colleges (AACJC), as well as state organizations such as the Illinois Council of Community College Administrators (ICCCA), through scanning current library and higher education publications, including *American Libraries, Community and Junior College Libraries, College & Research Libraries News*, and the *Chronicle of Higher Education*, through participating in campus staff development activities focusing on specific campuswide instructional issues, and more.

External College Information

External college information is more influential since it includes federal, state, and local regulations, requirements of regional and specialized accreditation agencies, membership criteria of consortia and cooperatives, as well as trends in higher education, economic conditions, etc. Community college enabling legislation and guidelines are found in state statutes and through the regulations of the state higher educational authority. The legal authority for the local board of trustees is based upon these state statutes. Consequently, information regarding changing state priorities and regulations provide direct influence.

Federal legislation affects community colleges through specific legal requirements, as those set forth in the Americans With Disabilities Act, the minimum wage act, and OSHA regulations, and through the withholding of federal funds unless the college complies with specific criteria, such as certification of a drug-free workplace. Local regulations affect the program through compliance with local fire regulations, etc.

Requirements for regional and specialized accreditation provide still other criteria for program review. The Middle States Commission on Higher Education is leading the trend among regional accreditation agencies to require the incorporation of information literacy into the total teaching/learning environment of the college. [Lutzker 14] Another trend among accrediting agencies is to focus on outcomes measures rather than only collection and circulation statistics. This emphasis on outcomes measures shifts to focus of the learning resources program from a repository of resources to the deliverer of information and instructional support. College self-study reports prior accreditation visits and subsequent evaluation team reports provide useful information regarding perceived strengths and weaknesses as well as agency priorities.

Membership criteria of consortia and cooperative additional external measures. For example, college membership in the Northern Illinois Learning Resources Cooperative requires not only payment of membership dues but also a specific minimal level of participation in cooperative leadership and activities. The Suburban Library System (IL) requires specific minimal reference staff coverage, ownership of telefacsimile equipment, annual updating of periodical holdings in the system union list, and compliance with systemwide resources sharing protocols for participation.

Collegewide Information

Collegewide information provides the most important data for the learning resources program review and planning cycle. The college mission and strategic plan as they respond to state, community, and other external influences provide the foundation for the learning resources program. The college president and chief academic officer provide leadership in interpreting the college mission and strategic plan in terms of college organization, program offerings, budget, staff, and facilities priorities. The chief learning resources administrator participates in campuswide strategic planning activities and, with cooperation of the institutional research office, has access to college mission and strategic planning documents, to demographic and economic data, to college annual reports and special studies, to curricular enrollment statistics, etc.

Since faculty and students are the primary customers of learning resources services, their satisfaction with and perceptions of the LRP provide important information. This information is gathered through informal conversations, "suggestion box" comments, focus group input, and user survey responses. Informal conversations and suggestion box comments provide informal, but haphazard, methods of obtaining user feedback. Focus group sessions require a neutral third party to lead and report on the sessions, groups of users and non-users of LRP services, and a set of questions to help establish what information is desired, and result in guided oral input. Formal surveys gather the broadest amount of information but most frequently require written response.

Van House et al's *Measuring Academic Library Performance* and Butler and Gratch's "Planning a User Survey: The Process Defined," provide specific guidance for gathering information through user surveys. The institutional research office assists with creating the surveys, obtaining authorization to conduct the project, and analyzing the results. For a general satisfaction survey, Van House et al recommend a return of 400 survey forms and estimate academic library response rates average 80 percent. [Van House 28] Once the survey project is complete and the data analyzed, the results are disseminated. Disseminating results of the survey beyond the program review and planning process is essential for maintaining good public relations and encouraging participation in future surveys.

Internal LRP Information

Internal LRP information includes a review of LRP budget, resources, services, facilities, and organization/staffing. Journal articles and books describing specific LRP evaluative criteria and techniques are available. A selective sampling follows. The LRP budget is reviewed historically as a percentage of the total instructional budget and by expenditure as subdivided among staff, materials, supplies, and capital equipment. Resources are reviewed in terms of usefulness based upon need for weeding, inventory accuracy and replacement plan, physical condition and the need for "merchandising," interlibrary loan requests, and faculty and student satisfaction. Services are reviewed through historic use patterns for circulation, telecourse support, interlibrary loan, equipment distribution, reference assistance, bibliographic instruction, etc., through user satisfaction with access and availability of resources, and through requests for additional or modified services. Facilities are reviewed through analysis of functional organization and space utilization, through physical environmental issues as HVAC and noise, and through availability, age, and reliability of instructional delivery equipment. LRP organization and staffing are reviewed through existing staffing patterns and workloads, professional development activities, availability of current written procedural guidelines. Internal LRP information also includes understanding of formal employee status and contractual agreements as well as individual abilities, attitudes, and ideas.

Once relevant information is gathered, LRP staff synthesize it into a self-study report identifying learning resources program strengths and weaknesses, critical issues to address, and future trends. This information summary serves as the foundation for reviewing the LRP mission and developing the LRP action plan. This information summary is discussed with the LRP Advisory Committee and LRP staff, is presented as an executive summary to the chief academic officer and then discussed, is orally shared with the Faculty Senate, and is reported campuswide through the student newspaper.

Reviewing the LRP Mission

Based upon the information summary and subsequent discussions, LRP staff begin the next stage of the program review and planning cycle by asking "What do we want the LRP to be in the future?", reviewing the LRP mission, developing general goals, and ensuring both the LRP mission and goals are compatible with the college's mission and strategic plan.

This review process may begin with LRP staff participating in problem-solving or brainstorming activities which encourage creative thinking. Through these activities, staff are asked to creatively freethink and to offer any ideas that come to mind in response to the question, "What would you like the LRP to be like in three to five years?". The ideas are recorded on cards or chalkboards or flip charts. No discussion or judgment of the ideas is permitted since an uninterrupted flow of creative ideas is sought. Since not everyone is comfortable with group brainstorming techniques, opportunities for individuals to submit creative ideas in the form of written cards or lists are also provided.

Once the ideas are compiled, they are reviewed for compatibility with the college mission and strategic plan. Those that are compatible are then synthesized into the LRP mission statement and general goals. The LRP mission is a philosophical statement which broadly defines what the LRP is and does. It states the purpose of the program and "serves as a mirror for the evaluation of services and the projection of future needs. As such it becomes an integral part of the planning process." [Standards 758] LRP goals, objectives, and subsequent action plan are predetermined by the LRP mission and its compatibility with the college's mission and strategic plan. Table 10.1 provides a sample mission statement with corresponding goal and activities.

The effective mission statement will "identify the community or communities the library (LRP) serves, describe the way in which it serves these communities, establish a vision of what the library (LRP) will become, provide a sound base for decentralized decision making, and stand without modification for a considerable period of time." [Jacob 61] In addition, it is "in congruence with its parent organization's mission." [Riggs 31]

While the LRP mission provides a broad philosophical description of what the program is and should be doing, goals provide a conceptual basis for the

TABLE 10.1   Sample Planning Components

Mission
The Learning Resources Program provides the resources and services necessary to serve the informational, learning, and developmental needs of its students, faculty, and administrators. In addition, the LRP supports the cultural, co-curricular, and recreational activities of the college community. To a lesser degree, the LRP extends its resources and services, as appropriate, to the general public and serves as a community and regional resources center.

Sample Goal
3. To provide assistance and instruction in the access to print and electronic information resources and their use through individualized assistance, point-of-use instruction, and formal class instruction.

Sample Objective
3.1 During FY93, point-of-use instructional aids will be created or updated for every print and electronic index.
   Activity: • List all print and electronic indexes.
         • Review existing point-of-use aids to determine need for revision.
         • Revise as necessary.
         • Create point-of-use aids for other indexes.
3.2 During FY93, extend bibliographic instruction into introductory programs in career programs.
   Activity: • Develop career specific pathfinders.
         • Create general instructional syllabus for career specific bibliographic instruction.
         • Invite classroom faculty to bring their introductory classes into Learning Resources Center for an orientation session.
         • Publicize the service.
3.3 During FY93, expand the Syllabus File to include minimally all liberal arts courses.
   Activity: • Compare existing syllabi on file with current course offerings.
         • Obtain copies of course syllabi for courses not on file from individual classroom faculty.
         • Ensure all LRP staff are aware of the file maintained at Reference.
         • Publicize the service.

---

operation of the learning resources program. They provide a direction or framework for planning by identifying the LRP's broad aims with respect to programs, resource management, and organization. Thus, goal statements may focus on the acquisition and delivery of resources, public services, staff development, etc. Goal statements reflect qualitative rather than quantitative aims and are stated in action terms, but are not specific enough to be operational.

The LRP mission and goals reflect the college's mission and strategic plan and are responsive to programmatic needs as identified through the information summary. This review and revision, as necessary, of the LRP mission and goals provide the framework for developing the LRP action plan.

Developing the Action Plan

Developing the action plan is the next stage of the LRP program review and planning cycle. Through this stage, after LRP staff review the information summary listing LRP strengths and weaknesses, critical issues, and key external trends and study the LRP mission and general goals, they begin to develop the action plan. The action plan consists of measurable objectives followed by specific activities which support each objective. The action plan should be "resultful, action oriented, fact-based and comprehensive, focused, consistent, flexible, and doable." [Virgo 22]

LRP staff again participates in problem-solving or brainstorming activities by responding to the question, "How can we develop a learning resources program responsive of existing LRP needs as well as planning toward future potentials?" Once the ideas are compiled, they are reviewed for compatibility with the LRP mission and goals. The remaining responses are analyzed with these questions: Is the idea consistent with external influences, such as the college strategic plan, state and federal regulations, accrediting agency requirements, professional trends, etc.? Is the idea appropriate in view of available human, equipment, supply, and operating budget resources? Is the amount of risk required in implementing the idea acceptable? Is the implementation timetable realistic? Is the idea workable? Based upon this process, specific objectives and activities for each LRP goal are developed creating the action plan.

Objectives relate directly to LRP goals and describe how the LRP will fulfill its mission. They are specific and state in measurable terms what particular result will be accomplished by a specific date. "Objectives are more internally focused than goals, and they imply a resource commitment, challenging library management to use necessary resources in order to achieve the desired results. They are purposeful, short-termed, consistent with goals, linked to other objectives, precise, measurable, verifiable, understandable, and flexible. Objectives could be described as the landmarks and milestones which mark the path toward the library's goal(s)." [Riggs 35]

Stueart lists criteria for objectives through a series of questions: "Is the objective suitable? Does it take the organization in the direction it wants to go? Does it support the overall mission? Is it compatible with other objectives? Is it acceptable to the majority who will be charged with implementing it? Can the organization afford it? Is it achievable? Is it ambitious enough to be challenging? Is it measurable?" [Stueart 36]

Activities are the specific courses of action or tasks necessary to accomplish goals and objectives. Most frequently, activities are developed through the formal program review and planning cycle, but on occasion, they emerge from ad hoc situations. Activities may be formally stated on an LRP Action Plan Form like Figure 10.2 which answers the questions of who, what, where, when, and how objectives are to be completed. The resulting action plan lists the general goal, measurable objectives, and activities necessary to achieve each objective including resources required (staff, facilities, budget), timeframe, and responsible individuals.

LEARNING RESOURCES PROGRAM ACTION PLAN FORM

GOAL:

Objective	Activity	Resources	When	By Whom

FIGURE 10.2   Learning Resources Program Action Plan Form

Implementing the Plan

Implementing the action plan involves publicizing the results of the program review and planning process, regularly assessing internal and external influences and their impact on the action plan, and adjusting the plan as necessary.

Since one purpose of the program review and planning cycle is to promote campuswide "ownership" of the learning resources program, communication is an essential part of implementation. Results of the program review and planning cycle are introduced, explained, and publicized through as many communication channels as possible. Potential audiences include LRP staff, LRP Advisory Committee, the chief academic officer, current and potential LRP users, the Faculty Senate, the Board of Trustees, and others. Information regarding LRP strengths and weaknesses, the mission and goals, as well as general strategies are shared. Special projects and significant accomplishments are publicized. In addition, visible, results-oriented activities demonstrate to everyone who participated in the process that their ideas were responsively considered and that the LRP wants to be accountable for serving the college's learning resources needs.

Another purpose of the program review and planning process is to provide a focus for the effective use of staff talents and fiscal resources. Therefore, activities included in the action plan are implemented by the individuals responsible. Their progress and the action plan itself are regularly asserted in light of internal and external influences which affect the learning resources program. The action plan is proactive looking toward the future, yet flexible in detail as change occurs.

Summary

Learning resources program review and planning is a cyclic process of determining where the program is and where it should be in the future and of developing a prescribed course of forward action. The process involves gathering information about existing resources and services, external influences, and future trends, reaffirming or updating the LRP mission and goals in response to the college's mission and strategic plan, developing an action plan, and implementing that plan.

The chief learning resources administrator coordinates the program review and planning cycle with the entire LRP staff, the LRP Advisory Committee, the college administration, and the broader college community participating. During the information gathering stage, existing legislation and criteria, trends and forecasts, college strategic planning data, and existing LRP resources and services are reviewed. Most importantly, user satisfaction data is gathered in both statistical and narrative form. Second, LRP staff review and update the LRP mission and goals and ensure that they are compatible with the college's mission and priorities.

Third, the LRP staff and advisory committee review all available information, determine where the program should be in three to five years, and develop an action plan. Existing and proposed resources, services, and facilities undergo a cost-benefit analysis through which cost in terms of labor and budget are compared with positive impact on the college. Some existing resources and services are rejustified, unnecessary or low priority resources and services are discontinued, new resources and services are added.

Finally, results of the program review and planning process are introduced, explained, and publicized at every group meeting and through as many communication channels as possible. The plan itself is implemented and assessed with program activities demonstrating to everyone who participated in the process that their input was responsively considered.

The program review and planning cycle serves as an educational tool for everyone involved and promotes campuswide "ownership" of the learning resources program, it provides a focus for the effective use of staff talents and fiscal resources, and adds credibility to the development and defense of a programmatic budget fitting the LRP into the collegewide mission and strategic plan.

Selected Bibliography

BUTLER, MEREDITH, and BONNIE GRATCH. "Planning a User Study: The Process Defined," *College & Research Libraries* 43 (July 1982): 320–330.

CHRISTIANSEN, DOROTHY E., ET AL. "Guide to Collection Evaluation through Use and User studies," *Library Resources & Technical Services* 27 (October/December 1983): 432–440.

DAHLGREN, ANDERS C., ED. "Library Buildings," *Library Trends* 36 (Fall 1987): 261–491.

FROHMAN, MARK A. "How to Improve Your Problem-Solving Capability," *Management Review* 69 (November 1980): 59–61.

GRATCH, BONNIE, and ELIZABETH WOOD. "Strategic Planning: Implementation and First-Year Appraisal," *Journal of Academic Librarianship* 17 (March 1991): 10–15.

JACOB, M.E.L. *Strategic Planning: A How-to-Do-It Manual for Librarians.* New York: Neal-Schuman, 1990.

LUTZKER, MARILYN. "Bibliographic Instruction and Accreditation in Higher Education," *College & Research Libraries News* 51 (January 1990): 14–18.

MAGRILL, ROSE MARY. "Evaluation by Type of Library," *Library Trends* 33 (Winter 1985): 267–295.

ORR, R.H. "Progress in Documentation: Measuring the Goodness of Library Services: A General Framework for Considering Quantitative Measures." In *Key Papers in the Design and Evaluation of Information Systems*, ed. Donald King. White Plains, NY: Knowledge Industry, 1979.

POST, RICHARD. "Longevity and Depreciation of Audiovisual Equipment," *TechTrends* 32 (November 1987): 12–14.

RIGGS, DONALD E. *Strategic Planning for Library Managers*. Phoenix: Oryx Press, 1984.

ROBBINS-CARTER, JANE, and DOUGLAS ZWEIZIG. "Are We There Yet? Evaluting Library Collections, Reference Services, Programs, and Personnel," *American Libraries* 16 (October 1985): 624–627); (November 1985): 724–727; (December 1985): 780–784; (January 1986): 32–36; and (February 1986): 108–112.

SCHLICHTER, DORIS J., and J. MICHAEL PEMBERTON. "The Emperor's New Clothes? Problems of the User Survey as a Planning Tool in Academic Libraries," *College & Research Libraries* 53 (May 1992): 257–265.

SIMAS, ROBERT J. *Assessment System for the Evaluation of Learning Resources Programs in Community Colleges*. Suisun, CA: Learning Resources Association of California Community Colleges, 1982.

Standards for College and University Learning Resources Programs: Technology in Instruction. Second Edition. Washington, DC: Association for Educational Communications and Technology, 1989.

"Standards for Community, Junior, and Technical College Learning Resources Programs," *College & Research Libraries News* 51 (September 1990): 757–767.

STEINER, GEORGE A. *Strategic Planning: What Every Manager Must Know*. New York: The Free Press, 1979.

STUEART, ROBERT D., and BARBARA B. MORAN. *Library Management*. Third Edition. Littleton, CO: Libraries Unlimited, 1987.

VAN HOUSE, NANCY A., ET AL. *Measuring Academic Library Performance: A Practical Approach*. Chicago, American Library Association, 1990.

VIRGO, JULIE A.C. *CE 111 Principles of Strategic Planning in the Library Environment*. Chicago: Association of College and Research Libraries, 1984.

11

The Learning Resources Budget

The learning resources program budget is directly related to the LRP program review and planning cycle. Through the cycle, relevant information is gathered, the LRP mission and goals are reviewed and correlated to the college mission and strategic plan, and an action plan is developed. As part of this cycle, existing resources and services are re-justified or discontinued and new resources and services proposed. The program review and planning cycle creates the foundation for developing a responsive learning resources budget fitting the LRP into the collegewide mission and strategic plan. The LRP budget proposal is a fiscal interpretation of the learning resources program.

The learning resources program receives its primary funding through an allocation of the collegewide budget. The adequacy of the LRP budget allocation is measured through its percentage of educational and general budget totals for the college or through a full-time student equivalent dollar basis. According to the "Standards," all community college LRP budgets should fall minimally 6 percent of the college's education and general expenditures or within a sliding scale of dollars per full-time equivalent (FTE) student for learning resources other than salaries. "Neither method includes capital expenditures. Technological changes, automation, replacement of equipment, and other capital expenditures will require additional funds." [Standards 761]

External sources, such as grants, entrepreneur activities, fines and fees, etc., provide secondary funding. Results of a American Library Association survey to determine how academic libraries are raising supplementary funds to augment the regular library budget found that only 24 percent of the two-year college respondents reported revenue exceeding $10,000 from alternative sources. [Lynch 1] These alternative sources of revenue included services, sales, and special events; computerized catalogs and databases, searching and printing; fines and replacement charges; gifts and grants; and library endowments. The survey also found that in many cases the revenue generated was not retained in the library operating budget but instead was passed on to its parent institution. This chapter focuses both on the internal learning resources budget and on the generation of external revenues.

The Internal Budget Process

The objective of the budget process is to provide the greatest amount of cost-effective, quality service to the largest number of people. Within the community college, a non-profit institution, budget emphasis is placed on determining what resources are necessary, how to best use those resources for achieving program objectives, and how to account for resources expended.

The budget, usually prepared on an annual basis, is a plan for allocating resources to the objectives of the learning resources program. It formalizes an expenditure plan based upon the availability of projected resources. The budget does not determine the full cost of operations, such as space, heating and cooling, utilities, etc. Instead, it assumes all budgeted dollars are controllable by the administrator receiving the allocation. Once the expenditure plan is established, it is monitored for compliance. The expenditure levels are not to be exceeded. [Smith, 1991, 55–56]

College budget processes reflect an annual cycle that parallels the cycle of governmental appropriations and funding. During this time, "plans and decisions are completed; operations are carried out; and reviews, reports, and audits follow. These recurring sequences of activities are necessary to procure financial resources, to expend them in support of program objectives, and to account for their use. The repetitive cycle does not always coincide with the calendar year (the federal fiscal year runs from October 1 through September 30), but the basic program and fiscal period is almost always twelve months long and is referred to as the Fiscal Year (FY)." [Vinter 24]

Budget Preparation

In most community college districts, the Board of Trustees approves the college budget with the President and the Vice President of Business Services responsible for developing the budget calendar and compiling the budget recommendation. The most frequently used budget techniques include the line item, program, PPBS (Planning Programming Budgeting System), and zero-based budgets.

The line item or incremental budget is the most common approach which divides expenditures into broad categories, such as personnel and fringe benefits, supplies and expenses, travel, and equipment, with further subdivisions within these categories. The line item budget process extrapolates the previous years spending levels into the next year, adjusts the costs for inflation, and further adjusts the spending level for any new projects or services.

The program budget identifies expenditures by area of service within the learning resources program, such as acquisitions, circulation, information services, etc. Within each program area, personnel, materials, supplies, equipment, among other things, are estimated to accomplish that service area's objectives and action plan. The total LRP budget is presented as a summary of each service area's budget needs.

PPBS (Planning Programming Budgeting System), introduced by the Department of Defense in the 1960s, was the first widely used version of program budgeting. PPBS begins the budgeting and planning process by identifying the goals and objectives to be accomplished. Next, alternative methods for achieving the objectives based upon the cost-benefit ratios for each are identified and evaluated and, finally, the appropriate alternative is implemented. PPBS is considered a combination of program budgeting and MBO (management by objectives).

Zero-based budgeting (ZBB) requires that each program must be presented and justified in detail from scratch. Through ZBB, a decision package for each program or project is developed. The decision package describes the program, its rationale, benefits, impacts, ramifications, and costs. The decision package also discusses alternative methods for accomplishing the same goals and explains why the alternatives have been rejected. Finally, the decision packages are ranked by priority and funded accordingly.

The effective chief learning resources administrator develops a positive working relationship with the Vice President of Business Services and adheres to the fiscal guidelines set forth by the college. Whatever the budget technique followed, the budget process is based upon the LRP program activity plan derived from the LRP program review and planning process. The activity plan lists the specific activities required to accomplish the goals and objectives set forth. For each activity, necessary resources are estimated. The planning process also suggests operational levels including the continuity budget with no increases except inflation, an incremental budget allowing for increases in addition to inflation, and an expansion budget for introducing new services.

Regardless of budget technique, the budget creator must arrive at a comprehensive list of how the budget allocation should be expended. The Budget Request Outline (Figure 11.1) provides generic guidance in establishing

```
                    BUDGET REQUEST OUTLINE


Department:_____    Requested by:_____

Budget     Description              Current   Proposed  Continuity
Code                                Budget    Budget    Incremental

100        Personnel
              Administrative
              Faculty
              Staff
              Part-time
              Student

400        External Services
              Repair & Maintenance
              Maintenance Contracts
              Equipment Rental
              Consortia Memberships
              Film Rental

460        Travel

500        Office Supplies

550        Printing

600        Learning Resources
              Books
              Standing Orders
              Periodicals
              Interlibrary Loan
              Database Searches
              Videocassettes
              Microcomputer Software
              Other Media Formats
              Miscellaneous

615        LRP Supplies
              Audiotape
              Videotape
              Photographic
              Transparency/Graphic
              Computer
              Library Circulation
              Library Processing
              AV Repair Parts
              AV Projector Lamps
              Miscellaneous

800        Capital Equipment
```

FIGURE 11.1   Budget Request Outline

that comprehensive list. While every college has its own unique procedures for budget preparation, Figures 11.1, 11.2, and 11.3 provide generic guidance. Capital equipment, frequently defined as equipment costing over $250, requires additional prioritization and justification through the Capital Equipment Request Form (Figure 11.2). Any special projects or program changes are outlined on the Special Project Proposal Form (Figure 11.3) and are submitted as a supplement to the LRP budget.

A separate budget narrative accompanies the budget preparation forms to describe how the proposed budget supports the college mission and strategic plan as reflected through the LRP review and planning process. This budget narrative succinctly explains and justifies the budget proposal as detailed on the accompanying forms. The LRP administrator also may be requested to orally explain, justify, and defend the budget proposal as submitted. If he thoroughly understands his total program and if the budget proposal is realistically based upon his program needs, he will successfully explain the budget proposal. If the budget proposal is based upon the program review and planning process, he can justify it through its relevance to the college as a whole. The effective LRP administrator never pads a budget proposal and never tries to hide costs. Instead, he develops a reputation for honesty and integrity with the welfare of the college as his primary concern.

Monitoring the Budget

Once the learning resources budget has been established, the learning resources administrator has a responsibility to prudently expend the funds and to monitor that expenditure to ensure the budget is neither overspent or underspent. This involves seeking the most cost-effective source of necessary supplies and services and maintaining appropriate bookkeeping records to account for all expenditures.

Locating the most cost-effective sources of supplies and services involves "comparison shopping" or determining what is needed and seeking alternative vendors for comparable items. Frequently, discounts are given for quan-

```
                    CAPITAL EQUIPMENT REQUEST FORM
    Department:_____    Requested by:_____

    Definition of Equipment:  Useful life > 3 years
                              Individual Items costing > $250

    Rank  Item Requested   Justification    Replace   #   Unit  Total
                                            Addnl.        Cost  Cost
    _____
```

FIGURE 11.2 Capital Equipment Request Form

SPECIAL PROJECT PROPOSAL FORM

Department:_____   Requested by:_____

CHECK ALL THAT APPLY:	PERSONNEL CHANGES REQUESTED:
____ Eliminate Program/Service	____ Create New Position
____ Expand Program/Service	____ Reallocate Postion
____ Decrease Program/Service	____ Eliminate Position
____ Add New Program/Service	____ Increase Hours--Current Emp.
____ Other	____ Decrease Hours--Current Emp.
	____ Other

DESCRIPTION OF PROPOSED CHANGE:

JUSTIFICATION:

RESOURCES REQUIRED:

_____ Personnel   Describe Special Needs:
                              (Space, facilities, etc.)
_____ External Services

_____ Travel

_____ Supplies

_____ Capital Equipment

_____ TOTAL EXPENSE

FIGURE 11.3   Special Project Proposal Form

tity purchases so quantity orders submitted once or twice per year are more cost-effective than more frequent smaller orders. Additional cost savings, due to consortia group purchase agreements or state contracts, also are considered prior to purchase. Other decisions, such as whether to repair or replace equipment and to rent or purchase equipment, must be made.

Once the purchase decision is made, a purchase requisition is created following established college procedures. The LRP bookkeeper will maintain an internal purchase record log like Figure 11.4 to ensure an up-to-date running balance is available for each budget line and to monitor the status of each purchase requisition. Thus, the LRP bookkeeper maintains a running balance of the amount of money budgeted in each budget line. As each purchase requisition is sent to the Business Office, it is logged and the funds are encumbered. By encumbering the funds, the bookkeeper is subtracting them from the budgeted amount and ensuring they will be available when the invoice arrives. Once the item arrives with invoice and approval for payment is sent forth, the encumbrance is released and the actual amount invoiced is expended. Through this process, a running balance for the budget line is maintained. Some spreadsheet programs, such as Lotus 1-2-3 or SuperCalc, simplify this procedure.

While the internal purchase record log provides immediate information regarding the status of a budget line, it must be reconciled regularly with the college's Business Office reports. (Figure 11.5) Any discrepancies should be discussed with Business Office personnel immediately. An increasing number of colleges have adopted online accounting systems which immediately encumber funds when the purchase requisition is created online in the LRP and monitor the status of encumbrances and expenditures. These online systems reduce the need for separate internal record keeping.

The need to monitor the budget is more critical as the end of the fiscal year approaches. Unexpended funds are forfeited. Encumbered funds are carried over only for a limited time period before they are charged against the next fiscal year. Thus, approximately three months before the end of the fiscal year, the bookkeeper checks with all vendors regarding outstanding orders. If they are unable to ship the item within the necessary timeframe, the order is cancelled and the funds are unencumbered. A new order for

INTERNAL PURCHASE RECORD LOG

Account Number_____

Vendor	PO#	$Encumbered	$Actual	Rcd	Inv	L

FIGURE 11.4   Internal Purchase Record Log

LEARNING RESOURCES BUDGET REPORT   Period Ending 10/31/92

Account No.	Description	Revised Budget	Actual To Date	Open Encumb	Balance
11763-400	External Svcs	23,000			
401	Repair		0	0	
402	Maint. Cont.		0	0	
403	Equip. Rent		0	0	
404	Consortia		11,000	0	
405	Film Rent		1,267	425	
	TOTAL	23,000	12,267	425	10,308
11763-460	Travel	1,500	28	0	1,472
11763-600	LRP Materials	135,000			
601	Books		18,298	5,363	
602	SO's		6,266	5,908	
603	Periodicals		12,349	0	
604	ILL		31	0	
605	Database		442	0	
606	Video		1,708	45	
607	Software		815	302	
608	Media		40	0	
609	Misc.		0	0	
	TOTAL	135,000	39,949	11,618	83,433
11763-615	LRP Supplies	18,000			
616	Audiotape		412	0	
617	Videotape		815	0	
618	Photo		1,100	614	
619	Graphic		0	0	
620	Computer		1,200	0	
621	Circulation		435	75	
622	Processing		977	62	
623	AV Repair		86	0	
624	Lamps		603	0	
625	Misc.		0	0	
	TOTAL	18,000	5,628	751	11,621

FIGURE 11.5   Sample Monthly Budget Report

necessary items which can be delivered within the necessary timeframe is created. The budget has been successfully monitored if the allocated funds have been spent in a cost-effective manner and if the budget lines are neither overspent or underspent.

External Revenues

Changing economic times, changing priorities, and expensive new technologies negatively affect the availability of internal budget allocations to support learning resources program needs. The learning resources administrator has an obligation to cooperate closely with the Director of Community Relations and the Vice President of Business Services to develop strategies to generate external revenues for the benefit of the LRP and the college as a whole.

Results of the 1991 ALA survey, *Alternative Sources of Revenue in Academic Libraries,* categorized external revenues into five categories: services, sales, and special events; computerized catalogs and databases, searching, and printing; fines and replacement charges; gifts and grants; and library endowments. Of the 113 public, two-year college respondents only 24 percent indicated that they received over $10,000 from external revenues. Of this 24 percent, most passed the revenue on to their parent institution. [Lynch 1]

Services, Sales, and Special Events

Of the two-year college respondents, 75 percent provided the following services, sales, and special events: interlibrary loan services, reference services to non-college clientele, borrowers cards, photocopy services, videocassette and film rental, and equipment rental. [Lynch 23–24] However, only 73 percent generated revenue from photocopier services, 41 percent from withdrawn or gift books, 39 percent from interlibrary loan photocopies, and 30 percent from workshops and/or teleconferences. [Lynch 25–26] Of these colleges, only four percent generated over $10,000 in revenue through services, sales, and special events. [Beaubien 574]

These statistics correlate with the community service aspect of the community college mission and with the learning resources program's role of providing service to the broader college community. Photocopier revenues, from ownership of the copier or as part of the photocopier site contract, are a primary source of revenues. In addition, microform printer and, possibly in the future, CD-ROM printer fees may be charged to defray costs and to subsidize subscription fees. Annual booksales of withdrawn and gift books provide both public relations events as well as revenue toward acquisition of new materials. Interlibrary loan photocopy charges pass along the fees which are charged by external providers and subsidize the service.

Entrepreneurial activities, contract services, and teleconferencing provide prime opportunities for community college learning resources programs to generate revenue while serving their community. Production of materials, access to specialized equipment and reference services, and satellite or ITFS telecommunications services provide possible sources of revenue from community corporations.

Computerized Catalogs and Databases

While approximately half of the two-year college survey respondents provide online, remote, or CD-ROM database searching and printing, most did not charge for the service. Of the respondents, 31 percent charged for remote database searching to recover costs. [Lynch 31–32]

These findings correlate with Johnston's survey of the membership of the Northern Illinois Learning Resources Cooperative (NILRC). Of the NILRC respondents providing online database search services, 100 percent provided services to faculty and administration or staff, 83 percent provided services to students, and 72 percent provided services to other patrons. "When asked, 'Do you charge a fee for reference database services?', 89% did not charge faculty or administration or staff, 61% did not charge students, and 1% did not charge other patrons. Among colleges charging fees, the fee structures varied, but most charged only direct expenses on a cost recovery basis." [Johnston 376] Johnston concluded that community colleges consider online search services as part of their overall library service in support of the college's instructional program and institutional mission.

Fines and Replacement Fees

The ALA survey found that 75 percent of the two-year college respondents assessed fines and 96 percent assessed replacement costs for damaged or lost materials. [Lynch 38] Of these assessments, fine income is passed on to the parent institution while replacement fees are deposited in the LRP materials budgets. [Beaubien 575]

When armed with statistics documenting revenue generated from fines and replacement fees, the LRP administrator may request his learning resources materials budget be increased to reflect the anticipated revenue generated from fines and replacement fees. Thus, the revenue will not return to the college general fund but instead will help acquire necessary resources.

Gifts and Grants

Only 36 percent of the ALA survey two-year college respondents generated revenue through gifts and grants. Eighteen percent of these were in amounts less than $10,000 with state grants, and gifts from individuals as primary sources. [Lynch 41–42]

Although on many campuses grant writing is coordinated through the Director of Community Relations or the Vice President of Business Services, the learning resources administrator finds grantsmanship skills a valuable asset. Successful grantsmanship includes creating a project idea which matches the college's mission and strategic plan, locating potential funding sources which are compatible with the project idea and the college, assessing the college's capability for sustaining its responsibilities with the project, and writing the proposal. The prime test of any proposal is whether the proposed project will contribute to achieving the goals or solving the needs of the college and the population it serves.

Library Endowments

Only 9 percent of the ALA survey's two-year college respondents reported having an endowment and only 2 percent received revenues in excess of $10,000 from endowments. Most community colleges have a collegewide foundation or alumni association and discourage separate "Friends" organizations or endowments.

Summary

The learning resources program is funded primarily through an allocation from the collegewide budget. The learning resources program review and planning cycle creates the foundation for developing a LRP budget which fits the learning resources program into the collegewide mission and strategic plan. The LRP budget proposal is a fiscal description of the learning resources program. Once the learning resources budget is allocated, the learning resources administrator is responsible for expending the funds in a cost-effective manner and for monitoring the LRP budget.

External revenues provide secondary funding. As economic times become more difficult, learning resources administrators must become more active in generating alternative sources of revenue. The community service aspect of the community college mission discourages the charging of fees for most traditional learning resources services. However, opportunities exist through grant writing, contract services, and distance learning.

The effective learning resources administrator is responsible for developing a responsive, service-oriented learning resources program serving the informational, instructional, and developmental needs of the college's students, faculty, administrators, and broader college community. He determines the necessary fiscal resources to implement this program, acquires them through internal and external sources, and monitors their expenditure in a cost-effective manner.

Selected Bibliography

BEAUBIEN, ANNE, and MARY JO LYNCH. "Alternative Sources of Revenue in Academic Libraries," *College & Research Libraries News* 52 (October 1991): 573–576.

BROWN, JAMES W., et al. *Administering Educational Media: Instructional Technology and Library Services.* Second Edition. New York: McGraw-Hill, 1972.

CAMPBELL, JERRY D. "Fundraising," *Show-Me Libraries* 38 (August 1987): 17–24.

DEVLIN, BARRY. "Basic Budget Primer: Choosing the Best Budget for Your Library." In *The Bottom Line Reader: A Financial Handbook for Librarians*, ed. Betty-Carol Sellen and Betty J. Turock. New York: Neal Schuman, 1990.

HALL, MARY. *Getting Funded: A Complete Guide to Proposal Writing.* Third Edition. Portland, OR: Portland State University, 1988.

JOHNSTON, WANDA K. "Online Search Services in the Community College," *College & Research Libraries News* 50 (May 1989): 375–377.

————. "Tips on Obtaining Grants for the Community College LRC," *Community & Junior College Libraries* 6 (1989): 43–52.

KOENIG, MICHAEL E. *Budgeting Techniques for Libraries and Information Centers.* New York: Special Library Association, 1980.

KOOI, JANA B. "Media Technology Begets Revenue." In *Alternative Funding Sources*, ed. James L. Catanzaro and Allen D. Arnold. San Francisco: Jossey-Bass, 1989.

LONG, SARAH ANN, and DONALD J. SAGER. "Management for Tough Times," *American Libraries* 20 (June 1989): 543–546 and 20 (July/August 1989): 663–666.

LUSKIN, BERNARD J., and IDA K. WARREN. "Strategies for Generating New Financial Resources." In *Strengthening Financial Management*, ed. Dale F. Campbell. San Francisco: Jossey-Bass, 1985.

LYNCH, MARY JO. *Alternative Sources of Revenue in Academic Libraries.* Chicago: American Library Association, 1991.

SMITH, G. STEVENSON. *Accounting for Librarians and Other Not-for-Profit Managers.* Chicago: American Library Association, 1983.

————. *Managerial Accounting for Libraries and Other Not-for-Profit Organizations.* Chicago: American Library Association, 1991.

"Standards for Community, Junior, and Technical College Learning Resources Programs," *College & Research Libraries News* 51 (September 1990): 757–767.

STUEART, ROBERT D., and BARBARA B. MORAN. *Library Management.* Third Edition. Littleton, CO: Libraries Unlimited, 1987.

TRUMPETER, MARGO C., and RICHARD S. ROUNDS. *Basic Budgeting Practices for Librarians.* Chicago: American Library Association, 1985.

VINTER, ROBERT D., and RHEA K. KISH. *Budgeting for Not-for-Profit Organizations.* New York: The Free Press, 1984.

VLCEK, CHARLES W., and RAYMOND V. WIMAN. *Managing Media Services: Theory and Practice.* Englewood, CO: Libraries Unlimited, 1989.

12

Human Resources Management

The greatest asset of the learning resources program is its human resources. As Peters and Waterman described in *In Search of Excellence,* the highly successful company emphasizes positive human resources management exhibiting respect for the individual. "We are talking about tough-minded respect for the individual and the willingness to train him, to set reasonable and clear expectations for him, and to grant him practical autonomy to step out and contribute directly to his job;" [Peters 239] Thus, human resources management includes the recruitment and selection, leadership and motivation, staff development, and performance appraisal.

The "Standards" recommend that "sufficient and qualified professional and support staff should be available to implement the services for which the program is responsible." [Standards 759] The "Standards" then charts appropriate community college LRP staffing levels based upon the full-time equivalent (FTE) student enrollment of the college. [Standards 760] If the college headcount enrollment is 50 percent more than the FTE enrollment, additional staff are recommended. A direct relationship exists between staff, budget, and services. Thus, if services or budget increase, staffing also should increase. The "Standards" also address staff qualifications and ongoing continuing education.

The chief learning resources administrator is a generalist, knowledgeable about all aspects of the learning resources program. He believes in the value of his staff and empowers them to effectively serve. He communicates the college mission and priorities, shares his vision, encourages staff ideas and questions, creates staff development opportunities, and, as feasible, enables job ownership and pride. He does not always set the agenda; instead, he encourages creative thinking and risk-taking.

He follows the "golden rule" of the workplace: "Treat your staff as you would like to be treated." He strikes a balance between organizational results and the needs of his staff. He creates a work climate of cooperation and teamwork. He realizes the efficiency and success of the learning resources program in meeting its goals is dependent upon his staff and the internal climate of the LRP.

The LRP administrator realizes that academic institutions tend to have two organizational structures. Faculty follow a laissez-faire, or collegial, structure while non-faculty follow a semi-autocratic, hierarchial structure. The administrator faces the comparative inflexibility and adversarial nature of collective bargaining and Civil Service regulations. His staff includes both those energized and enthusiastic about their careers and those long-tenured staff who are marking time. He applies the practical aspects of management theory, leadership studies, and communications theory to accomplish LRP goals by working with and through his staff.

To be successful, he develops a close working relationship with the Director of Personnel. He learns the college's organizational structure and climate. He studies staff contracts, collective bargaining agreements, and personnel handbooks. He follows established college personnel procedures and guidelines. He reviews state and federal regulations which relate to employee selection, job performance, and performance appraisal. For example, the Equal Employment Opportunity Commission (EEOC) Guidelines protect the right of all people to be hired and to advance in a job on the basis of merit or ability. Title VII of the Civil Rights Act of 1964 prohibits discrimination based on race, color, religion, sex, or national origin in all employment practices including hiring, firing, promotion, compensation, and other conditions or privileges of employment. In 1935, the National Labor Relations Act, also commonly called the Wagner Act, gave employees the right to organize unions and to bargain collectively. It also established the National Labor Relations Board which has the authority to establish rules, regulations, and procedures necessary to fulfill the provisions of the Wagner Act.

This chapter focuses on human resources management which includes the staff recruitment and selection, leadership and motivation, staff development, and performance appraisal.

Recruitment and Selection

The LRP administrator holds responsibility for recruiting and selecting the most qualified candidate for the position. Whether a newly created position or a recently vacated one, the recruitment and selection process begins with an in depth position analysis. The newly created position is defined and justified through the budget review process. The vacated position requires analysis of the position responsibilities, its role in the organization, work schedule, etc. prior to initiating the search. It is much easier to create change through the innovative use of a position vacancy than to redirect the responsibilities of an existing employee. Thus, the ideal time to modify a position is while it is vacant.

The result of the job analysis is the creation of or updating of the position description. The position description summarizes job information which is necessary for recruiting, selecting, and orienting a new staff member. In addition, it provides basic guidelines for job evaluation, affirmative action and EEO reporting, and staff development.

Although position descriptions vary from college to college, they generally include the position title, position summary, specific responsibilities, relationships with others, and minimum qualifications. The position summary provides a thumbnail sketch of the position describing its major functions, purpose, and scope. The specific responsibilities list each of the major duties that comprise the job. The list is ranked in order of importance. Duties are stated in terse, direct statements preceded by action verbs. The statement of relationships names immediate supervisor, staff supervised, and cooperative relationships. Minimum qualifications state required and desired educational background, experience, and special skill/ability characteristics necessary for success in the position. Several sample position descriptions are included in Appendix IV.

Once the position description has been created or updated and the authorization to fill the position has been granted, the recruitment process begins. Recruitment involves the attracting of a pool of qualified applicants for the position. The position announcement is written incorporating wording from the position summary, statements on qualifications, salary, standard benefits, and application instructions. The announcement is distributed in a manner dependent upon the nature and level of the position with the goal of attracting as large a pool of qualified candidates as possible. Affirmative action procedures require a wide enough distribution of the announcement to ensure that minority groups are aware of the opening. The position announcement may be distributed to professional area joblines, selected graduate library/media programs, regional learning resources consortia and networks, peer community colleges, and through classified advertisements in local or regional newspapers, the *Chronicle of Higher Education*, and professional journals and newsletters.

The selection process consists of choosing the person who is most likely to be successful in the position. The objective of selection is to determine which applicant has the qualifications to best "fit" into the specific requirements of the position. The LRP administrator usually enlists the assistance of a search committee with the selection process. "A goal is to appoint those who have a real need to be represented because of their working relationship with the person who fills the job." [Birdsall 277]

The LRP administrator clarifies what level of participation and subsequent decision is expected from the search committee. Minimally, the committee will screen applications, interview likely prospects, and offer an assessment of each without ranking them. The consultative approach is for the committee to rank candidates and provide justification for their decision. Finally, some committees assume the prerogative of making the final selection decision. The LRP administrator provides each committee member with a packet of information including the committee's charge, the position description, interview evaluation report criteria, and other general information.

The selection process follows the procedures established by the Director of Personnel. Each applicant may be requested to complete the official college application form, to submit a current resume with appropriate letter of interest, and to send college transcripts. These documents not only provide information about the applicant's meeting the minimum qualifications but also provide subjective impressions, such as quality of written communication skills and the care taken with the resume. In addition, applicants for professional positions may be requested to submit "a written statement on, for example, the applicant's philosophy of service or leadership. This request separates the serious candidates from the casual ones and also allows an assessment of written and thinking skills." [Birdsall 278] Finally, applicants will be requested to provide references. Frequently, reference checks are completed only for the candidates selected for interview or for the ranking finalists after the interview.

The on-site interview is the most important aspect of the selection process. The interview schedule permits time for applicants to be introduced to the college, the learning resources program as a whole, and the specific work area in detail. Interview sessions with the search committee, supervisors, future co-workers, and appropriate others are scheduled. Everyone participating in the interview process is provided in advance with the interview schedule, the applicant's resumes, and the position description. An Interview Evaluation Report such as Figure 12.1, designed to reflect the desired qualifications of the applicant, may be distributed to gather feedback for the search committee.

```
                        INTERVIEW EVALUATION REPORT
                        Information Services Librarian


      CANDIDATE:

      QUALIFICATIONS:
            Rate the candidate on a scale of 1 (Low) to 5 (High) for
            required and desired qualifications listed.
            Education:
            _____ MLS degree from accredited program
            _____ Program included relevant coursework
            Experience:
            _____ Minimum 3 years reference service
            _____ Experience with CD-ROM & online database searching
            _____ Experience with bibliographic instruction
            _____ Experience in an automated environment
            _____ Experience with collection development
            _____ Experience in a community college setting
            Skills and Abilities:
            _____ Oral and written communication skills
            _____ Strong public service orientation
            _____ Ability to work in a team environment
            _____ Problem-solving skills
            _____ Positive interpersonal skills

      STRENGTHS                        | WEAKNESSES
                                       |
                                       |
                                       |
                                       |
                                       |
                                       |
                                       |
                                       |
                                       |
                                       |
      OVERALL SUMMARY




      OVERALL RATING:   Poor     Average     Excellent


      Evaluated by_____Date_____
```

FIGURE 12.1   Sample Interview Evaluation Report

During the interview, the applicant is made as comfortable as feasible. The interview scheduling and questions must be similar for each applicant and must fall within affirmative action guidelines. Questions relating to education, training, work history, and work-related skills related to the position description are acceptable. Conversations which are legally out-of-bounds, such as age, child care, or religion, must not be introduced or pursued. The interviewers actively listen during the interview and encourage the applicant to do most of the talking while the interviewer observes body language, semantics, and uses creative silence.

The final decision to hire the person is based upon the affirmative answer to the question, "Will this individual add strength to the staff and increase the overall caliber and effectiveness of the staff?" [Birdsall 282] If so, the applicant of choice is offered the position at a specified starting salary and other terms of employment. The applicant will accept, refuse, or negotiate. Once the offer is accepted, the unsuccessful applicants are also notified.

With the LRP chief administrator's goal of attracting and hiring the best staff, "management of the search process must also be based on a respect for candidates as guests and professional colleagues. Cordial treatment and simple courtesies should not have to be itemized on a checklist, but their absence in any phase of recruitment will place all efforts in jeopardy." [Birdsall 283]

Leadership and Motivation

Weiss defines individual job performance through an equation:

"Job Performance = Motivation × Ability (Behavior + Skills and Knowledge), where

Job Performance = the achievement of goals required if the job is to make its contribution to the organizational success and performance,

Motivation = the sustained desire to achieve goals—the want-to-do aspect, and

Ability = the capacity to apply the requisite skills and knowledge to achieve goals—the can-do aspect." [Weiss 153]

The effective administrator leads in a manner which motivates the individual and ensures he has the ability to successfully perform his job. This effective leadership and motivation requires the practical application of the leadership studies, management theory, and communication theory discussed in Chapter 9.

In *Leaders: The Strategies for Taking Charge* (1985), Bennis and Nanus cite the four types of interpersonal skills which all the leaders they surveyed embodied:

1. Attention through vision. "Leaders are the most results-oriented individuals in the world, and results get attention." [Bennis 28] "Leadership is also a transaction, a transaction between leaders and followers. Neither

could exist without the other. So what we discovered is that leaders also pay attention as well as catch it." [Bennis 32]

2. Meaning through communication. "Success requires the capacity to relate a compelling image of a desired state of affairs—the kind of image that induces enthusiasm and commitment in others." [Bennis 33]

3. Trust through positioning. "We trust people who are predictable, whose positions are known and who keep at it; leaders who are trusted make themselves known, make their positions clear." [Bennis 44]

4. Deployment of self through positive self-regard. Positive self-regard reflects itself in the way people relate to others. It enables the acceptance of others as they are, the approach to relationships and problems in terms of the present, the bestowing of similar courtesies on everyone, the trust in others, and the ability to do without constant approval and recognition. [Bennis 66–67]

Thus, the effective administrator is a leader who has a vision and shares it, who is predictable and trustworthy, and who is self-secure enough to demonstrate positive interpersonal relations.

Focusing on Maslow's Hierarchy of Needs, Weiss encourages administrators to empower their employees to climb the hierarchy by:

1. Selecting people with the right capabilities and behaviors;
2. Providing autonomy and freedom from excessive controls;
3. Demonstrating trust that employees' skills, knowledge, and judgment are appropriate;
4. Providing requisite resources;
5. Providing consistent, reliable, and predictable leadership;
6. Communicating clearly, honestly, and frequently;
7. Exemplifying the behaviors and values you wish to establish. [Weiss 161]

The effective administrator delegates authority and responsibility, empowers staff to stretch and grow on the job, and gives them credit when credit is due. He establishes a healthy problem-solving climate where conflict is permissible and is considered a resolvable difference of opinion. He praises in public and reprimands in private, each time promptly addressing the specific actions. He is a good listener employing active listening skills and encouraging open communication. He follows the "golden rule of the workplace" by being sensitive to the needs of his staff, by encouraging fair play, and by encouraging the participation of every staff member. He values the positive strengths of every staff member and motivates them to perform to their maximum.

Staff Development

If "job performance equals motivation multiplied by ability," the effective administrator is responsible not only for motivating his staff, but also for staff development. "Organizations want productivity, improved service, and effective use of resources. Individuals seek opportunities to learn, to keep up, to be recognized. A staff development program brings these needs together and seeks to improve the effectiveness of library personnel." [Lipow, 53] The General Libraries at the University of Texas at Austin define staff development as "a continual process used to guide and encourage staff members to develop their skills, capabilities, knowledge and attitudes in order to mutually benefit both the organization and the individual." [Lipow 61]

Implementation of a staff development program begins with the creation of a definition along with associated procedures and policies. "This involves many of the same steps which one follows in developing the mission statement and strategic plan of the organization. The definition should recognize all employees as potential career employees." [Robinson 9] In *Staff Development: A Practical Guide*, Lipow provides a checklist of questions to ask when developing an ongoing program. These questions summarized include: 1) Is there agreement about a definition of staff development? 2) What and whose needs have been identified and assessed? 3) What types of programs would fill the need(s) and achieve the desired outcome(s)? 4) Where are the experts, speakers, presenters found? 5) How is transfer of learning to on-the-job performance promoted? 6) What budget exists? [Lipow 3–5]

Staff development is an ongoing process. It begins through pre-employment training and experience. Applicants for positions bring with them formal training offered through Masters in Library Science and Educational Technology programs or Library Technical Assistant programs. They bring with them the practical learning from on-the-job experience and workshops from previous employment. They bring special skills, knowledge, and observations.

Each new staff member participates in an orientation program designed to ensure his understanding of the college culture and his role within the institution. The program introduces him to the community college philosophy and mission, to college procedures and regulations, to the learning resources program (mission, goals, objectives, organizational structure), and to his specific responsibilities. His position description is discussed in depth and amplified. Relevant procedure manuals and equipment manuals are provided to ensure consistency in explanation. Specific tasks are introduced and demonstrated. A senior staff member is assigned to mentor him.

The LRP administrator considers every employee a career employee and creates staff development opportunities for everyone. Thus, he encourages all staff members to identify their strengths and weaknesses and to request appropriate staff development activities for themselves or for the Division. He monitors the needs of each staff member and creates appropriate staff development opportunities. These opportunities include continuing education workshops, formal courses, staff exchanges both within the LRP and with other colleges, participation in professional organizations, and the availability of professional materials. He encourages technical and clerical staff to participate in organizations, such as the Council on Library/Media Technicians (COLT), the ALA Library Support Staff Membership Intitiative Group (MIG), and the Association of Audio-Visual Technicians (AAVT). He enables all staff to participate in LRP committees and taskforces as well as in campuswide activities. He organizes group activities for the entire learning resources staff and he sends individuals to external activities. Whatever the format, he supports a staff development program responsive to LRP staff needs and requests. He ensures that every staff member ranks high on "ability" in the job performance equation.

Performance Appraisal

Performance appraisal provides an opportunity to enhance job performance by providing both feedback and direction. It ties performance expectations to the position goal and provides feedback. Following McGregor's "Theory Y," the administrator views LRP staff members as individuals who enjoy working, seek responsibility, and are capable of self-control. He, consequently, clarifies the goals and parameters of the position and provides support and feedback as appropriate. He implements lessons from *The One Minute Manager* by setting clear, succinct goals, promptly praising and reprimanding specific actions, encouraging staff members, speaking the truth, and enjoying life. [Blanchard 101]

Thus, the rationale for performance appraisal is to maintain and improve the learning resources program, to identify and resolve problems, to specify expected work performance, and to provide regular feedback. Helpful feedback is descriptive, not evaluative, is specific, not general; and is relevant to the self-perceived needs of the receiver. Helpful feedback is provided in a timely, ongoing and regular basis, focusing on specific accomplishments or problems.

The annual, formal, performance appraisal follows the format and procedures established by the Director of Personnel. It is based upon the individual's goals and work responsibilities during the preceding twelve months. Thus, the appraisal begins with the position description and focuses on the specific responsibilities. It focuses on work performance, not personality. It summarizes successes and disappointments, strengths and weaknesses, and results in a mutually acceptable action plan for the future. When feedback has been provided in an ongoing and regular basis, this formal performance appraisal holds no surprises. Instead, it provides an opportunity to review the progress of the past year and to plan toward the future. It encourages creative problem-solving and establishes a commitment of both administrator and employee to take specific steps toward improvement.

Common errors with performance appraisal ratings include the halo effect when a supervisor gives a favorable rating to all evaluation categories based upon the impressive performance in only one, the central tendency effect when the supervisor rates everyone as average, the loose rater or tight rater effect when the supervisor rates everyone either high or low, and the recency bias effect when the supervisor places too much reliance on recent events rather than the entire year. Some administrators maintain an "incident file" which includes personal notes regarding successes and weaknesses discussed during the year to ensure their ratings reflect the entire year. (Note: If an incident file is created, it must be maintained for every staff member and must include positive as well as negative notes.)

The performance appraisal conference is scheduled in advance giving the evaluee time to read the appraisal and to prepare a response if desired. The conference is held in a private setting without interruptions. Some administrators meet in a conference room, or other private neutral area, to encourage the evaluee to relax. The conference focuses on work related facts with specific examples of both high performance as well as areas that need improvement. A specific improvement/development action plan, including how to use current strengths or resources to improve weaknesses, is established. The conference ends with a restatement of positive points, review of the action plan, restatement of the administrator's commitment to help, and a positive look toward the future.

The performance appraisal provides an opportunity to provide both impromptu and formal feedback to an employee. It evaluates the result of motivation multiplied by ability resulting in job performance. It provides a systematic evaluation of an employee's strengths and weaknesses as reflected in job performance and results in a positive growth plan.

Summary

The foundation of the learning resources program rests with its human resources. The chief learning resources administrator holds responsibility for positive human resources management which includes staff recruitment and selection, leadership and motivation, staff development, and performance appraisal. He follows established college personnel procedures as well as state and federal guidelines. He recruits and selects the most qualified candidate for each position. Through this process, he conducts a job analysis, creates or updates the position description, and then recruits, interviews, and selects the best applicant.

He defines job performance as the achievement of goals required if the job is to make a contribution to the organization. This job performance is the result of motivation or the "want-to" aspect multiplied by ability or the "can-do" aspect. Consequently, he demonstrates the practical applications of leadership studies with management and communications theory to motivate and lead his staff. He develops ongoing staff development opportunities for all staff members, encouraging each individual to develop the skills and knowledge for the mutual benefit of the learning resources program and the individual. He ties performance appraisal to the position responsibilities, providing frequent informal and formal feedback, summarizing strengths and weaknesses, and creating a mutually acceptable action plan for the future.

The chief learning resource administrator appreciates and promotes the strengths of the individuals in his staff. He empowers them to effectively serve. He shares his vision, encourages staff ideas and questions, enables job ownership and pride, and follows the "golden rule" of the workplace: Treat your staff as you would like to be treated. He creates a work climate of cooperation and teamwork. He realizes the efficiency and success of the learning resources program in meeting its goals is dependent upon his staff and the internal climate of the LRP.

He is secure enough to follow Lao Tzu's wisdom: "Fail to honor people, they fail to honor you; but of a good leader, who talks little, when his work is done, his aim fulfilled, they will say, 'We did this ourselves.'" [Bennis 152]

Selected Bibliography

BACON, DONALD C. "See You in Court," *Nation's Business* 77 (July 1989): 17–26+.

BENNIS, WARREN, and BURT NANSU. *Leaders: The Strategies for Taking Charge.* New York: Harper & Row, 1985.

BIRDSALL, DOUGLAS G. "Recruiting Academic Librarians: How to Find and Hire the Best Candidates," *Journal of Academic Librarianship* 17 (November 1991): 276–283.

BLANCHARD, KENNETH, and SPENCER JOHNSON. *The One Minute Manager.* New York: Berkeley Publishing Group, 1984.

BOONE, MORELL, et al. *Training Student Library Assistants.* Chicago, American Library Association, 1991.

CUBBERLEY, CAROL W. "Write Procedures That Work," *Library Journal* 116 (September 15, 1991): 42–45.

EDWARDS, JOHN D. "A Staff Exchange Program: Mid-America's Experience," *Law Library Journal* 76 (Spring 1983): 402–413.

EVERED, JAMES F., and J. ERICH EVERED. *Shirt-Sleeves Management.* Second Edition. New York: AMACOM, 1989.

GLOGOFF, STUART, and JAMES P. FLYNN. "Developing a Systematic In-House Training Program for Integrated Library Systems," *College & Research Libraries* 48 (November 1987): 528–536.

GUY, JENIECE, and MARGARET MEYERS. *Writing Library Job Descriptions: T.I.P. Kit #7.* Chicago: American Library Association, 1985.

JONES, MARK A. "Job Descriptions Made Easy," *Personnel Journal* 63 (May 1984): 31–34.

KATHMAN, MICHAEL D., and JANE McGURN KATHMAN. *Managing Student Workers in College Libraries: CLIP Note #7.* Chicago: American Library Association, 1986.

LIPOW, ANNE GRODZINS. *Staff Development: A Practical Guide.* Chicago: American Library Association, 1988.

MARTIN, PHYLLIS. "Hire Smart, Hire Right," *Working Woman* 14 (March 1989): 71–76.

McCONKEY, DALE D. *No Nonsense Delegation.* New York: American Management Association, 1986.

PETERS, THOMAS J., and ROBERT H. WATERMAN, JR. *In Search of Excellence: Lessons from America's Best-Run Companies.* New York: Warner Books, 1984.

PREECE, BARBARA G. "Paraprofessional Training in Technical Services," *Illinois Libraries* 72 (September 1990): 503–505.

ROBINSON, RICK. "Training the Paraprofessional Staff: The Library Director's Role," unpublished paper, 1992.

ROOKS, DANA C. *Motivating Today's Library Staff: A Management Guide.* Phoenix: Oryz Press, 1988.

RUBIN, RICHARD E. *Human Resource Management in Libraries: Theory and Practice.* New York: Neal-Schuman, 1991.

RUMMLER, GEARY A., and ALAN P. BRACHE. *Improving Human Performance: How to Manage the White Space on the Organization Chart.* San Francisco: Jossey-Bass, 1990.

"Standards for Community, Junior, and Technical College Learning Resources Programs," *College & Research Libraries News* 51 (September 1990): 757–767.

STUEART, ROBERT D., and BARBARA B. MORAN. *Library Management.* Third Edition. Englewood, CO: Libraries Unlimited, 1987.

STUEART, ROBERT D., and MAUREEN SULLIVAN. *Performance Analysis and Appraisal: A How-to-Do-It Manual for Librarians.* New York: Neal-Schuman, 1991.

VEANER, ALLEN B. *Academic Librarianship in a Transformational Age: Program, Politics, and Personnel.* Boston: G.K. Hall, 1990.

VLCEK, CHARLES W., and RAYMOND V. WIMAN. *Managing Media Services: Theory and Practice.* Englewood, CO: Libraries Unlimited, 1989.

WEISS, ALAN. *Managing for Peak Performance: A Guide to the Power (and Pitfalls) of Personal Style.* New York: Harper & Row, 1989.

ZIOLKOWSKI, DARLENE M. "Common Sense, Integrity, and Expectations of Excellence: Practical Advice on Dealing with Employee Problems," *Library Administration & Management.* 7 (Winter 1993): 24–29.

13

Facilities Management

Facilities management involves providing "space for housing collections, for study and research, for public service and staff needs, and for basic production." [Standards 765] Thus, the chief learning resources administrator works closely with the Director of Physical Plant and serves on the campus facilities committee to ensure the appropriate creation and maintenance of functional, yet aesthetic, user and resource facilities. User facilities are those that are used directly by faculty, students, and the broader college community. These include the public areas of the learning resources center as well as classrooms, laboratories, auditoriums, etc. Resource facilities include those spaces which are necessary to provide print and nonprint resources. These include the collection storage areas, access services work areas, staff production areas, and office spaces. [Vlcek 287]

Space allocated to the learning resources program is directly related to the mission, goals, and objectives of the program as well as to projected student enrollments. The "Standards" chart assignable square feet per full-time equivalent (FTE) student enrollment for various learning resources services including stack, staff, user, media production, and viewing and storage areas. In addition, recommended numbers of user stations are charted. These charts provide recommended guidelines. Exact patterns of use and spatial needs vary from college to college.

In addition, the "Standards" state, "the space for user activities should accommodate a wide variety of learning and study situations, should be attractive, comfortable, designed to encourage use." [Standards 766] Space for appropriate access and utilization of resources by individuals and groups, including the differently-abled, is essential. A bibliographic instruction classroom is necessary to meet the mission of the LRP. Optimally, the learning resources center is centrally located on campus and housed in an inviting, functional facility.

As a facilities manager, the LRP administrator holds responsibility for working closely with the Director of Physical Plant to ensure the day-to-day maintenance of LRP facilities. The LRP administrator also monitors changing space requirements due to changing user needs and technological developments. He ensures that the LRP program review and planning process and subsequent budget address learning resources facilities issues. He learns about ergonomics to protect his staff's physical welfare and complies with requirements of the Americans With Disabilities Act (ADA). This chapter discusses facilities planning and introduces ergonomics and ADA compliance requirements.

Facilities Planning

Quoting the "Standards," "facilities must be planned on a long-term basis, including space for an expanding collection, workspace, machines and other equipment, storage, and the needs of users. Space planning must take into account the need for computer workstations, for transmission and retrieval of information by telecommunications, for media production, and for related requirements within the building for electrical and conduit connections." [Standards 765–766]

McAdams summarizes trends in academic library facilities with these observations. "Whether concerned with existing space or new, library planning continues to follow the well-established principles of centrality of the library to its clientele, access to services and collections, protection of library materials through environmental and egress control, spatial and operational efficiency, and accommodation of growth and change. Of equal importance to current planners is compliance with governmental and regulatory requirements (codes and standards) and fiscal prudence." [McAdams 297]

Facilities planning may involve building a new building, expanding or renovating an existing facility, or modifying a space within an existing facility. Whatever the scope of the project, it relates directly to the LRP program review and planning process. Facilities planning requires reviewing current LRP program strengths and weaknesses, forecasting future user needs, researching and evaluating options, and developing an implementation plan. This process ranges in scope from creating the formal building program (out-

lining furniture and equipment needs for each area in square-foot requirements) for an architect to creating a simple, scale floorplan and work request
for physical plant workers.

Researching facilities design options includes reading the literature, visiting other community colleges, and possibly hiring a consultant. *Facilities
Planning: The User Requirements Method* provides a list of common user
requirements and includes sample forms for evaluating needs. The *Checklist
of Library Building Design Considerations, Effective Audio-Visual: A User's
Handbook,* and *Criteria for Planning the College and University Learning
Resources Center* are samples of many works which outline general spatial
and other facility planning considerations. Other works, such as *CD-ROM
in the Library* and *Public Access to Online Catalogs,* include chapters and
diagrams addressing more specific work areas.

Another source of facilities design information is the ALA Library and
Information Center collection which includes entries from the joint ALA-
American Institute of Architects awards program for the recognition of excellence in architectural design and planning in libraries. This collection
contains several hundred notebooks comprised of photographs, plans,
statistical information, slides, and drawings from individual libraries. The
collection is available for browsing at the ALA Headquarters or through interlibrary loan. (For more information, call 800-545-2433, ext. 2153.)

The objective of facilities planning is to create functional, yet aesthetic,
spaces resulting in an inviting, responsive service-oriented program. Thus,
the facilities plan includes the following considerations:

• general space allocations including area relationships, seating space, and
  travel patterns;
• maintenance, supervision, and security of people and resources;
• electrical and telecommunications lines to support current and future technology;
• acoustics reducing people and equipment noises;
• lighting which is adequate for the local task, anti-glare in consideration for
  health, and economical;
• color to unify or to differentiate work functions and to encourage appropriate activities;
• environmental controls including heat, ventilation, and cooling as well as
  humidity control for preservation of materials;
• general aesthetics making the facility attractive and inviting as well as functional.

Cargill and Webb cite the impact of the new technologies on facilities
planning as requiring the creative use of existing space and demanding better planning for the future use of existing space. "At the minimum, managers

will see the addition of electrical power poles in order to place outlets where they are needed, conduits placed along existing walls and columns, raised flooring to provide space for adequate wiring of electrical and data lines, and utilization of work stations rather than standard desks and offices." [Cargill 16]

They further describe microcomputer and terminal workstations. "If used by multiple operators, the workstations should have shelving for manuals; space for the terminal or micro; adjacent space for a printer; work space for data sheets or the materials being processed; or space for a book truck. Lighting should be shielded to reduce glare or the terminals should have (or be modified for) nonglare screens. If noise from printers or group work in an area is a problem, acoustic partitions should be used." [Cargill 16]

As a part of the annual learning resources program review and planning process, the chief learning resources administrator continually monitors the trends in education including group and individual user needs as well as the impact of technology on user and staff needs. He then ensures a creative and responsive facilities plan which addresses current issues but also looks toward the future.

Ergonomics

"Also referred to as human factors engineering, ergonomics is the study of furniture, tool, and office designs that keep people comfortable and healthy while they work." [Cummings 330] Although visual or video display terminals (VDTs) have improved staff productivity and the potential for LRP services, their use can be harmful. Inappropriate design of the workstation, the work environment (lighting and acoustic), and the organization of work can contribute to stress, musculoskeletal problems, and vision difficulties among those who use VDTs. With the expanding use of VDTs, the LRP administrator is obligated to ensure the health of his staff.

The VDT user typically is sitting at a terminal, viewing a cathode ray tube (CRT) and source document, and using a keyboard. To alleviate neck and arm problems and carpal tunnel syndrome, appropriate design of the workstation and seating is essential (Figure 13.1). Generally, the viewing distance to the CRT is adjustable so the top of the screen is eye level and the screen is approximately 19 inches from the eyes. The keyboard height enables the operator's arms to form an angle equal to or greater than 90 degrees at the elbow. The chair has an adjustable seat height, adjustable backrest height, and adjustable tension on the backrest. The keyboard is 23–28 inches high and detached to provide flexibility in the workstation. The keyboard is thin, with a palm rest, and neural in color. [Miller, 1983, 154–155]

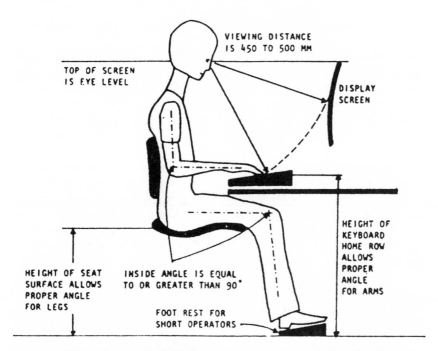

VIEWING DISTANCE
IS 450 TO 500 MM

TOP OF SCREEN
IS EYE LEVEL

DISPLAY
SCREEN

HEIGHT OF
KEYBOARD
HOME ROW
ALLOWS
PROPER
ANGLE
FOR ARMS

HEIGHT OF SEAT
SURFACE ALLOWS
PROPER ANGLE
FOR LEGS

INSIDE ANGLE IS EQUAL
TO OR GREATER THAN 90°

FOOT REST FOR
SHORT OPERATORS

FIGURE 13.1 Ergonomic Guidelines   Source: R. Bruce Miller. "Radiation, Ergonomics, Ion Depletion, and VDTs: Healthful Use of Visual Display Terminals," *Information Technology and Libraries* 2 (June 1983): 155. Reprinted with permission.

Environmental issues include lighting and acoustics. Illumination in the room and at the workstation and screen glare affect visual effectiveness. The addition of anti-glare screens and screen hoods reduce screen glare reflected from external sources, such as windows, light fixtures, etc. The creation of uniform lighting between the screen and work documents is accomplished through adjusting the screen brightness and adding an appropriately placed, supplementary lighting unit near the document holder. In addition, frequent visual breaks reduce visual strain.

Accoustical factors include the noise irritations or distractions from background noise, equipment noise, and speech privacy. Printers are the single largest equipment noise factor, although voices frequently are found more annoying. Sound mufflers for printers reduce printer noise. In addition, acoustical treatments to ceilings and vertical surfaces adjacent to and part of the workstation reduce noise. If necessary, background noise masking systems are added. [Wright 17]

Organization of work is another issue affecting ergonomics. This includes the intensity of work, frequency of rest periods, and the operator's autonomy over work. "The National Institute for Occupational Safety and Health (NIOSH) recommends: a 15-minute work-rest break should be taken after two hours of continuous VDT work for operators under moderate visual demands and/or moderate work load and a 15-minute work-rest break should be taken after one hour of continuous VDT work for operators under high visual demands, high work load, and/or those engaged in repetitive work tasks." [Miller, 1983, 156] Regular exercises for the upper back, wrist, lower back, head and neck, shoulders, fingers and hands, and legs are recommended in addition to deep breathing. [Working 7]

"Even if a major renovation of work areas and replacement of all equipment is not possible, some incorporation of good ergonomic ideas is essential. This may be accomplished by acquisition of comfortable and appropriate seating, purchase of workstations of the proper height for terminals, placing of terminals to minimize glare, addition of utility poles where outlets are needed, replacement of desks as finances allow, regrouping of work areas to accommodate the new technology and the utilization of different tools to accomplish new tasks." [Cargill 18]

Americans with Disabilities Act

Service to everyone, including the differently-abled, has been a concern among library/LRP professionals for many years. Decades of legislation reflect this concern. On March 3, 1931, President Hoover signed into law the Pratt-Smoot Act mandating that embossed books be provided to adult blind residents of the United States and that these books be circulated through a number of regional libraries. This Act was subsequently amended to inaugurate the talking books program as well as to create a library of musical scores, instructional texts, and other specialized materials. In 1966, President Johnson extended the service to anyone physically disabled and unable to use conventional printed material. [Velleman 158] Through cooperation with regional multi-type library systems, community college learning resources programs offer these services to their students and staff.

Section 504 of the Rehabilitation Act of 1973 sets forth minimum guidelines and requirements to ensure buildings and facilities are accessible to individuals with disabilities in terms of architecture, design, and communication. This Act provides specific accessibility standards outlined in the *Uniform Federal Accessibility Standards* (1988) and later incorporated into the Americans with Disabilities Act.

The Americans with Disabilities Act of 1990 (ADA) was signed into law by President Bush on July 26, 1990. It's purpose is "to extend to people with disabilities civil rights similar to those now available on basis of race, color, sex, national origin, and religion through the Civil Rights Act of 1964. It prohibits discrimination on the basis of disability in the private sector and in state and local governments, public accommodations and services, including transportation, provided by public and private entities. It also includes provisions for telecommunications relay services." [President's 2] *The Americans With Disabilities Act Handbook* includes the text of the law, architectural guidelines, and the regulations for implementing the major components of the ADA. (Contact the U.S. Department of Justice at 202-514-0301 or the Equal Employment Opportunity Commission at 800-669-3362 for ordering information.)

Summarizing the ADA, Title I of the ADA outlaws employment discrimination against Americans with disabilities. Title II mandates equal provision of services and programs for everyone in all public entities, including public community colleges. Gunde interprets Title II, in this manner: "For libraries that receive state or local public funds, this means that any resident, student, or otherwise eligible patron with a disability must be able to receive and benefit from all services available from their library." [Gunde 808] Thus, if a library provides the service of book circulation, it must provide an appropriate selection of books in alternate formats, such as large print, Braille, spoken word, etc. If videocassette loans are offered, the collection must include closed-captioned videocassettes. If telephone reference service is provided, it must provide telecommunications services for the hearing impaired. [Gunde 808]

Title III of the ADA addresses discrimination against individuals with disabilities by private entities, but also includes a variety of public accommodations. It states that "no individual shall be discriminated against on the basis of disability in the full and equal enjoyment of the goods, services, facilities, privileges, advantages, or accommodations of any place of public accommodation by any person who owns, leases . . . or operates a place of public accommodation. [section 302a]" [Gunde 809]

Specific accessibility guidelines for buildings and facilities are published in the July 26, 1991, *Federal Register,* pages 35606–35691. Although these guidelines are to be applied during the design, construction, and alteration of buildings and facilities, they provide guidance to the LRP administrator. Sample general accessibility guidelines follow: The learning resources center should have at least one primary entrance accessible by an individual in a wheelchair; door thresholds should be flush with the floor or bevelled for easy wheelchair access; all doors should have a clear opening no less than 32″ when open and operable by a single effort; the entrance should be at a level that makes elevators, as appropriate, accessible and useable by physically disabled; corridors and aisles should be a minimum of 36" wide and kept free of obstacles; for wheelchairs to pass or to turn around, a width of 60" is advised; a minimum of 80" clear headroom should be provided; floor-coverings should not be slippery or carpeted with thick pile making wheelchair access difficult; appropriate identification signage, such as raised letters or numbers for tactile reading, should be provided; warning signals must be both visible and audible.

Sample specific library guidelines include the following: At least 5 percent or a minimum of one of each element of fixed seating, tables, or study carrels shall be provided; tables and carrels should be overheight at 29" with the apron removed or recessed for wheelchair access; the circulation counter must have at least one station no higher than 36" from the floor; bookstacks must have a minimum 36" aisle and should not dead end; shelf height in stack areas is unrestricted; however, the preferred heights are no higher than 67" and no lower than 12"; the card catalog should be between 18" and 48" high and an OPAC station should be 29" high.

In addition, learning resources programs should be equipped with large print books, television magnifiers, talking book machines, Braille typewriters/computers, Edna Lite magnifiers, optacons, Kurzweil reading machines, etc. LRP staff should be oriented to serving differently-abled people.

Because each college serves a different population and because the needs of each individual with a disability differ, no one list of ADA requirements for every LRP exists. Thus, the ADA regulations provide guidelines instead of an inclusive catalog of all possible required accommodations and modifications. The LRP administrator must evaluate the elements of the learning resources program and the needs of LRP users with disabilities and strive to comply with the ADA guidelines to ensure equal service to all.

Summary

The chief learning resources administrator holds responsibility for ensuring the creation and maintenance of functional, yet aesthetic, user and resource facilities. The space allocated to the LRP is directly related to the mission, goals, and objectives of the program as well as to projected student enrollments.

Facilities planning is responsive to the current strengths and weaknesses and future projections as identified through the learning resources program review and planning process. The LRP administrator views the learning resources program as a dynamic organization with evolving needs and technology. He envisions future service needs as a blending of traditional resources with the new electronic resources.

The administrator is concerned for the physical well-being of his staff and, consequently, implements an ergonomically sound work environment. Thus, he ensures ergonomically designed workstations, appropriate lighting and acoustics, and the flexible organization of work. He teaches his staff to effectively use the equipment provided, to exercise, and to monitor their health.

He believes in accessibility to resources and services for everyone. Thus, he ensures the accessibility of the learning resources program to the differently-abled as well as able bodied students and staff. His learning resources program complies with the guidelines set forth through the Americans with Disabilities Act.

He studies the trends in education and the impacts of technology on the learning resources program. In cooperation with the Director of Physical Plant and the campuswide facilities committee, he develops and implements a facilities program responsive of current needs while looking toward the future.

Selected Bibliography

An Architectural Dictionary for Librarians: A Glossary of Frequently Used Terms in Design and Construction of Buildings. Denton, TX: HBW Associates, 1991.

BELCHER, M. CLAY, and RONALD N. HELMS. "Visual Concerns for the VDT Environment," *Missouri Journal for Educational Technology* 14 (Spring 1991): 17–20.

BOSS, RICHARD. *Information Technologies and Space Planning for Libraries and Information Centers.* Boston: G.K. Hall & Co., 1987.

BRAUER, ROGER L. *Facilities Planning: The User Requirements Method.* New York: AMACOM, 1986.

BRAY, JESSICA ADAMS. "The Americans with Disabilities Act of 1990: New Questions," *RQ* 31 (Spring 1992), 315–324.

CARGILL, JENNIFER, and GISELA M. WEBB. *Managing Libraries in Transition.* Phoenix: Oryx Press, 1988.

CLABAUGH, SUE, ed. *Design of General Purpose. Classrooms, Lecture Halls, and Seminar Rooms.* College Park, MD: University of Maryland, 1993.

COHEN, ELAINE. "Talking to Architects," *American Libraries* 20 (April 1989): 299.

Comments on the California Community Colleges' Library Space Study. Sacramento, CA: California Post-Secondary Education Commission, 1985.

CONN, DAVID R., and BARRY McCALLUM. "Design for Accessibility," *Canadian Library Journal* 39 (June 1982): 119-125.

CUMMINGS, STEVE "Workstations Tailored to Fit," *PC World* (November 1987): 330–335.

Department of Justice. "28 CFT Part 36: Nondiscrimination of the Basis of Disability by Public Accommodations and in Commercial Facilities; Final Rule," *Federal Register* (July 26, 1991): 35544–35691.

Disaster Planning and Recovery. Washington, DC: Special Libraries Association, 1989.

DUBIN, FRED. "Mechanical Systems and Libraries," *Library Trends* 36 (Fall 1987): 351–360.

DUGGAN, MARY K. "CD-ROM for Reference: Making the Electronic Library Work for Users." In *CD-ROM in the Library: Today and Tomorrow*, ed. Mary Kay Duggan. Boston: G.K. Hall & Co., 1990.

EPSTEIN, SUSAN BAERG. "Technology, Buildings, and the Future," *Library Journal* 116 (December 1991): 112–114.

Equal Opportunity Employment Commission and U.S. Department of Justice. *Americans with Disabilities Act Handbook.* Washington, DC: U.S. Government Printing Office, 1991.

General Services Administration et al. *Uniform Federal Accessibility Standards.* Washington, DC: U.S. Government Printing Office, 1988.

GUNDE, MICHAEL G. "What Every Librarian Should Know about the Americans with Disabilities Act," *American Libraries* 22 (September 1991): 806–809.

KASER, DAVID. "Current Issues in Building Planning," *College & Research Libraries* 50 (May 1989): 297–304.

LEIGHTON, PHILIP D., and DAVID C. WEBER. "The Influence of Computer Technology on Academic Library Buildings." In *Academic Librarianship: Past, Present, and Future*, ed. John Richardson, Jr. and Jinnie Y. Davis. Englewood, CO: Libraries Unlimited, 1989.

MATTHEWS, JOSEPH R. *Public Access to Online Catalogs.* Second Edition. New York: Neal-Schuman, 1985.

MCADAMS, NANCY R. "Trends in Academic Library Facilities," *Library Trends* 36 (Fall 1987): 287–298.

MERRILL, IRVING R., and HAROLD A. DROB. *Criteria for Planning the College and University Learning Resources Center.* Washington, DC: Association for Educational Communications and Technology, 1977.

MILLER, R. BRUCE. "Libraries and Computers: Disaster Prevention and Recovery," *Information Technology and Libraries* 7 (December 1988): 349–358.

———. "Radiation, Ergonomics, Ion Depletion, and VDTs: Healthful Use of Visual Display Terminals," *Information Technology and Libraries* 2 (June 1983): 151–158.

President's Committee on Employment of People with Disabilities and the U.S. Architectural and Transportation Barriers Compliance Board. *The Americans with Disabilities Act: ADA in Brief.* Washington, DC: U.S. Government Printing Office, 1990.

ROHLF, ROBERT H. "Library Design: What NOT to Do," *American Libraries* 17 (February 1986): 100–104.

SANWALD, WILLIAM W. *Checklist of Library Building Design Considerations.* Second Edition. Chicago: Library Administration and Management Association, 1991.

SIMPSON, ROBERT S. *Effective Audiovisual: A Users Handbook.* Boston: Focal Press, 1987.

SMITH, LESTER, ed. *Planning Library Buildings: From Decision to Design*. Chicago: Library Administration and Management Association, 1986.

"Standards for Community, Junior, and Technical College Learning Resources Programs," *College & Research Libraries News* 51 (September 1990): 757–767.

THOMPSON, GODFREY. *Planning and Design of Library Buildings*. Third Edition. London: Butterworth Architecture, 1989.

UTZ, PETER. "Video Presentation Ergonomics: The Basics of Screen and Audience Placement," *AV Video*. 14 (October 1992): 70–88.

"VDTs in the 1990's: Advancing Technologies, Mounting Concerns," *BNA's Employee Relations Weekly* 8 (July 30, 1990, Special Supplement): 5–15.

VEATCH, LAMAR. "Toward the Environmental Design of Library Buildings," *Library Trends* 36 (Fall 1987): 361–376.

VELLEMAN, RUTH A. *Meeting the Needs of People with Disabilities: A Guide for Librarians, Educators, and Other Service Professionals*. Phoenix: Oryx Press, 1990.

VLCEK, CHARLES W., and RAYMOND V. WIMAN. *Managing Media Services: Theory and Practice*. Englewood, CO: Libraries Unlimited, 1989.

WATERS, BRADLEY A., and WILLIS C. WINTERS. "On the Verge of a Revolution: Current Trends in Library Lighting," *Library Trends* 36 (Fall 1987): 327–349.

Working with VDTs: The Human Interface. Daly City, CA: Krames Communications, 1984.

WRIGHT, CAROL, and LINDA FRIEND. "Ergonomics for Online Searching," *Online* 16 (May 1992): 13–27.

14

Public Relations
and Outreach

The effective learning resources administrator focuses on the community college mission and that of the learning resources program. Through the learning resources program review and planning cycle, he ensures the LRP is responsive to the college's educational goals, curricula, student population, size and complexity, and special needs. He orchestrates college priorities, service needs, staff productivity, and physical and fiscal resources into a successful program. His responsibility is not only to ensure the smooth internal operation of the learning resources program, but also to create a positive external environment.

This chapter introduces the administrator's external roles, or responsibilities, which affect the learning resources program's relationship with its external environment. These external responsibilities include promoting positive public relations throughout the college community and participating in cooperative networks and consortia activities beyond.

Public Relations

The chief learning resources administrator determines the philosophy of learning resources services. Through his leadership, the image and tone of the learning resources program are established. Public relations manages image. Positive public relations activities influence public opinion by conveying information through a variety of techniques that will result in a favorable image. This favorable image, in turn, affects the external environment both campuswide and beyond resulting in a healthy learning resources program.

Public relations efforts tie closely to the LRP program review and planning process. Its functions as outlined by Kotler include "1) identifying the organization's relevant publics, 2) measuring images and attitudes of the relevant publics toward the organization, 3) establishing image and attitude goals for the key publics, 4) developing cost-effective public relations strategies, and 5) implementing actions and evaluating results." [Kies 58] The public relations plan identifies the audience, the goal, the expectations, and the communication vehicle. Public relations efforts succeed when implemented with consistency and frequency.

To achieve positive public relations, the LRP administrator follows Drucker's advice in the *Effective Executive* by focusing his vision on outward contribution, making strengths productive, concentrating on the major areas where superior performance can bring outstanding results, and making effective decisions. [Drucker 23–24] He focuses on customer service, campuswide interaction, publications, and special events.

Customer Service

Business research has found that it takes five times more effort to attract a new customer than it does to keep one. At any given time, as many as one customer in four is dissatisfied enough to start doing business with someone else—if he can find someone who can provide the same service in a more satisfying manner. Only one of twenty-five dissatisfied customers will ever state his dissatisfaction. [Anderson 7–8]

According to findings at Texas A&M, customers evaluate service quality on five factors:

1. Reliability. The ability to provide what was promised, dependably, and accurately.
2. Responsiveness. The willingness to help customers promptly.
3. Assurance. The knowledge and courtesy you show to customers, and your ability to convey trust, competence, and confidence.
4. Empathy. The degree of caring and individual attention you show customers.
5. Tangibles. The physical facilities and equipment, and your own (and others') appearance. [Anderson 9]

Thus, the most important aspect of positive public relations is positive customer service. Everyone who uses learning resources services is a customer. Every learning resources staff member interacting with a LRP user has a responsibility to make that interaction a positive experience by meeting expectations and satisfying needs in such a way that the learning resources services are easy to obtain. The result is positive public relations for both the staff member and the department.

Unfortunately, LRP staff encounter LRP service users who have complaints about LRP services or have encountered problems. On such occasions, the staff member listens sympathetically while the user states the problem, does not offer an explanation or justification, restates the problem clearly and concisely and seeks alternative solutions, agrees on a course of action, and implements that action. A complaint resolved effectively generates additional LRP user respect and positive public relations.

To promote positive customer service, LRP administrators survey LRP users to ensure their needs are met. Satisfaction surveys incorporated into the program review and planning process provide customer service input. A suggestion box or suggestion notebook encourages LRP users to share their concerns in writing to the administration rather than in person to the desk staff. Feedback demonstrating responsive action based upon LRP user suggestions promotes positive public relations.

The physical environment of the Learning Resources Center also affects public relations. An image of organized, functional service combined with an aesthetic, inviting atmosphere results in a positive image. Directional signage, point-of-use aids, posters, and exhibits contribute to positive image and public relations.

Campuswide Interaction

Campuswide interaction includes both informal and formal public relations activities. This form of public relations effort emphasizes two-way, face-to-face communication rather than the written memo or publication. "Walking the halls," informally visiting with discipline faculty and administrators, results in valuable information sharing and positive visibility for the LRP. A caution of this outreach method is to ensure visits are made to all faculty and administrators rather than only those who are personal friends. Participation on campuswide committees, organizations, and activities also encourages informal information sharing and builds a positive image for the LRP.

More formal interaction occurs through liaison programs in which LRP faculty are paired with subject disciplines. The LRP faculty member participates informal department meetings, informal conversation, and other activities to determine ways the LRP can augment the educational process. Another formal interaction occurs through the LRP Advisory Committee which is composed of campus representatives interested in LRP services. Through this advisory committee's input, the development and evaluation of the LRP is more responsive to the college community and enhanced communication occurs.

Formal presentations to student and faculty/staff groups further promote positive public relations. The LRP administrator or representative plans the presentation following effective communication models, such as Berlo's *Source Message Channel Receiver* model, tailoring the message to the target audience. Thus, formal presentations may be given to the Student Government, African American Student Organization, Women in New Goals, etc. or to the Faculty Senate, English Department, or Board of Trustees.

Publications

All LRP publications for distribution must follow the college's public information guidelines. At most colleges, internal publications, defined as those distributed on campus to faculty and staff, may be created and distributed by LRP staff. However, publications, other than teaching aids, to be distributed to students and the general public must be approved through the Director of Community Relations. The most common publication ideas include handbooks, newsletters, annual reports, instructional aids, and press releases; however, only the imagination limits the possibilities.

Faculty/staff handbooks, the LRP newsletter, and the annual report are internal publications. Faculty/staff handbooks provide a brief introduction to LRP services and procedures and list who to call for what service. As a cost savings, an increasing number of colleges are consolidating this information with that from other areas into a campuswide Faculty Handbook. LRP newsletters are designed to draw faculty/staff attention to new or special services, personnel and facilities changes, and special events. For economic reasons, many colleges prefer only one newsletter, or house organ, for the college which is produced by the Director of Community Relations. When this occurs, LRP staff provide LRP news by writing a LRP column on a regular basis or by frequently submitting positive news. LRP flyers listing services also provide a vehicle for promoting the learning resources program and building positive public relations.

Annual reports serve two different purposes. The official annual report fulfills the requirements set forth by the higher administration. A briefer summary version of the official annual report is prepared for public relations purposes. "The annual report can be useful when it tries to inform the public of the value of library services and to be a vehicle for the discussion of library problems and potentials." [Oberembt 1] It summarizes the events of the year, includes a compendium of statistics documenting LRP services, and emphasizes the strengths and weaknesses of the program. It provides a vehicle through which learning resources services are documented for public review.

Instructional aids provide positive public relations by demonstrating the goal of helping the user successfully use LRP resources. For example, point-of-use instructional aids, effective online public access computer (OPAC) help screens, and information pathfinders demonstrate the service goal of LRP staff. Special bibliographies introduce resources on specific topics and may supplement campus forums and colloquia. "Book Alert!" forms notify discipline faculty of the acquisition of new materials supporting their discipline or special interests. Bookmarks with LRP hours, phone numbers, services, or other useful information also contribute to a positive image.

The college's Director of Community Relations welcomes ideas for positive publicity for the college. LRP staff provide ideas for positive news regarding special services or events which would impact the broader college community. The community relations staff prepare the official press release and make the appropriate contacts with the media.

Special Events

Special events promoting the LRP include workshops, receptions, book-sales, and more. Typical workshops include new faculty or student orientations, curriculum development strategies, introductions to electronic resources, or other topics which benefit the college. LRP staff may present workshops themselves or host them as staff development or enrichment activities. Orientations for college secretaries and administrators also publicize LRP services in a positive manner.

Receptions honoring faculty authors, campus leaders, or featured speakers, or celebrating special events, such as GED Graduation or National Library Week, also promote the image of the LRP. Booksales provide publicity by demonstrating collection development activities and by drawing in additional potential LRP users. Contests, such as designing the bookmark or naming the OPAC, heighten awareness of the LRP. Whatever the event, or public relations format, LRP staff seek to positively influence public opinion regarding the learning resources program. Customer service, campuswide interaction, publications, and special events all affect this positive image.

External Cooperation and Outreach

The learning resources administrator seeks "to enlarge access to the services available at the college and in the community through networking, resource sharing, online information services, and technological advances." [Standards 762] Efforts to expand services during tight economic times as well as to fullfill the community service role of the community college encourage cooperation. No LRP can afford to be self-sufficient or totally autonomous. The LRP administrator holds responsibility for developing and managing resources beyond the learning resources center, for participating in external resource sharing agreements and consortia.

Person surveyed 200 community colleges to discover the level of cooperative efforts undertaken with other area libraries and non-library agencies. Of the respondents, "ninety-nine percent of the LRCs in the present study reported some level of inter-library cooperation, and eighty percent reported interagency activities. This cooperation ranged from what one respondent characterized as 'just a friendly work-together attitude on the part of practically all individual librarians whatever their location' to the formalized efforts represented by regional community college LRC organizations and public-school-community college combined facilities. Interagency cooperation ranged from providing materials about community groups to housing museum facilities and space for the Internal Revenue Service." [Person 57]

In 1987, Schuman estimated that, in addition to the three major bibliographic utilities (OCLC, WLN, RLIN), nearly 500 local, state, and regional networks, systems, cooperatives, and consortia exist in the United States. [Schuman 33] A single community college learning resources program participates in a national bibliographic utility, in regional resource sharing and reciprocal access agreements, in general community college and multi-type cooperatives, and in special purpose cooperative agreements and consortia. In addition, learning resources staff network through professional and special interest organizations and share ideas through publication.

Resource Sharing Agreements

Successful cooperative resource sharing agreements require availability of desired resources, bibliographic information describing ownership and availability, and an effective access system either through direct access or a delivery system. In addition, resource sharing agreements may include cooperative collection development. Resource sharing does not save money through reduced acquisitions or staffing; however, it does make learning resources programs more cost effective and increases availability of resources.

"A bibliographic utility is an organization which maintains a large online bibliographic database and provides customer libraries products and services (on and offline) using that database." [Matthews 262] "OCLC (The Online Computer Library Center, Inc.) is our largest network and both the Washington Library Network (WLN) and the Research Libraries Information Network (RLIN) have an important influence on our networking environment. OCLC and RLIN are private, nonprofit corporations." [Schuman 33] Through access to such a bibliographic database, community colleges can locate and access, through interlibrary loan, desired resources.

Regional and state cooperative network agreements enhance resource sharing activities by providing bibliographic control and access to collections within the network. In addition, services of networks include "1) arranging contracts with the major bibliographic utilities, and in so doing, acting as a director in negotiating terms between the utilities and the individual members of the regional network; 2) holding down the cost of services because of a large membership base; 3) providing for the training of librarians and consulting with libraries which wish to modify existing database services; 4) arranging new services for members developing those services at the local, regional, and national levels; 5) determining the authority control of records for the members and improving circulation and acquisition databases; and 6) helping members to change or even drop bibliographic brokers who serve the local system." [Katz 164] AMIGOS, SOLINET, CLASS, and BCR are examples of regional systems. Ohio's OHIONET, Illinois' ILLINET, and Pennsylvania's PALINET are examples of state systems.

Local resource sharing networks range from exchanging periodicals holdings lists to sharing common or linked bibliographic databases. Access may be through traditional library-to-library interlibrary loan or through direct access to the patron via reciprocal borrowing agreements. Delivery may be through UPS delivery, telefacsimile transmission, or a formal delivery system. These networks may be informal agreements developed through daily cooperation among LRPs and libraries or formal cooperatives with membership agreements and dues.

A benefit of effective resource sharing agreements is cooperative collection development (CCD). "The principal objective of a shared collection/ shared resources program should be to increase access to specialized materials or to materials users request which are not available in local collections. The aim, then, is to put into place shared collection/shared resources programs that maximize the number of materials which can be brought to the attention of and delivered to faculty and students." [Dougherty 291]

Through CCD, the community college LRP first identifies and develops a core collection of resources essential to the needs of the local institution. This core collection includes materials needed to support the instructional and developmental needs of its students. Next, it identifies collections of resources which had been previously purchased, but need not be purchased if made available in a timely basis through resource sharing. Finally, it identifies resources "needed and not owned." By cooperating, the LRP would choose to borrow some resources previously purchased in order to buy materials formerly not purchased. For such CCD plans to succeed, each participating LRP "would have to develop a written materials selection policy which would detail these areas: 1) an essential local core collection, 2) material no longer purchased in favor of borrowing, 3) previously unpurchased materials now acquired for local and regional needs. This would entail using a common comprehensive method for describing materials collections." [Haselhuhn 5]

Cooperatives and Consortia

Cooperatives and consortia exist to bring together member organizations to work toward their common welfare. The Northern Illinois Learning Resources Cooperative (NILRC) provides a model of a successful community college learning resources cooperative. NILRC was established in 1975 by eight suburban Chicago community colleges "to facilitate the cooperative exchange of locally produced instructional materials and, therefore, to prevent duplication of effort. Program objectives were established to identify the available materials and determine the legal ramifications of duplicating and distributing them." [Steinke 475] Today the cooperative, consisting of forty-four member institutions, engages in a wide range of activities revolving around cooperative purchasing, information and resource sharing, and staff development.

Steinke attributes NILRC's success to the cooperative effort of its member institutions. "Along with the human element, a learning resources cooperative must have other foundation stones. Those supports include a common philosophy—the comprehensive community college and learning resources concept. Bylaws and membership agreements help to define organizational structure. Additionally, the supports encompass focal points that provide meaningful direction: cooperative purchasing, information and resources sharing, and staff development. Finally, methods for coping with successful growth insure a cooperative's ability to adjust to sociological as well as technological change." [Steinke 485]

Multi-type library systems also provide avenues for cooperation. One example is the Suburban Library System (SLS) consisting of 180 suburban Chicago public, school, academic, and special libraries voluntarily working together to provide materials and services. Services include reciprocal borrowing and interlibrary loan agreements among all SLS member libraries and ILLINET access, reference assistance, audiovisual services, staff development activities, cooperative purchases, and other joint projects. Through participation in the multi-type system, all members gain an appreciation for the commonalities and differences among each type of institution and collectively benefit every member.

To become a SLS member, the community college must agree to fulfill all requirements of the Illinois State Library and Information Network (ILLINET) in terms of collection, bibliographic access, and interlibrary loan compliance and of the Suburban Library System in terms of staffing, collection, hours open, financial support, facilities, reciprocal access, annual reports, and reference standards. Upon acceptance, SLS agrees to provide full system services and access to ILLINET.

Networks and consortia also exist for the purpose of cooperatively serving special needs of their members. For example, MITCO, (Missouri Telecourse Cooperative), facilitates group negotiations with telecourse contracts. SUNYnet, (State University of New York Network), coordinates satellite receive sites throughout the state of New York to enhance educational communication.

Other formal and informal networks encourage cooperation between community colleges and public schools, local museums, art institutes, science centers, zoos, etc. In the tradition of *Building Communities*, the LRP seeks to build cooperation among the community college and the community it serves.

Computer Networks

Computer networks enable the connectivity through computers to the information resources in the world. These networks are the backbone to the concept of the "virtual library," a library that provides access to electronic and print materials from many sources, both local and remote. As the dependence upon electronic publications and electronic bibliographic access grows, the interests and expertise of discipline faculty, the computing center, and the learning resources program become intertwined. Research and special librarians lead this movement; however, community college professionals must become active participants in the development of these networks.

The analogy of a highway system, a general purpose system for carrying traffic, independent of the services that can be offered by third parties, has frequently been used to describe a computer network. Unlike a single purpose network, such as OCLC, linking terminals to a host computer, the computer network provides the linkage, or "data highway" moving information resulting in computer-to-computer communication. The National High-Performance Computer Technology Act of 1989, known as the Gore Bill, charges the National Science Foundation with establishing a three-gigabit/second National Research and Education Network (NREN) by 1996. The bill specifies that the network link government, industry, and the higher education community. While NREN is a proposal, the Internet, on which it is based is a reality. [Arms 20]

BITNET and Internet are the two major international computer networks. BITNET (Because It's Time NETwork) is a research network for electronic mail and file transfers. Network use has expanded to include electronic journals and interest group forums linking users in the United States, Canada, Europe, Asia, and South America. BITNET was established in 1981 with the first link installed using leased telephone lines between IBM mainframes in computer centers at Yale and City University of New York. In 1989, BITNET, Inc. became the Corporation for Research and Educational Networking (CREN), which also operates the CSNET using the TCP/IP computer communications protocol.

Internet is a world-wide network of over five thousand separately run networks that use TCP/IP protocol in 39 countries. Internet was established in 1969 through a project funded by the Department of Defense to explore the feasibility of a long-distance packet switching network resulting in the creation of ARPANET, or the Defense Data Network. "Both the technological capabilities and the concept have matured since then, with today's Internet comprising a network of networks that provides global access to computing and information resources. The Internet topology now consists of the NSFNET backbone." [Britten 104] "NSFNET is a very high speed backbone (currently 1.5 megabits/second, but soon to be raised to 45 megabits/second) that links the supercomputer centers and a number of mid-level networks. Mid-level networks are independently funded and operated (although several had some initial support from NSF) and most are state or regional networks. Attached to the mid-level networks are campus networks; universities are responsible for providing access to the network facilities for their communities." [Arms 17]

The Internet is used for three broad types of computer to computer interactivity. Electronic mail provides the ability to communicate with anyone who has an Internet address. These may be to an individual or through a list-serve discussion group. Remote log-in enables connection to almost any computer on the Internet, with some password restrictions, and allows browsing of data files. Thus, over 250 library online catalogs and special databases may be accessed. File transport protocol (FTP) allows the transfer of files from remote computers on the Internet back to the home computer.

Because the underlying communications protocols between Internet and BITNET are very different, a merger has been challenging. Mail "gateways" allow the exchange of mail messages between Internet and BITNET users; however, direct file transfer is not possible. "NSF is the National Science Foundation, charged with supporting scientists and maintaining the nation's leadership role in science and engineering. CREN's aim is for networks to reach the widest community possible, supporting university faculty, staff, and students in all disciplines and all aspects of research and education." [Arms 18–19] The Gore Bill creating NREN will promote the convergence of the two networks.

Learning resources professionals have a responsibility to learn about and to participate in the development of these "data highways" and to introduce them to LRP users. To more effectively participate in this information network, they understand the information flow process. "The information flow process consists of the creation of information by authors, publishers, sponsors, composers, artists, directors, producers, editors, translators, and a host of others. It includes the consignment of information to a medium (such as print or other media) in a variety of formats—visual, audio, graphic, tactile, books, journals, electronic display, etc.; access, which can be bibliographic or textual, including the act of finding-out-about, of evaluating and identifying; and transfer, the process of display or getting for eventual processing." [Billings 40] LRP professionals explore existing computer networks and are involved in shaping the information network of the future.

Professional Networking

Active participation in professional organizations enables the LRP administrator to network with his colleagues by sharing ideas, issues, and successes. This networking occurs informally before and after consortia meetings, at regional and national conferences, and via the telephone. In addition, he builds contacts through giving presentations at conferences, participating in discussion groups, and serving on committees. Through touring library and audiovisual convention exhibits, visiting other colleges, and actively reviewing the literature, he gathers ideas which help him improve the learning resources program or look toward the future. He, in turn, has an obligation to welcome colleagues to his college and to share his expertise through publication in professional literature.

Professional networking also involves forging links with non-library organizations. This may involve giving presentations to area organizations. More importantly, it involves proactively communicating the role of learning resources to discipline faculty and administrators. This requires becoming active in professional organizations of mutual interest, such as AACJC, the American Society for Training and Development, or State organizations. By becoming an active member in the organization and providing a positive, learning resources professional's presence, the partnership with discipline faculty, administrators, and other members will be forged.

Summary

The chief learning resources administrator fulfills many roles. He not only ensures the smooth internal operation of the learning resources program, but also actively develops positive external relationships. He promotes positive public relations throughout the college community through adopting a "customer service" attitude, promoting formal and informal face-to-face communication and interactions campuswide, creating effective LRP publications which adhere to college guidelines, and encouraging special events which promote the learning resources program image. He also initiates and participates in resource sharing agreements, cooperatives and consortia, and professional networks beyond the campus. The effective learning resources administrator integrates his internal and external responsibilities to ensure the learning resources program is an integral part of the college and the broader college community.

Selected Bibliography

ANDERSON, KRISTIN, and RON ZEMKE. *Delivering Knock Your Socks Off Service.* New York: AMACOM, 1991.

ARMS, CAROLINE R. "A New Information Infrastructure," *Online* 14 (September 1990): 15–22.

BENEFIEL, CANDACE R., et al. "Fun, Friends, and Good P.R.: Celebrating National Library Week in an Academic Library," *College & Research Libraries News* 53 (February 1992): 85–89.

BRITTEN, WILLIAM A. "BITNET and the Internet: Scholarly Networks for Librarians," *College & Research Libraries News* 51 (February 1990): 103–107.

CLEWIS, BETH. "Scholarship and the Community College Librarian," *Journal of Academic Librarianship* 17 (September 1991): 220–222.

DOUGHERTY, RICHARD M. "A Conceptual Framework for Organized Resource Sharing and Shared Collection Development Programs," *Journal of Academic Librarianship* 14 (November 1988): 287–291.

DRUCKER, PETER F. *The Effective Executive.* New York: Harper & Row, 1966.

EVANS, G. EDWARD. *Developing Library and Information Center Collections.* Second Edition. Littleton, CO: Libraries Unlimited, 1987.

GETAZ, JOHN. "Library Orientations for College Secretarial Staff," *College & Research Libraries News* 51 (May 1990): 427–428.

HASELHUHN, RONALD P., and HENRY R. STEWART. "Proposed Method for Describing the Collection in Two-Year Materials Selection Policy Statements." In *Enter, Save, Delete . . .: Libraries Pioneering into the Next Century,* ed. Douglas G. Birdsall. Emporia, KS: Emporia State University, 1989.

KATZ, WILLIAM A. *Introduction to Reference Work, Vol II.* Fifth Edition. New York: McGraw Hill, 1987.

KIES, COSETTE. *Marketing and Public Relations for Libraries.* Metuchen, NJ: Scarecrow Press, 1987.

LEERBURGER, BENEDICT A. *Promoting and Marketing the Library.* Rev. Edition. Boston: G.K. Hall & Company, 1989.

MATTHEWS, JOSEPH R. "Understanding the Utilities," *American Libraries* 11 (May 1980): 262–264.

MOSHER, PAUL H., and MARCIA PANKAKE. "A Guide to Coordinated and Cooperative Collection Development," *Library Resources & Technical Services* 27 (October/December 1983): 417–431.

OBEREMBT, KENNETH J. *Annual Reports for College Libraries: CLIP Note #10.* Chicago: ACRL, 1988.

PERSON, RUTH J. "Community College LRC Cooperative Efforts: A National Study," *Community & Junior College Libraries* 3 (Winter 1984): 53–64.

RUBIN, RHEA JOYCE. "Anger in the Library: Defusing Angry Patrons at the Reference Desk (and Elsewhere)," *Reference Librarian* 31 (1991): 39–51.

SCHAEFFER, MARK. *Library Displays Handbook.* New York: H.W. Wilson, 1991.

SCHUMAN, PARTICIA GLASS. "Library Networks: A Means, Not an End," *Library Journal* 112 (February 1, 1987): 33–37.

SLOAN, BERNARD G. *Linked Systems for Resource Sharing.* Boston: G.K. Hall & Company, 1991.

"Standards for Community, Junior, and Technical College Learning Resources Programs," *College & Research Libraries News* 51 (September 1990): 757–767.

STEINKE, RALPH G. "Learning Resources Cooperation: It Can Be Successful," *Library Trends* 33 (Spring 1985): 473–485.

TENNANT, ROY, JOHN OBER, and ANNE G. LIPOW. *Crossing the Internet Threshold: An Instructional Handbook.* Berkeley, CA: Library Solutions Press, 1933.

"Tip Sheet for Involvement in Non-Library Associations," *College & Research Libraries News* 51 (July/August 1990): 632.

VAUGHAN, GEORGE B. "The Community College Mission," *AACJC Journal* 58 (February/March 1988): 25–27.

WOODSWORTH, ANNE, and THOMAS B. WALL. *Library Cooperation and Networks: A Basic Reader.* New York: Neal-Schuman, 1991.

15

Leading Toward the Future

The chief learning resources administrator is responsible for leading the learning resources program toward the future. He is committed to the mission of the community college and to the priorities of his own college. He accepts Vaughan's five constants describing the mission of the community college: 1) It is an institution of higher education; 2) It mirrors society; 3) It emphasizes teaching instead of research; 4) It provides access to higher education regardless of race, age, or station in life; and 5) It provides a comprehensive instructional program supported by student advising, guidance, and counseling. [Vaughan 25–26]

He studies community college literature to enhance his awareness of the issues and trends affecting community colleges. For example, from *Campus Trends 1990*, he learns that college administrators cite leadership and governance, finance and politics, faculty issues, program quality, facilities and technology, enrollment issues, and diversity as the primary issues facing community colleges. He understands how external influences, such as the state legislature, regional and specialized accrediting agencies, the district Board of Trustees, and the local community, impact the college and the LRP.

He believes the mission of the learning resources program is to provide the resources and services necessary to serve the informational, learning, and developmental needs of its students, faculty, administrators, and broader college community. Each LRP has the responsibility to "promote learning through the academic program of the institution," by providing "the best possible access to wanted information in printed, media, or electronic format, and have the means for delivering the information to an individual user or distributing it to campus classrooms." [Standards 762]

Since no two community colleges are identical, he is cognizant of his own college's organizational chart and governance structure, faculty composition, student demographics, and comprehensiveness of its programs and services. Based upon the learning resources program review and planning process, he develops a learning resources program reflecting the college's educational goals, curricula, student population, size and complexity, and special issues.

He fulfills many roles. He not only ensures the smooth internal operation of the learning resources program but also actively develops positive external relationships. He develops a leadership strategy and style resulting in the fulfillment of the learning resources program mission and goals. With his leadership, the learning resources program is an integral part of the college.

This chapter describes the LRP administrator's leadership toward the future. It summarizes trends as described by futurists and challenges as described by colleagues. It addresses the "change agent" status of the LRP administrator in which he encourages his staff to think creatively and to develop problem solving skills.

Futurists' Visions

Futurists consistently address the impact of the information technologies on education and learning resources programs. Parnell in *Dateline 2000*, finds similarities between the technological advances made during the turn of the twentieth century and those anticipated for the twenty-first. "Advances in technology and the creation of new inventions offer colleges and universities many exciting new possibilities, but these same advances carry with them some new challenges. Rapid technological developments are pushing higher education institutions of all kinds into a search for synergy, for systems and disciplines to work together. There will be a merging of media utilizing voice, video, text, and graphics." [Parnell 251]

More specifically, Parnell envisions textbooks with accompanying interactive video discs, increased responsibilities with fewer staff, routine acceptance of distance learning through telecommuting, educational simulators that enable students to be application literate, interactive video disc to help serve different learning styles, and fiber-optic cable commonplace. In addition, he sees increased cooperation among colleges, universities, and schools, among disciplines as interdisciplinary teaching increases, and between liberal arts and technical education. Technology will be utilized to individualize teaching and learning. Graphics, text, video, and voice will be integrated by faculty who are routinely developing instructional materials. [Parnell 249–250] Parnell's future directly impacts the role of the community college learning resources program.

Library futurists describe the electronic library with digital texts and electronic mail delivery to scholar workstations. Some envision the library as decentralized with service focused on the user, wherever he may be. The emphasis will change from ownership of materials to access of information and shared use. Information resources and responsibilities will integrate as divisions between the library, computer, and telecommunications departments merge. The role of the learning resources specialist will change as information literacy and critical thinking are emphasized. Still other visionaries see the future as a moderate blend integrating the present learning resources center with remote access from off-site workstations. The LRP administrator holds responsibility for leading toward the future in a manner sensitive to his college community.

Challenges for the Future

Hisle identifies five challenges that must be faced if excellence in learning resources services are to be achieved. First is focus. While the "Standards" provide a situational definition for learning resources programs by accepting the local program as long as library and audiovisual services are represented, "a clearer and more consistent definition will facilitate program comparison, foster better training programs for LRS professionals, and make easier the task of explaining to administrators, accrediting bodies, associated professional organizations, and legislative overseers what the LRS program does." [Hisle 620]

Instructional involvement is second. The successful learning resources program is integrally involved with the instructional program. This involvement is achieved through developing partnerships with discipline faculty. Such partnerships may include integrating bibliographic instruction into every curriculum, through introducing new learning methods and materials, and through assisting with curriculum development.

Adapting to technology is third. Advances in technology will continue. LRP staff have responsibility to keep abreast of new developments and provide leadership in introducing technology which will more effectively serve students, faculty, and staff. Examples include introducing telefacsimile systems, electronic mail, and telecommunications technologies. Another example is the use of technology to expand beyond the walls of the campus for purposes of resource sharing.

Service to nontraditional students is fourth. Part of the community college mission is to provide access to higher education regardless of race, age, or station in life. This results in a nontraditional student population including increasing numbers of educationally disadvantaged students, adult learners, and students enrolled in distance education. Distance learners may be telecommuters, employees in the workplace, or students still in high schools. LRP staff must serve the needs of this nontraditional student population.

Professional commitment and liaison is fifth. LRP professionals have an obligation to remain current in their profession. Thus, they must actively read professional journals, participate in library and media conferences and continuing education activities, and promote their profession through publication, presentations, and professional involvement. The LRP administrator not only demonstrates his own professional commitment but also provides staff development opportunities for members of his staff.

Managing Change

The learning resources administrator realizes that to lead the learning resources program toward the future, he must manage change. He is sensitive to the psychological aspects of change including fear, mourning, and social inertia. He encourages his staff to think creatively, to take risks, and to solve problems. He develops a cooperative teamwork to tap the collective strength and wisdom of the staff.

He facilitates the implementation of quality circles and collegiality to address challenges. He encourages individual and group problem solving which includes: 1) identifying the perceived and expressed dissatisfaction or problem to be addressed; 2) describing, analyzing, and defining the problem; 3) proposing and evaluating alternative solutions and identifying the "best" solution; 4) developing strategies to implement the proposed solution and implementing it; and 5) evaluating the resolution of the problem. If the selected solution when implemented does not resolve the problem or challenge, the process is repeated until the desired resolution is reached.

He integrates his internal and external responsibilities as a proactive "change agent" leading the learning resources program toward the future. He is adaptable to cope with the unexpected and to plan toward the future.

Conclusion

"Like a well-built bridge, a healthy institution is a balanced combination of stiffness and resilience—sturdy enough to resist the static force of its own dead weight and flexible enough to bend under highly variable dynamic loads. If leadership is unimaginative, stiffness gains ascendance over resilience, making it possible for external change to bring the whole organization crashing down with catastrophic suddenness. The administrator's responsibility is to protect the institution's health by maintaining its stability, while at the same time designing and implementing changes that enhance its capacity to respond to external developments." [Veaner 452–453]

Administering the community college learning resources program requires the understanding and acceptance of the community college mission. It requires the leadership to orchestrate budgets, personnel, resources, and facilities into a responsive, service-oriented program which is an integral part of the instructional program of the college. It requires the ability to forge positive working relationships both within the college and beyond. And most importantly, it requires the vision toward the future and the courage to design and implement positive change. With effective LRP leadership, the learning resources program is an integral part of the college today and into the future.

Selected Bibliography

BILLINGS, HAROLD. "The Bionic Library," *Library Journal* 116 (October 15, 1991): 38–42.

BREIVIK, PATRICIA SENN, and E. GORDON GEE. *Information Literacy: Revolution in the Library.* New York, Macmillan, 1989.

BREIVIK, PATRICIA SENN, and WARD SHAW. "Libraries Prepare for an Information Age," *Educational Record* 70(Winter 1989): 13–19.

BUCKLAND, MICHAEL K. "Foundations of Academic Librarianship," *College & Research Libraries* 50 (July 1989): 389–396.

FROHMAN, MARK A. "How to Improve Your Problem-Solving Capacity," *Management Review* 69 (November 1980): 59–61.

GORMAN, MICHAEL. "The Academic Library in the Year 2001: Dream or Nightmare or Something in Between?" *Journal of Academic Librarianship* 17 (March 1991): 4–9.

HANKS, NANCY, and STAN WADE. "Quality Circles: Realistic Alternatives for Libraries," *Show-Me Libraries* 36 (June 1985): 6–11.

HISLE, W. LEE. "Learning Resources Services in the Community College: On the Road to the Emerald City," *College & Research Libraries* 50 (November 1989): 613–625.

JOHNSTON, WANDA K. "Future Directions of Information Technologies as Projected in the Literature," *Illinois Libraries* 73 (February 1991): 187–190.

KEEN, PETER G. W. "Information Systems and Organizational Change," *Communications of the ACM* 24 (January 1981): 24–33.

LYMAN, PETER. "The Library of the (Not-So-Distant Future," *Change* 23 (January/February): 34–41.

PARNELL, DALE. *Dateline 2000: The New Higher Education Agenda.* Washington, DC: AACJC, 1990.

VEANER, ALLEN B. *Academic Librarianship in a Transformational Age: Program, Politics, and Personnel.* Boston: G.K. Hall & Company, 1990.

APPENDIX I

Standards for Community, Junior, and Technical College Learning Resources Programs

The New Standards, Approved by ACRL and AECT

Reprinted with permission from *College & Research Libraries News* 51 (September 1990): 757–767.

These standards apply to two-year or three-year academic institutions awarding an associate degree or certificate. They are intended to assist in evaluating and developing learning resources programs. With approval by the Association for Educational Communications and Technology and the Association of College and Research Libraries, the document replaces "Guidelines for Two-Year College Learning Resources Programs (Revised)" and "Quantitative Standards for Two-Year Learning Resources Programs."

Two-year colleges colleges make a significantly different contribution than other academic institutions. The public institutions, because of community control, are generally more responsive to local needs. Moderate costs and open-access allow greater flexibility to students who would not otherwise be able to attend college. Emphases on vocational and adult programs and continuing education provide employable skills to many adult students through responsiveness to changing vocational needs. At the same time, while allowing for remedial work to remove deficiencies, academic programs in private and community colleges parallel education in the arts and sciences in four-year institutions. Reflecting the combination of availability of opportunity and expectation of excellence in performance, more than half of the students pursuing higher education are enrolled in community, technical and junior colleges nationwide.

The emphasis being made by the American Association of Community and Junior Colleges, especially for community colleges but also applicable to other two-year institutions, upon the building of communities, upon partnerships for learning, and upon excellence in teaching, requires resources and services which must be provided in accordance with these standards if the vision is to become reality. (See American Association of Community and Junior Colleges, *Building communities: A Vision for a New Century*, a report of the Commission on the future of community colleges, 1988.)

In most two-year institutions an expanded concept of learning resources provides services to the college community. The term "learning resources" is applied in these standards to an organizational configuration which provides library and media materials and services. In addition, learning resources programs can provide various specialized services and perform other instructional responsibilities.

The structure and function of a learning resources program in each institution obviously has been determined by the role assigned within the institutional structure. This role must be consistent with the stated mission of the institution. It must also be related realistically to the institution's educational goals, curricula, size and complexity, as well as the diversity of resources needed to accommodate different modes of learning.

As an educational entity, the learning resources program with audiovisual responsibilities must provide the needed services in a technological environment which requires a substantial proportion of the campus budget. The combination of a number of related responsibilities under the title of a learning resources program is an effective and reasonable way to make the maximum use of the budget. This will expand the role and structure of the learning resources center, and, thereby, create an organizational unit which can provide all major instructional requirements needed to support the diverse educational programs.

Contents

- Standard One. Objectives.
- Standard Two. Organization.
- Standard Three. Administration and staff.
- Standard Four. Budget.
- Standard Five. Services.
- Standard Six. Collections.
- Standard Seven. Facilities.
- Appendix A. Checklist of basic library services.
- Appendix B. Checklist of basic audiovisual and learning technology services.
- Appendix C. Checklist of special services components.

Standard One: Objectives

1.0 The college shall develop a comprehensive statement of the mission of the learning resources program based on the nature and purpose of the institution.

Commentary. A clear and unambiguous statement of the role of the learning resources program is essential for accountability, administration, and review regardless of the organizational structure. Where there are public multi-college districts, separate mission statements should be developed for each campus; multi-campus community college districts may either develop mission statements for each campus or prepare a comprehensive statement for the district-wide learning resources program components.

1.1 The mission statement shall be developed by the learning resources staff, in consultation with the widest possible representation of the college community. The statement or statements shall be endorsed by the governing board and shall be reviewed periodically.

Commentary. Assignment of responsibility to the learning resources staff for the development of the statement and for its utilization and review is appropriate.

1.2   The mission statement shall be used, along with institutional educational goals, in the annual planning process.

Commentary. The mission statement serves as a mirror for the evaluation of services and the projection of future needs. As such it becomes an integral part of the planning process.

1.3   All component units of the learning resources program, whether administered centrally or administered by other campus units, should be clearly defined.

Commentary. The learning resources program should include essential and basic library and media services as identified in the lists in Appendices A and B. There must be explicit understanding of the units which comprise the centralized services. The learning resources program may include other special components such as those listed in Appendix C. To standardize statistical data nationally, decentralized service units (those that report to other departments) should provide needed information about staff and expenditures for reporting to external agencies.

1.4   The learning resources program shall be an integral part of the institution's process for the improvement of instruction.

Commentary. An effective learning resources program is and must be immediately and intimately involved in the entire educational program. There must be participation in curriculum development and approval because the identification and acquisition of resources to support any curricular changes requires time for planning services that may be needed, reading lists that could be provided, bibliographical instruction that must be given, and priorities on use of resources that should be established. Introduction of new models of instruction that require student use of self-paced materials and equipment in centrally-administered facilities require lead time for planning equipment acquisition, development of procedures, and preparation of materials and staff.

Standard Two: Organization

2.0   The responsibilities and functions of the component units of the learning resources program within the institutional structure shall be clearly defined.

Commentary. The services provided are directly related to the quality of the educational program. When restricted to only a small number of basic services, the quality of the instructional program is inhibited; when too vaguely defined, valuable resources will be poorly utilized. Clarity in identifying functions and specificity in assigning responsibilities will provide a learning resources program potentially capable of meeting the needs of the college. Institutional manuals, procedures, and job descriptions confirm the status of the program.

2.1 The duties and responsibilities of the chief administrator of the learning resources program shall be clearly defined within the institutional structure.

Commentary. The chief administrator is responsible for administering the program and for providing leadership and direction so that mission of the program is fulfilled. The administrator should report to the chief academic officer and should have the same administrative rank and status as others with similar institution-wide responsibilities; a title such as Dean of Instructional Services or of Learning Resources is appropriate.

2.2 The comprehensive learning resources program shall include a variety of services which are organized into functional units.

Commentary. The type of component units needed and included will vary from institution to institution and campus to campus. Some possibilities are: technical services, library services, media services, learning development, reprographic services, professional materials services, video production, graphics production, learning laboratories, and computer services. A listing of many of these can be found in the Appendices. Services which are not administratively under the supervision of the program's chief should have a secondary relationship to the learning resources program to allow comprehensive planning and reporting and to avoid duplication.

2.3 The administrator and professional staff should be involved in all areas and at all levels of academic activities and institutional planning.

Commentary. The professional staff members should be involved in major college committees and participate in faculty affairs to the same extent as other faculty. The chief administrator must meet regularly with college administrators and department heads and, along with the professional staff members, must be involved in planning, implementing, and evaluating the instructional program of the college.

2.4 Advisory committees should be formed to provide essential information to the staff and to serve as a link with users.

Commentary. Advisory committees are appointed, elected, or selected by the appropriate faculty, staff or student constituencies. The development and evaluation of services can be more effective because of their responses.

2.5 Internal administration of the learning resources program should be based on staff participation in decisions on policies, procedures, and personnel.

Commentary. While the chief administrator is ultimately responsible, the basis for internal administration should be participatory governance through regular staff meetings and internal communication. The administrator is responsible for reporting to the staff on institutional plans, anticipated curriculum changes, and matters affecting the internal effectiveness of the learning resources program; in turn the administrator will report concerns and recommendations of the learning resources staff to the college administrator.

Each professional and supportive staff member must be provided with a position description which clearly identifies the duties and responsibilities of the position and superior and subordinate relationships. Performance appraisal standards must be clearly defined and understood by all staff members. In addition to a general administrative manual, each unit may require a supplementary manual which provides policy and procedural statements, duty assignments, other organizational matters, and items of general information pertaining to its particular unit. Policy and procedures manuals covering internal library governance and operational activities shall be made available to all staff members.

Standard Three: Administration and Staff

3.0 Sufficient and qualified professional and support staff should be available to implement the services for which the program is responsible.

Commentary. Table A evaluates the requirements for adequate numbers of staff on a single campus. The figures are for full-time positions at two levels, basic and excellent, based on full-time equivalent student enrollments. The table does not include services listed in Appendix C as peripheral; if any of these services are assigned, additional staff will be needed in addition to the positions in the table. There is a direct relationship between staff, budget, and services. When staff level and funding level increase, the number of services possible will also increase; the reverse is also a dangerous possibility which should be avoided. If enrollment is 50% greater than FTE, additional staff will be needed. Another factor which affects staff requirements is the ratio of total enrollment to full-time equivalent students. The higher the ratio the greater will be the need for additional staff beyond the formulas in Table A. If there is a regular summer session at the college, the positions in Table A should be based on an eleven or twelve month equivalency. If, in a multi-campus or multi-college district, some services are centralized, additional personnel will be needed.

3.1 The chief administrator shall be professionally trained and knowledgeable about all types of library and media materials and services.

Commentary. The training and experience of the chief administrator shall be as a librarian, a media specialist, or an information specialist with cross-training desirable. The minimal professional degree and prerequisite for the

TABLE A*. Staffing Requirements for Services (excluding those in Appendix C**) ***

FTE Students	Administrators Min. and Excel.	Professionals Min.	Professionals Excel.	Technicians Min.	Technicians Excel.	Other Staff**** Min.	Other Staff**** Excel.	Total Staff Min.	Total Staff Excel.
Under 200	1		2	1	2	1	2	3	7
200–1,000	1	2	4	2	4	2	3	7	12
1,000–3,000	1	3	5	3	6	3	6	10	18
3,000–5,000	1	5	7	5	8	4	8	15	24
5,000–7,000	1	7	9	7	12	6	11	21	33
7,000–9,000	1	8	11	9	17	7	14	25	43
9,000–11,000	1	10	15	11	20	9	17	31	53
11,000–13,000	2	14	21	13	24	11	20	40	67
13,000–15,000	2	16	24	16	28	13	24	47	78
15,000–17,000	2	18	27	19	32	16	28	55	89
17,000–19,000	2	20	30	21	36	18	32	61	100

*Does not include student assistants.
**Most will require 3–8 additional positions.
***Additional staff will be needed if enrollment is 50% greater than FTE.
****Secretaries, clerks, lab aides, etc.

223

position is a master's degree in educational technology or library services. In order to interact with other administrators and the learning resources staff the chief administrator should demonstrate knowledge of effective management. To make decisions on costly new information services, the administrator should have continuous experience with new technologies.

3.2 The professional staff shall have a graduate degree from an accredited institution and shall have faculty status, benefits, and obligations.

Commentary. The complexity of the learning resources program may require considerable differentiated staffing by individuals with widely varied professional education and areas of specialization. All should have the same status and recognition as other instructional faculty; where faculty rank exists they should meet the same requirements for promotion and tenure as the other instructional family.

3.3 Professional staff should belong to library, media, and other appropriate associations, and professional development should be encouraged through direct financial support of attendance and participation in those local, state, and national organizations.

Commentary. The mark of a professional is not only performance on the job but also awareness of professional trends and technological developments learned at professional meetings and workshops, and from professional journals.

3.4 Technical and classified personnel should have appropriate specialized training or experience; classification, status, and salary should be equivalent to those provided for other institutional employees with similar qualifications.

Commentary. Requirements for training and experience needed should relate to the duties assigned. The relative importance of each type of skill will vary across organizational levels. Supervisors should be selected on the basis of knowledge, experience, and human relations skills.

3.5 Student assistants are employed to perform a variety of tasks, but they should not be used in place of full or part-time staff personnel.

Commentary. The tasks performed by student assistants are usually of a routine nature. However, second-year students in some technical programs may bring skills of a more advanced nature which may supplement the skills of the staff. Student assistants are valuable sources of student opinion of services. They should be treated with respect by all other staff, encouraged to work responsibly on a job, and be given training for doing their tasks successfully.

3.6 The changing nature of the learning resources programs and technological changes which impact such programs mandate regular continuing education participation by all persons, professional and staff alike.

Commentary. Duty schedules should be flexible enough for staff to occasionally pursue further training during working hours. The institutional budget should include provision for travel to meetings and conferences, for registration fees, released time for in-service training, and participation in teleconferences.

Standard Four: Budget

4.0   The budget for the learning resources program should be developed within the mission statement as part of the institutional planning process; the annual objectives should be developed by the learning resources staff.

Commentary. The significance of the mission statement and the annual defined objectives forms the basis for the fiscal process for all of the budget except acquisitions. Stable funding for acquisitions based on the collection development policy is necessary for effective service. Unfortunately consistent funding is the element least congenial to the development of annual objectives and is most affected by decreases; care must be taken to provide adequate information about the significance of stability.

4.1   An ample and stable budget should be based either on a percentage of educational and general budget totals for the institution as shown in Table B for a full-time student equivalent dollar basis as shown in Table C.

Commentary. Basing the learning resources budget totals on a percentage of the educational and general funds is the preferred approach, but, because this percentage represents the final stage in the budget process, it is difficult to determine during the budget planning. Capital funds are not included in the percentage except for acquisition of library materials.

An alternative which uses a per full-time student equivalent dollar figure will allow planning of collections and services upon a more stable basis. Table C is based on 1987 dollars; when there is inflation these figures should be adjusted upward accordingly. There is a correlation between services,

TABLE B*.   Learning Resources Budget as % of
Educational & General Expenditures

Size	Minimum	Excellent
All	6%	9%

*Appendix C activities and services will require additional funding.

TABLE C*.   Dollar Expenditure per FTE Student
for Learning Resources Other Than Salaries

FTE	Minimum	Excellent
Under 200	211	450
200–1,000	225	400
1,000–3,000	190	375
3,000–5,000	190	375
5,000–9,000	190	375
9,000–12,000	200	400
12,000–15,000	210	410
15,000–19,000	220	425

*Appendix C activities and services will require additional funding.

collection, and staff size and the level expenditures. Neither table includes capital expenditures. Technological changes, automation, replacement of equipment, and other capital expenditures will require additional funds. Neither table involves capital expenditures except for library materials.

4.2   Local level processes should be developed so that all expenditures other than payroll originate within the learning resources program and all invoices should have the approval of the chief administrator.

Commentary. Management involves full responsibility for expenditures; no payments should be made without such written approval. Cost analyses and financial planning depend upon the control of adequate records, but these are not always the same records needed by the business offices. To the legal extent possible and to make the greatest financial savings, purchases of materials should be exempt from restrictive annual bidding and should permit online ordering and standing orders for continuations.

4.3   Internal accounts shall be maintained for evaluating the flow of expenditures, monitoring encumbrances, and approving payment of invoices.

Commentary. An accurate account of expenditures in categories that are meaningful is necessary for fiscal accountability, for monitoring status of accounts, for decision making, and for planning.

4.4   The learning resources budget should provide stable funding for contractual services, equipment, and materials replacement (of three to five percent), and for maintenance of automated public and technical services.

Commentary. Many services are based on continuing support. They cannot be interrupted without serious constraint on the ability to perform effectively. The materials in the collection will become stagnant without a three to five percent replacement of older materials each year.

Standard Five: User Services

5.0 The learning resources program should provide a variety of services to support and expand the instructional capabilities of the institution.

Commentary. Learning resources exist to facilitate and improve learning by supporting and expanding classroom instruction and to perform the instructional function of teaching students the information-seeking skills for self-directed studies and life-long learning. As an integral part of the total educational program of the institution, learning resources provide classroom instructional as well as support services to students, faculty, and staff. In some institutions regular classroom instruction in media and bibliographic subjects and service to the community are also provided.

The primary purpose of the learning resources program is to promote learning through the academic program of the institution. To do this the program should provide the best possible access to wanted information in printed, media, or electronic format, and have the means for delivering the information to an individual user or distributing it to campus classrooms. Access in the first instance is provided from the institutions own collection of materials, paired with supportive equipment and efficient service delivery systems to ensure that the available physical resources are deployed for the engagement of students with information and ideas. To integrate new resources of information and new instructional technologies into the ever-changing curriculum, access and delivery systems must be extended through such means as cooperative borrowing or renting materials from other institutions, online searching of large databases, and employing the power of electronic transmission. Most, but not all, potential services are listed in the Appendices.

Students should have access to professional assistance at all times the central facility is open as well as access to materials. Faculty members should have access to basic media production assistance and to assistance in research projects.

5.1 Priority should be given to basic services in accordance with the mission statement; when the program includes special service components, additional staff and funding must be provided.

Commentary. Staff and budget must relate to basic services if service goals are to be met. Special services components listed in Appendix C can and do provide significant support to a learning resources program if the institution is able to afford to provide them, but they must be recognized as supplementing, not replacing, basic services. Table D shows basic services in Appendices A and B which budget and available staff make possible.

5.2 The program should seek to enlarge access to the services available at the college and in the community through networking, resource sharing, online information services, and technological advances.

TABLE D.   Number of Possible Services* from
Ranking of Staff and Budget

FTE Students	Minimum	Excellent
Under 200	16	28
200–1,000	19	30
1,000–3,000	22	35
3,000–5,000	26	40
5,000–7,000	30	44
7,000–9,000	34	48
9,000–11,000	37	52
11,000–13,000	40	54
13,000–15,000	43	56
15,000–17,000	45	58
17,000–19,000	47	60

*From services listed in Appendices A and B only.

Commentary. Institutional self-sufficiency is no longer possible today; provision must be made to utilize new delivery systems. Timely access is the key to services. Table D provides a basis for evaluating the number of services which realistically can be provided based on the level of funding and staff. New technology and new services should be adopted as they become useful in meeting institutional goals. The administrator should be prepared to bring to the attention of the faculty and administration new information formats and services as they emerge.

5.3 The services provided should meet the instructional and informational needs of students, faculty, staff, and administration, should provide professional assistance in interpretation, and should include provision for students in off-campus locations.

Commentary. Successful performance is indicated when the needs of students are met. Professional staff as part of the instructional faculty must be accessible to students and must help them gain the skills needed to become self-reliant and critical users of information services. Close cooperation with the classroom faculty is mandatory. Off-campus instruction at a multi-use center must be supported by branch services or by contract services with an accessible library in accordance with ACRL's "Guidelines for Extended Campus Library Services."

5.4 Services are provided for all levels of user: students and other members of the college community.

Commentary. The two-year college has a heterogeneous population with widely different needs. Care must be taken that services provided will meet the needs of every individual. This means that the gifted and the remedial student, the recent high school graduate and the mature adult, the physically handicapped and the limited English student can each receive the services that individual student requires. Other campus groups have differing research and informational requirements which should be given careful consideration.

5.5 Necessary instructional equipment is available and managed in the most efficient manner to insure effective utilization.

Commentary. Equipment must be available when and where it is needed; some equipment may be kept permanently in appropriate classrooms or where materials are found. Equipment must be maintained in operating condition and should be replaced on a scheduled basis, taking into consideration obsolescence, operating condition, and age. Capital funds should also be available to insure that advantage can be taken of new technological advances.

5.6 Provision should be made for instructional support production services.

Commentary. Production services should consist, at a minimum, of visualization services, such as production of overhead transparencies, and audio services, such as recording of lectures and speeches, and duplication of these. As staff and budget allow additional production capabilities should be added to meet institutional requirements.

5.7 There shall be a program to provide to students bibliographic instruction through a variety of techniques enabling them to become information literate.

Commentary. One responsibility of the learning resources program is to provide instruction in the use of the materials and equipment available. In addition to general orientation programs, bibliographic instruction may use many different methods, including group and individual instruction and even credit courses. Traditional reference services should be geared to the provision of individualized instructional assistance at all open hours. The student should be prepared to use new information resources for a lifetime.

Standard Six: Collections

6.0 The learning resources program shall make available an organized collection of materials and diversified forms of information useful in the educational process, including various forms of print and non-print media, computer software, optical storage, technologies, and other formats.

Commentary. The college must be prepared to utilize new technologies for securing information as these are developed. All types of materials conveying intellectual content, artistic and literary works, programmed texts and packaged instruction are considered resources of information that may be used as tools of effective teaching and learning along with books, periodicals, newspapers, government documents, and microform equivalents. There is not a substitute for a well-selected, immediately accessible collection.

Media materials, including those locally produced, play a vital role in the instructional program of most two-year colleges. The increasing volume of specialized, high quality information recorded on videotape at relatively low cost gives videocassette formats a leading role in delivering current information across all disciplines. Computer software must be treated as a curricular resource for programmed learning, development of basic skills, creative research activities, and preparation for the job world. Online computer services are increasingly important as information resources along with the CD-ROM laser technologies.

Table E provides collection goals using definitions from the Integrated Postsecondary Education Data System (IPEDS) of the Office of Education. The table combines some of the items which are separately reported in the IPEDS, but otherwise they are consistent with it. Quantities under the various columns can be interchanged according to the mission of the institution. For example, an institution with a very strong music program may need to develop a strong collection of sound recordings or videorecordings much in excess of these quantitative standards but may need less of some other items. The basis for evaluation in such a case would be the total holdings for that size institution.

6.1 A collection development policy statement shall serve as the basis for selection and acquisition of materials.

Commentary. Acquiring materials based on a written policy with clear guidelines for selection is the nature of collection development. The statement should be developed in consultation with instructional faculty, students, and administrators. Although there are many alternative ways of writing a collection development policy, the following essentials should be included:

a. The purpose for which resources are required.
b. The primary clientele who are to be served.
c. The kinds of materials which are to be acquired.
d. The various factors of cost and usability which will be considered in determining acquisition priorities.
e. The procedures for handling new types of materials, such as computer software and videocassettes, in conformance to copyright law.
f. The process for leasing or renting materials not readily available or too expensive to purchase.
g. Any arrangements with other institutions for cooperative collection, production, or distribution activities.

h. A statement in support of intellectual freedom and the Library Bill of Rights.

i. A policy on the acceptance and incorporation of gifts into the holdings which recognizes the inherent processing and storage costs.

6.2 The selection of materials should be coordinated by the professional staff, working closely with the campus community; final management decisions as to the order in which materials are to be purchased and what gifts should be accepted and processed is the responsibility of the chief administrator or designee.

Commentary. Professionally trained librarians and information specialists, because of their knowledge of the collection, are best able to give systematic attention to collection development. The importance of knowledge about existing holdings, identifying weaknesses, and determining what should and can be acquired requires systematic attention of professionals. They should have access to bibliographical tools and reviewing sources for effective collection development.

6.3 The collection shall be of sufficient scope and currency to support the curriculum as well as meet individual information needs of students and faculty.

Commentary. The mission of the college will determine the complexity of the collection but an institutional commitment to excellence should mean building and maintaining collections that adequately support: liberal arts and sciences programs to prepare students fully for transfer to four-year colleges and universities; programs that have specialized accreditation (fields such as nursing, radiologic technology, etc.); vocational and technical programs; special programs for job training, retraining, or upgrading of skills in continuing and community education services; and needed remedial programs for non-traditional or under-prepared learners. Materials must be available to meet term paper assignments and classroom student reports and self-paced learning in a broad spectrum of knowledge.

6.4 Obsolete, worn-out, and inappropriate materials should be removed based on a policy statement.

Commentary. Deselection and weeding on a regular basis is indispensable to a useful collection and should be done systematically. A written policy should govern what should be removed, what should be replaced, and what should be permanently retained. Not only do obsolete and inappropriate materials occupy expensive storage space but they also distract from other current materials containing important information. From three to five percent of the collection should be replaced annually. The condition of the collection should be reviewed regularly and needed repairs should be made.

6.5 The reference collection shall include a wide selection of standard works, with subject bibliographies and periodical indexes in print and electronic formats.

TABLE E. Size of Collection for a Single Campus

Minimum Collection

FTE Students	Volumes*	Current Serial Subs.	Video & Film	Other Items**	Total Collection
Under 200	20,000	200	125	1,400	21,725
200–1,000	30,000	230	140	2,500	32,870
1,000–3,000	40,000	300	400	5,100	45,800
3,000–5,000	60,000	500	750	8,000	69,250
5,000–7,000	80,000	700	1,250	10,000	92,550
7,000–9,000	95,000	850	1,600	12,000	109,450
9,000–11,000	110,000	900	1,800	14,800	127,500
11,000–13,000	125,000	1,000	2,000	17,400	145,400
13,000–15,000	140,000	1,200	2,200	19,800	163,200
15,000–17,000	155,000	1,500	2,400	22,000	180,900
17,000–19,000	170,000	1,800	2,600	24,000	198,900

*Does not include microforms; an annual replacement of 3–5% is anticipated.
**Includes microforms, cartographic, graphic, audio, and machine-readable materials.

232

Excellent Collection

FTE Students	Volumes	Current Serial Subs.	Video & Film	Other Items	Total Collection
Under 200	30,000	350	525	3,400	34,275
200–1,000	45,000	400	560	5,000	50,960
1,000–3,000	60,000	600	800	8,000	69,400
3,000–5,000	85,000	800	1,300	11,600	98,700
5,000–7,000	112,000	1,000	2,250	18,000	124,240
7,000–9,000	136,000	1,200	3,000	21,000	161,200
9,000–11,000	166,000	1,400	3,300	26,000	196,700
11,000–13,000	200,000	1,600	4,000	31,000	236,600
13,000–15,000	240,000	1,800	4,500	36,000	282,300
15,000–17,000	285,000	2,100	5,000	41,000	333,100
17,000–19,000	320,000	2,400	5,600	50,000	378,000

Commentary. Reference is the core of every learning resources center and the beginning point for research. The reference collection should be of sufficient breadth and depth to serve the research and informational needs of the campus community.

6.6 Materials which document the history of the institution should be available.

Commentary. Each institution should collect all available publications and internal documents relating to the institution itself. These could include publications by the faculty as well as materials relating to the history of the college. If other institutions or libraries are not collecting materials about the history and life of the local community in which the college is located, these could also become part of the materials to be collected.

6.7 Collections should be organized to provide users with full, efficient, and direct access.

Commentary. The choice of a classification system, the type of catalog, and the arrangement of materials are important decisions. Nationally approved systems (such as LC or Dewey) and formats (such as MARC) should be used. Uniform and multiple access through a public catalog is essential to make available information in all types of formats. The public catalog should include all print and non-print items.

Standard Seven: Facilities

7.0 The learning resources program should provide space for housing collections, for study and research, for public service and staff needs, and for basic production.

Commentary. Flexibility is essential to cope with technological developments. Most services should be housed in a central location managed by the chief administrator. When components are located elsewhere, these should be located for the most efficient and effective access to these services. Facilities must be planned on a long-term basis, including space for an expanding collection, workspace, machines and other equipment, storage, and the needs of users. Space planning must take into account the need for computer workstations, for transmission and retrieval of information by telecommunications, for media production, and for related requirements within the building for electrical and conduit connections. Space needs of basic components require as a minimum the space indicated in Table F. Additional space should be provided when special services (such as are found in Appendix C) are included in the responsibilities of the learning resources program.

TABLE F.   Assignable Square Feet (ASF) for Learning Resources Excluding Corridors, Stairs, Rest Rooms, etc.)*

Minimum ASF for Learning Resources Facilities

FTE Students	Stack	Staff	User	Media Production	Viewing, Storage & Other	Total Space	Users Stations
To 200	2,000	890	1,925	3,800	4,561	13,176	70
200–1,000	3,000	1,380	4,125	5,000	7,625	21,130	150
1,000–3,000	4,000	1,800	9,625	8,000	15,285	38,710	350
3,000–5,000	6,000	2,500	14,575	9,500	22,065	54,640	530
5,000–9,000	9,500	3,900	26,474	12,500	35,625	87,500	720
9,000–12,000	10,200	5,300	33,500	13,250	44,445	106,695	960
12,000–15,000	14,000	6,980	43,259	14,000	53,265	131,504	1,200
15,000–19,000	17,000	8,940	51,225	15,000	65,025	157,190	1,520

Excellent ASF for Learning Resources Facilities

FTE Students	Stack	Staff	User	Media Production	Viewing, Storage & Other	Total Space	Users Stations
To 200	3,000	1,380	2,340	4,100	5,020	15,920	85
200–1,000	4,500	2,080	4,800	5,500	8,390	25,270	175
1,000–3,000	6,000	2,920	11,000	8,800	16,820	45,540	400
3,000–5,000	8,500	3,760	16,775	10,450	24,270	63,755	610
5,000–9,000	12,000	6,000	22,825	13,750	39,180	93,765	830
9,000–12,000	17,000	8,100	30,250	14,575	48,890	118,815	1,100
12,000–15,000	24,000	10,200	48,950	15,400	58,590	157,140	1,780
15,000–19,000	29,000	13,280	59,125	16,500	71,530	189,435	2,150

*Based initially on legal formulas for California community colleges; these formulas are based on current enrollment statistics. Since enrollments fluctuate and buildings are planned for long-term usage, these tables were adapted for a range, modified by the provisions in other portions of these standards.

235

7.1 The space for user activities should accommodate a wide variety of learning and study situations, should be attractive, comfortable, designed to encourage use.

Commentary. Proper arrangement and sufficient space for utilization of instructional equipment and materials, for the needs of the physically handicapped, and for both isolated individual study and for conference and group study is essential. Space should also be provided for group bibliographic instruction.

Display and exhibit space, preview space, and study areas for faculty are desirable. With technological developments, planning for use of specialized equipment requires consideration in terms of electrical connections, cables, conduits, lights, environmental control, fire protection, security, and other factors which affect service. The increase in telecommunications may justify cable linkage to faculty offices, classrooms, and to outside locations.

7.2 Space assigned to learning resources should be restricted to the functions for which designed.

Commentary. Space designed for learning resources use should not be filled by other campus activities when these will adversely impact the learning resources program.

Appendix A: Checklist of Basic Library Services and Activities

Listed below are specific services which are considered to be normal and basic services in learning resources program budgets in two-year colleges. Inclusion does not mean that an institution must or should have every activity or service listed.

Acquisition of computer software.
Acquisition of microforms.
Acquisition of non-print materials.
Acquisition of print materials.
Automated online catalog.
Bibliographic instruction.
Circulation of print materials.
Circulation of non-print materials.
Collection management.
Computer reference searching.
Government document borrowing.

Government document selective depository.
Independent study guidance.
Institutional publications reference collection.
Instructional television individualized access.
Interlibrary borrowing.
Interlibrary lending.
Laser optical/reference searches.
Literacy training materials.
Local history collection.
Machine-assisted cataloging of books.
Machine-assisted cataloging of audiovisuals.
Microcomputers for public use.
Microform cataloging.
Microform print service.
Online public access catalog.
Participation in bibliographic networks.
Physical access to materials.
Preparation of bibliographies.
Processing of audiovisuals.
Processing of microforms.
Processing of print materials.
Reference services.
Reserve book service.
Selection of materials.
Self-service copy machine.
Special collections services.
Telefacsimile service.
Telephone reference service.
Term paper counseling.
Union card catalog.
User-available typewriters.

Appendix B: Checklist of Basic Instructional Media Activities and Services

Listed below are services which are considered to be normal and basic services in two-year college learning resources program budgets. This list may not include future technologies and services. Inclusion does not mean that an institution should have every activity or service listed.

Adult literacy laboratory.
Audiocassette duplication.
Audiocassette editing.
Audiocassette recording.
Audiovisual equipment maintenance.
Audiovisual equipment distribution.
Closed circuit television.
Copyright consultation.
Darkroom services.
Equipment distribution.
Equipment maintenance.
Equipment repair.
Equipment specifications.
Graphic art layouts.
Group presentations.
Group television viewing.
Identification photography.
Instructional design and development counseling.
Instructional film and video renting and borrowing for classroom use.
Instructional materials scheduling.
Interactive television.
Inventory of audiovisual equipment.
Listening services.
Microcomputer literacy.
Media orientation and instruction.
Motion picture photography.
News photography.
Photography for slides.
Preview services for faculty.
Production of instructional materials.
Production of sound slide programs.
Satellite communication downlink.
Scripting of audiovisual presentations.
Scripting of television modules.
Self-paced learning assistance.
Telecourse availability information.
Television off-air video recording.
Television off-site video recording.

Videotape editing.
Videotape multi-camera production.
Videotape one-camera production.

Appendix C: Checklist of Special Services Components

This list includes technologies and roles which, if assigned to the learning resources program, will require capital funds, space, personnel, and operational budgets in excess of those included in Tables A to F. Inclusion of programs in this list is not advocacy for these services as part of the learning sources program but recognition that some institutions have included them in the supervisory responsibilities of the chief administrator.

Adult literacy program direction.
Auto-tutorial laboratory.
Career counseling.
College catalog production.
College press.
Community cable television instruction.
Computer center.
Copy shop (not self-service)
Cross-divisional programs.
Government document full depository.
Institutional records center and archives.
Instructional design office.
Library technician curricular program.
Materials preservation laboratory.
Media technician curricular program.
Print shop.
Public library branch services.
Public museum.
Radio on-air broadcasting station.
Records management.
Satellite communications uplink.
Special learning laboratory operation.
Teleconference and distant learning.
Telecourse administration.
Television on-air broadcasting.

Television course broadcast-level production.
Television station maintenance.
Testing.
Text-book rental service.
Tutoring program supervision.

APPENDIX II

DeKalb College Learning Resources Program Collection Development Policy

Courtesy of DeKalb College, Georgia. (Adopted: October 1987; Revised: February 1988; September 1990; February 1991; March 1992)

I. Philosophy and Mission Statement

The philosophy of the DeKalb College Learning Resources Program reflects and supports the stated educational purpose of DeKalb College. The Mission Statement of DeKalb College follows.

DeKalb College Mission Statement

DeKalb College is an evolving two-year college servicing the eastern metropolitan area of Atlanta by providing broad access to high quality undergraduate programs. Emphasizing the University System core curriculum in the liberal arts tradition, DeKalb College offers academic opportunities in the fine arts, the humanities, the sciences, the social sciences, and the professional fields of business and health sciences.

DeKalb College values excellence in teaching and seeks to create an academic environment that supports effective teaching and encourages personal and intellectual growth along with the pursuit of lifelong learning.

To become an exemplary two-year institution, DeKalb College is dedicated to the following goals:

1. To specialize in general education courses for individuals interested in the first two years of college work leading to an associate degree.
2. To offer a transfer program that prepares students for completion of the baccalaureate degree at a senior college or university.

In addition, DeKalb College offers selected career programs, cultural programs, and continuing education.

DeKalb College Learning Resources Program Mission Statement

The DeKalb College Learning Resources Program is designed to provide comprehensive learning resources and instructional support for the academic programs of the College. The Learning Resources Program includes library services, media services, and instructional support services. Because of its direct relationship to the educational objectives of the College, the Learning Resources Program has the following as its mission:

1. To create an environment that supports effective teaching, intellectual growth, and lifelong learning;
2. To provide a variety of services as an integral part of the instructional process, and to provide assistance to both students and faculty in the use of all learning resources;

3. To provide organized and readily accessible information resources and equipment to meet instructional, institutional, and individual needs;
4. To provide a staff qualified, concerned, and involved in serving the needs of the College and the community.

II. Intellectual Freedom

The Learning Resources Program upholds and supports a series of policy statements by the American Library Association and the Educational Film Library Association concerning the responsibilities of librarians and libraries in making materials available to the public. Copies of these documents are included in Appendix A, "Freedom to Read Statement"; Appendix B, "Library Bill of Rights"; Appendix C, "Intellectual Freedom Statement"; Appendix D, "Freedom to View"; and Appendix E, "Guidelines for Off-Air Recording of Broadcast Programming for Educational Purposes."

III. Standards

The Learning Resources Program accepts the *Criteria for Accreditation* as published by the Southern Association of Colleges and Schools to achieve overall effectiveness in all areas of its growth and to ensure the quality of its components. Further, the standards as published by the Association of College and Research Libraries of the American Library Association and of the Association for Educational Communications and Technology are accepted as measurements for ensuring excellence in all program units.

IV. Copyright

The Learning Resources Program abides by all regulations of relevant sections of the Copyright Revision Act of 1976, and the "Guidelines for Off-Air Recording of Broadcast Programming for Educational Purposes."

V. Description of Clientele

The collection of the DeKalb College Learning Resources Centers is designed primarily to serve students, faculty, and staff of DeKalb College. The LRC provides access to library resource materials for physically handicapped individuals by architecturally planning for ease of access and use.

The LRC staff works closely with the Special Academic Support staff to provide an area, in the LRC, to house equipment used by special needs students.

Borrowing privileges are extended to faculty, research staff, and students of the University System of Georgia who possess a valid University System Borrower's Card. Borrowing privileges are also extended to other groups through formal agreement between DeKalb College and those groups as approved by the Board of Regents.

Any citizen is permitted to use the College's Learning Resources Centers' facilities, materials, and services on the campus. The LRC staff reserve the right to attend to the needs of DeKalb College students above all others.

VI. Responsibility for Selection

The building of an outstanding learning resources collection in a two-year college is the joint responsibility of the professional LRC staff and the faculty.

Since faculty members are most directly involved with the teaching programs of the College, it is appropriate that they play a major role in selecting materials which directly support the curriculum. Funds are not allocated among the various divisions. The collection development librarians are responsible for guarding against an imbalance by frequently surveying the collection and relating holdings to circulation and enrollment figures.

Faculty requests for materials in support of courses taught will have priority, but faculty will also be urged to recommend purchases which will develop all major areas of their discipline.

While faculty recommendations are welcomed and faculty help is solicited, the professional LRC staff have the primary responsibility for selecting materials in academic and other areas not specifically represented in the curriculum. It is also the responsibility of the LRC staff to develop a well-balanced collection. In addition, when the professional staff perceive weaknesses in any area of the collection, it is their responsibility to work with the appropriate department in correcting the deficiencies.

Students are encouraged to submit requests which will be given serious consideration if material requested meets the guidelines of this policy statement.

VII. Criteria for Selection

A. *General Collection.* Priority for book and non-print materials to be purchased for the Learning Resources Centers is given to those materials which meet the curriculum needs of the students in the courses offered. Duplicate copies may be purchased in areas of high circulation.

Materials may be selected that best fulfill the previously stated objectives. The following criteria will be followed in the selection process:

1. Author's/Editor's reputation and significance
2. Importance of the subject matter to the collection
3. Scarcity of materials on the subject
4. Timeliness or permanence of the title
5. Appearance of the title in special bibliographies or indexes
6. Authoritativeness
7. Reputation of the publisher
8. Price
9. Anticipated future needs
10. Appropriateness for use in a junior college program
11. Frequency of requests through intracampus/interlibrary loans

B. *Reference Collection.*   Books will be selected in all areas in which factual information may be desired. This is a noncirculating collection of general and specialized books providing quick access to factual information or overviews of subject areas. An attempt is made to provide basic reference works in subject areas contained in the curriculum as well as those subject fields common to general information requests. The materials in the reference collection are reviewed regularly, and outdated resources are removed or updated. A concerted effort is made not to duplicate expensive reference sets at the various campuses. Only those reference sets which are deemed necessary will be duplicated; otherwise, current editions of expensive reference materials are rotated among the campuses.

C. *Serials/Periodicals Collection.*   Serial/Periodical titles are considered for inclusion in the collection if they meet the previously stated objectives, can be accessed through indexes available in the LRC, and are likely to be utilized by more than a few readers. Title exceptions to index availability will be made by the LRC staff on a case-by-case basis. Generally microform is purchased to represent periodical backfiles. It is the policy of the LRC to maintain a collection of general interest journals, library professional journals, and journals that are considered strictly for relaxation and enjoyment.

D. *Popular Book Collection.*   The Popular Book Collection includes current fiction and non-fiction titles selected for their general interest and possible later addition to the permanent collection. The *New York Times* bestseller list serves as a guide in selecting some titles, but the collection also includes works of local and regional interest and other titles of potential high interest among college clientele.

E. *Textbooks.*   As a general rule, approved textbooks for current course offerings are not acquired by the LRC.

F. *Vertical File.*   The vertical file collection is comprised of inexpensive pamphlets and some newspaper clippings. These materials are used to supplement the collection by providing current and often difficult-to-find information in a concise format.

G. *College Catalogs.*   College catalogs are available for the use of students, faculty, and staff.

H. *Audio Recordings.*   The LRC selects recordings of both music and the spoken word in various formats. The emphasis in this collection is placed on materials that support the curriculum although recordings are also purchased for leisure listening.

I. *Databases.*   The Learning Resources Program currently contracts for access to the DIALOG retrieval system. In addition, the LRC is a member of the OCLC/SOLINET Database. Several periodical and newspaper databases are available via the WIZARD on-line catalog and on CD ROM workstations.

J. *Non-Print Collection.*   The following types of audiovisual formats are presently included in the non-print collection although some may/may not be acquired in the future: 16mm motion picture films, slide/tape programs, filmstrips/tape programs, and videotapes in VHS and inch format.

The following criteria will be followed in the selection process:

1. Importance of the subject matter to the collection
2. Scarcity of materials on the subject matter
3. Timeliness and permanence of the title
4. Technical quality
5. Physical quality
6. Price
7. Audience viewing level
8. Favorable preview by faculty members

VIII. Fine Arts Collection

The Fine Arts collection supports the Fine Arts curriculum of the College. The collection consists of scores, plays, reference books, phonograph records, and compact discs. This collection is frozen and no materials are being added. All items acquired to support the Fine Arts curriculum are currently added to the Central Campus Library collection. When the new building is completed, the current Fine Arts collection will be integrated into the main collection.

IX. Gift Policy

All gifts of print and non-print materials to the LRC are accepted with the understanding that they are added after they have met the same criteria as materials which are to be purchased. The LRC will not accept gifts with conditions as to their disposition or location. The LRC retains the right to dispose of any unneeded materials regardless of how they are acquired.

The LRC will acknowledge but cannot legally appraise gifts for tax purposes. Any appraisal for income tax purposes of a gift of books or other materials to the LRC is the responsibility of the donor.

X. Interlibrary Cooperation

Interlibrary loan service, by which needed materials are obtained from and loaned to other libraries, provides the LRC with a valuable means of supplementing resources and sharing its resources with other libraries. Interlibrary loan service supports the philosophy of resource sharing which enhances information sharing throughout the county, state, region, and country. Types of materials borrowed include books, periodical articles, and microforms. There may be a service charge assessed for the supply of photocopies of journal articles borrowed from other libraries.

The LRC abides by all regulations of relevant sections of the Copyright Revision Act of 1976 and the National Interlibrary Loan Code and the Georgia Interlibrary Loan Code.

XI. Collection Maintenance

A. *Deselection.* The LRC recognizes the need to continually evaluate its collection in response to the changing nature and needs of the college curriculum through the deselection, replacement, and repair of its titles.

Deselection is a necessary component of selection since it systematically provides the following results:

1. Gives the LRC a reputation for reliability
2. Gives the LRC a fresh, inviting appearance
3. Creates a collection which is up-to-date
4. Identifies books which need repairing, rebinding, or replacing
5. Gives the best library service through a collection of quality

A unique set of withdrawal criteria is used for each type of library material and is listed later in this section. The following criteria are considered in deselecting materials from the collection:

1. Poor physical condition; not suitable for rebinding
2. Obsolescence of information
3. Replacement by later edition
4. Duplicate copies of a title no longer in demand
5. Lack of space for materials
6. Insufficient use
7. Materials determined as missing
8. Broken files of unindexed journals/microfilm

Major withdrawal decisions will be jointly discussed by the library staff of the three centers. In some situations, such as academic program relocation, materials may be transferred from one LRC to the other. The guidelines for withdrawal of titles in specific collection areas are listed below.

General Collection. All superseded editions of the General Collection become candidates for withdrawal. Decisions to withdraw are made by the Collection Development Librarians on a title-by-title basis.

All damaged, lost, and long overdue General Collection titles become candidates for withdrawal. Decisions to withdraw or replace are made on a title-by-title basis by the Collection Development Librarians.

All General Collection titles which have not circulated for ten years become candidates for withdrawal.

Reference Materials. The Reference Department has established specific withdrawal policies for many of the reference titles for which revised or superseded editions are regularly received. Decisions to withdraw other titles are made by the Head of the Reference Department in consultation with the Collection Development Librarian.

Serial and Standing Orders. Each year the Collection Development Librarians review serial holdings and evaluate titles which receive infrequent use. Recommendation for cancellation and retention are made in light of curriculum needs and budgetary considerations.

Non-print Materials. All damaged non-print materials become candidates for withdrawal. Decisions to withdraw or replace are made on a case-by-case basis by the Non-Print Librarian.

Fine Arts Materials. All damaged, lost, and long overdue Fine Arts titles become candidates for withdrawal. Decisions to withdraw or replace are made on a title-by-title basis by the Central Collection Development Librarian in consultation with the Head of the Fine Arts Department.

B. *Replacements.* Resources that are missing, lost, or withdrawn because of wear will not automatically be replaced.

The merit of the book, serial, or non-print material must be considered by the librarian before replacement copies are authorized.

The following criteria are used when making decisions on replacements:

1. The continued value of the particular title
2. The demand for the specific title
3. The number of copies held
4. Existing coverage of the subject
5. The availability of newer or better materials on the subject
6. Price of the replacement copy

C. *Binding.* Decisions will be made continually on how to handle worn books—whether to mend, bind, or withdraw them. In making decisions on binding, the following considerations should be made:

1. Value and use of the title
2. Cost of rebinding versus cost of replacement
3. Number of duplicate copies in the collection

D. *Duplication.* More than one copy of a title may sometimes be required to meet special needs of the instruction program. While not encouraged because of budget and space restrictions, purchase of duplicate copies may occur in accordance with the following guidelines:

1. *Print Materials*
   a. Multiple demand and heavy continual use of individual titles
   b. Reference titles that are in heavy demand
2. *Non-Print Materials*
   a. Multiple demand and heavy continual use of individual titles
   b. Non-Print is needed in a different format (e.g., 16mm film to VHS)

The cost of any given publication, together with the acquisitions budget of the LRC, will be the overriding factor in applying these guidelines and in making ultimate duplication decisions.

XII. Procedure for Handling Complaints

Should an objection be raised regarding Learning Resources materials used in the College's educational program, the following procedure should be followed:

A. The College official or staff member receiving a complaint regarding materials shall try to resolve the issue informally. The materials shall remain in use until the complaint is resolved.

1. The College official or staff member receiving a complaint shall explain to the complainant the LRC selection procedure, criteria, and qualifications of those persons selecting the materials.
2. The College official or staff member initially receiving a complaint shall explain to the best of his/her ability the particular place the objected material occupies in the educational program, its intended educational usefulness, and refer the complaining party to someone who can identify and explain the use of the material.

B. In the event that the person making an objection to material is not satisfied with the initial explanation, the person raising the question should be referred to the Dean for Learning Resources.

XIII. Review of Collection Development Policy

This policy will be periodically reviewed by the LRC staff to ensure that it is responsible to the changing needs and objectives of the DeKalb College Learning Resources Program.

Library Bill of Rights

The American Library Association affirms that all libraries are forums for information and ideas, and that the following basic policies should guide their services:

1. Books and other library resources should be provided for the interest, information, and enlightenment of all peoples of the community the li-

brary serves. Materials should not be excluded because of the origin, background, or views of those contributing to their children.

2. Libraries should provide materials and information presenting all points of view on current and historical issues. Materials should not be prescribed or removed because of partisan or doctrinal disapproval.

3. Libraries should challenge censorship in the fulfillment of their responsibility to provide information and enlightenment.

4. Libraries should cooperate with all persons and groups concerned with resisting abridgement of free expression and free access to ideas.

5. A person's right to use a library should not be denied or abridged because of origin, age, background, or views.

6. Libraries which make exhibit spaces and meeting rooms available to the public they serve should make such facilities available on an equitable basis, regardless of the beliefs or affiliations of individuals or groups requesting their use.

The Freedom to Read

The freedom to read is essential to our democracy. It is continuously under attack. Private groups and public authorities in various parts of the country are working to remove books from sale, to censor textbooks, to label "controversial" books, to distribute lists of "objectionable" books or authors, and to purge libraries. These actions apparently rise from a view that our national tradition of free expression is no longer valid: that censorship and suppression are needed to avoid the subversion of politics and the corruption of morals. We, as citizens for disseminating them, wish to assert the public interest in the preservation of the freedom to read.

We are deeply concerned about these attempts at suppression. Most such attempts rest on a denial of the fundamental premise of democracy: that the ordinary citizen, by exercising his critical judgment, will accept the good and reject the bad. The censors, public and private, assume that they should determine what is good and what is bad for their fellow citizens.

We trust Americans to recognize propaganda, and to reject it. We do not believe they need the help of censors to assist them in this task. We do not believe they are prepared to sacrifice their heritage of a free press in order to be "protected" against what others think may be bad for them. We believe they still favor free enterprise in ideas and expression.

We are aware, of course, that books are not alone in being subjected to efforts at suppression. We are aware that these efforts are related to a larger pattern of pressures being brought against education, the press, films, radio, and television. The problem is not only one of actual censorship. The shadow of fear cast by these pressures leads, we suspect, to an even larger voluntary curtailment of expression by those who seek to avoid controversy.

Such pressure toward conformity is perhaps natural to a time of uneasy change and pervading fear. Especially when so many of our apprehensions are directed against an ideology, the expression of a dissident idea becomes a thing feared in itself, and we tend to move against it as against a hostile deed, with suppression.

And yet suppression is never more dangerous than in such time of social tension. Freedom has given the United States the elasticity to endure strain. Freedom keeps open the path of novel and creative solutions, and enables change to come by choice. Every silencing of a heresy, every enforcement of an orthodoxy, diminishes the toughness and resilience of our society and leaves it the less able to deal with stress.

Now as always in our history, books are among our greatest instruments of freedom. They are almost the only means for making general available ideas or manners of expression that can initially command only a small audience.

They are the natural medium for the new idea and the untried voice from which came the original contributions to social growth. They are essential to the extended discussion which serious thought requires, and to the accumulation of knowledge and ideas into organized collections.

We believe that free communication is essential to the preservation of a free society and a creative culture. We believe that these pressures towards conformity present the danger of limiting the range and variety of inquiry and expression on which our democracy and culture depend. We believe that every American community must jealously guard the freedom to publish and to circulate, in order to preserve its own freedom to read. We believe that publishers and librarians have a profound responsibility to give validity to that freedom to read by making it possible for the readers to choose freely from the variety of offerings.

The freedom to read is guaranteed by the Constitution. Those with faith in free men will stand firm on these constitutional guarantees of essential rights and will exercise the responsibilities that accompany these rights.

We therefore affirm these propositions

1. It is in the public interest for publishers and librarians to make available the widest diversity of views and expressions, including those which are unorthodox or unpopular with the majority.

> Creative thought is by definition new, and what is new is different. The bearer of every new thought is a rebel until his idea is refined and tested. Totalitarian systems attempt to maintain themselves in power by the ruthless suppression of any concept which challenges the established orthodoxy.

The power of a democratic system to adapt to change is vastly strengthened by the freedom of its citizens to choose widely from among conflicting opinions offered freely to them. To stifle every nonconformist idea at birth would mark the end of the democratic process. Furthermore, only through the constant activity of weighing and selecting can the democratic mind attain the strength demanded by times like these. We need to know not only what we believe but why we believe it.

2. Publishers, librarians, and booksellers do not need to endorse every idea or presentation contained in the books they make available. It would conflict with the public interest for them to establish their own political, moral, or aesthetic views as a standard for determining what books should be published or circulated.

Publishers and librarians serve the educational process by helping to make available knowledge and ideas required by the growth of the mind and the increase of learning. They do not foster education by imposing as mentors the patterns of their own thought.

The people should have the freedom to read and consider a broader range of ideas then those that may be held by any single librarian or publisher or government or church. It is wrong that what man can read should be confined to what another thinks proper.

3. It is contrary to the public interest for publishers or librarians to determine the acceptability of a book on the basis of the personal history or political affiliations of the author.

A book should be judged as a book. No art or literature can flourish if it is measured by the political views or private lives of its creators. No society of free men can flourish which draws upon lists of writers to whom it will not listen, whatever they have to say.

4. There is no place in our society for efforts to coerce the taste of others, to confine the adults to the reading matter deemed suitable for adolescents, or to inhibit the efforts to writers to achieve artistic expression.

To some, much of modern literature is shocking. But is not much of life itself shocking. We cut off literature at the source if we prevent writers from dealing with the stuff of life. Parents and teachers have a responsibility to prepare the young to meet the diversity of experiences in life to which they will be exposed, as they have a responsibility to help them learn to think critically for themselves. These are affirmative responsibilities, not to be discharged simply by preventing them from reading works for which they are not yet prepared. In these matters taste differs, and taste cannot be legislated; nor can machinery be devised which will suit the demands of one group without limiting the freedom of others.

5. It is not in the public interest to force a reader to accept with any book the prejudgment of a label characterizing the book or author as subversive or dangerous.

> The idea of labeling presupposes the existence of individuals or groups with the wisdom to determine by authority what is good or bad for the citizen. It presupposes that each individual must be directed in making up his mind about the ideas he examines. But Americans do not need others to do their thinking for them.

6. It is the responsibility of publishers and librarians, as guardians of the people's freedom to read, to contest encroachments upon that freedom by individuals or groups seeking to impose their own standards or tastes upon the community at large.

> It is inevitable in the give and take of the democratic process that the political, the moral, or the aesthetic concepts of the individual or group will occasionally collide with those of another individual or group. In a free society each individual is free to determine for himself what he wishes to read, and each group is free to determine what it will recommend to its freely associated members. But no group has the right to take the law into its own hands, and to impose its own concept of politics or morality upon other members of a democratic society. Freedom is no freedom if it is accorded only to the accepted and the inoffensive.

7. It is the responsibility of publishers and librarians to give full meaning to the freedom to read by providing books that enrich the quality and diversity of thought and expression. By the exercise of this affirmative responsibility, bookmen can demonstrate that the answer to a bad book is a good one, the answer to a bad idea is a good one.

> The freedom to read is of little consequence when expended on the trivial; it is frustrated when the reader cannot obtain matter fit for his purpose. What is needed is not only the absence of restraint, but the positive position of opportunity for the people to read the best that has been thought and said. Books are the major channel by which the intellectual inheritance is handed down, and the principle means of its testing and growth. The defense of their freedom and integrity, and the enlargement of their service to society, requires of all bookmen the utmost of their faculties, and deserves of all citizens the fullest of their support.
>
> We state these propositions neither lightly nor as easy generalizations. We here stake out a lofty claim for the value of books. We do so because we believe that they are good, possessed of enormous variety and usefulness, worthy of cherishing and keeping free. We realize that the application of these propositions may mean the dissemination of ideas and manners of expression that are repugnant to many persons. We do not state these prop-

ositions in the comfortable belief that what people read is unimportant. We believe rather that what people read is deeply important; suppression of ideas is fatal to a democratic society. Freedom itself is a dangerous way of life, but it is ours.

This statement was originally issued in May 1953 by the Westchester Conference of the American Library Association and the American Book Publishers Council, which in 1970 consolidated with the American Educational Publishers Institute to become the Association of American Publishers.

Intellectual Freedom Statement

An Interpretation of the Bill of Rights

The heritage of free men is ours.

In the Bill of Rights to the United States Constitution, the founders of our nation proclaimed certain fundamental freedoms to be essential to our form of government. Primary among these is the freedom of expression, specifically the right to publish diverse opinions and the right to unrestricted access to those opinions. As citizens committed to the full and free use of all communications media and as professional persons responsible for making the content of those media accessible to all without prejudice, we, the undersigned, wish to assert the public interest in the preservation of freedom of expression.

Through continuing judicial interpretations of the First Amendment to the United States Constitution, freedom of expression has been guaranteed. Every American who aspires to the success of our experiment in democracy—who has faith in the political and social integrity of free men—must stand firm on those Constitutional guarantees of essential rights. Such Americans can be expected to fulfill the responsibilities implicit in those rights.

We, therefore, affirm these responsibilities:

1. We make available to everyone who needs or desires them the widest possible diversity of views and modes of expression, including those which are strange, unorthodox or unpopular.

Creative thought is, by its nature, new. New ideas are always different and, to some people, distressing and even threatening. The creator of every new idea is likely to be regarded as unconventional—occasionally heretical— until his idea is first examined, then refined, then tested in its political, social, or moral applications. The characteristic ability of our governmental system to adapt to necessary change is vastly strengthened by the option of the people to choose freely from among conflicting opinions. To stifle nonconformist ideas at their inception would be to end the democratic process. Only through continuous weighing and selection from among opposing views can free individuals obtain the strength needed for intelligent, constructive decisions and actions. In short, we need to understand not only what we believe, but why we believe as we do.

2. We do not endorse every idea contained in the materials we produce and make available.

We serve the educational process by disseminating the knowledge and wisdom required for the growth of the mind and the expansion of learning. For us to employ in our own political, moral, or aesthetic views as standards for determining what materials are published or circulated conflicts with the public interest. We cannot foster true education by imposing on others the structure and content of our own opinions. We must preserve and enhance the people's right to broader range of ideas than those held by any librarian or publisher or church government. We hold that it is wrong to limit any person to those ideas and that information another believes to be true, good, and proper.

3. We regard as irrelevant to the acceptance and distribution of any creative work the personal history or political affiliations of the author or others responsible for it or its own publication.

A work of art must be judged solely on its own merits. Creativity cannot flourish if its appraisal and acceptance by the community is influenced by the political views or private lives of the artists or the creators. A society that allows blacklists to be compiled and used to silence writers and artists cannot exist as a free society.

4. With every available legal means, we will challenge laws or governmental action restricting or prohibiting the publication of certain materials or limiting free access to such materials.

Our society has no place for legislative efforts to coerce the taste of its members, to restrict adults to reading matter deemed suitable only for children, or to inhibit the efforts to creative persons in their attempts to achieve perfection. When we prevent serious artists from dealing with truth as they see it, we stifle creative endeavor as its source. Those who direct and control the intellectual development of our children—parents, teachers, religious leaders, scientists, philosophers, statesmen—must assume the responsibility for preparing young people to cope with life as it is and to face the diversity of experience to which they will be exposed as they mature. This is an affirmative responsibility that cannot be discharged easily, certainly not with the added burden of curtailing one's access to art, literature, and opinion. Tastes differ. Taste, like morality, cannot be controlled by government, for governmental action, devised to suit the demands of one group, thereby limits the freedom of all others.

5. We oppose labeling any work of literature or art, or any persons responsible for its creation, as subversion, dangerous, or otherwise undesirable.

> Labeling attempts to predispose users of the various media of communication, and to ultimately close off a path to knowledge. Labeling rests on the assumption that persons exist who have a special wisdom, and who, therefore, can be permitted to determine what will have good and bad effects on other people. But freedom of expression rests on the premise of ideas vying in the open marketplace for acceptance, change, or rejection by individuals. Free men choose this path.

6. We, as guardians of intellectual freedom, oppose and will resist every encroachment upon the freedom by the individuals or groups, private, or official.

> It is inevitable in the give-and-take of the democratic process that the political, moral, and aesthetic preferences of a person or group will conflict occasionally with those of others. A fundamental premise of our free society is that each citizen is privileged to decide those opinions to which he will adhere or which he will recommend to the members of a privately organized group or association. But no private group may usurp the law and impose its own political or moral concepts upon the general public. Freedom cannot be accorded only to selected groups for it is then transmitted into privilege and unwarranted license.

7. Both as citizens and professionals, we will strive by all legitimate means open to us to be relieved of the threat of personal, economic, and legal reprisals resulting from our support and defense of the principles of intellectual freedom.

> Those who refuse to compromise their ideals in support of intellectual freedom have often suffered dismissals from employment, forced resignations, boycotts of products and establishments, and other invidious forms of punishment. We perceive the admirable, often lonely, refusal to succumb to threats of punitive action as the highest form of true professionalism: dedication to the cause of intellectual freedom and the preservation of vital human and civil liberties.
>
> In our various capacities, we will actively resist incursions against the full exercise of our professional responsibility for creating and maintaining an intellectual environment which fosters unrestrained creative endeavor and true freedom of choice and access for all members of the community.
>
> We state these propositions with conviction, not as easy generalizations. We advance a noble claim for the value of ideas, freely expressed, as em-

bodied in books and other kinds of communications. WE do this in our belief that a free intellectual climate fosters creative endeavors capable of enormous variety, beauty, and usefulness, and thus worthy of support and preservation. We recognize that application of these propositions may encourage the dissemination of ideas and forms of expression that will be frightening or abhorrent to some. We believe that what people read, view, and hear is a critically important issue. We recognize, too, that ideas can be dangerous. It may be, however, that they are effectually dangerous only when opposing ideas are suppressed. Freedom, in its many facets, is a precarious course. We espouse it heartily.

Freedom to View

The FREEDOM TO VIEW, along with the freedom to speak, to hear, and to read, is protected by the First Amendment to the Constitution of the United States. In a free society, there is no place for censorship of any medium of expression. Therefore, we affirm these principles

1. It is in the public interest to provide the broadest access to films and audiovisual materials because they have proven to be among the most effective means for the communication of ideas. Liberty of circulation is essential to ensure the constitutional guarantee of freedom of expression.
2. It is in the public interest to provide for audiences, films, and other/ audiovisual materials which present a diversity of views and expression. Selection of a work does not constitute or imply agreement with or approval of the content.
3. It is our professional responsibility to resist the constraint of labeling or prejudging a film on the basis of the moral, religious, or political beliefs of the producer or film maker or on the basis of controversial content.
4. It is our professional responsibility to contest vigorously, by all lawful means, every encroachment upon the public's freedom to view.

Guidelines for Off-Air Recording of Broadcast Programming for Educational Purposes

1. The guidelines were developed to apply only to off-air recording by nonprofit educational institutions.
2. A broadcast program may be recorded off-air simultaneously with broadcast transmission (including simultaneous cable retransmission) and re-

tained by a non-profit educational institution for a period not to exceed the first forty-five (45) consecutive calendar days after date of recording. Upon conclusion of such retention period, all off-air recordings must be erased or destroyed immediately. "Broadcast programs" are television programs transmitted by television stations for reception by the general public without charge.

3. Off-air recordings may be used once by individual teachers in the course of relevant teaching activities, and repeated once only when instructional reinforcement is necessary, in classrooms and similar places devoted to instruction within a single building, cluster or campus, as well as in the homes of students receiving formalized home instruction, during the first ten (10) consecutive school days in the forty-five (45) calendar day retention period. "School days" are school session days—not counting weekends, holidays, vacations, examination periods, or other scheduled interruptions—within the forty-five (45) calendar day retention period.

4. Off-air recordings may be made only at the request of and used by individual teachers, and may not be regularly recorded in anticipation of requests. No broadcast program may be recorded off-air more than once at the request of the same teacher, regardless of the number of times the program may be broadcast.

5. A limited number of copies may be reproduced from each off-air recording to meet the legitimate needs of teachers under these guidelines. Each such additional copy shall be subject to all provisions governing the original recording.

6. After the first ten (10) consecutive school days, off-air recordings may be used up to the end of the forty-five (45) calendar day retention period only for teacher evaluation purposes, i.e., to determine whether or not to include the broadcast program in the teaching curriculum, and may not be used in the recording institution for student exhibition or any other non-evaluation purpose with authorization.

7. Off-air recordings need not be used in their entirety, but the recorded programs may not be altered from their original content. Off-air recordings may not be physically or electronically combined or merged to constitute teaching anthologies or compilations.

8. All copies of off-air recordings must include the copyright notice on the broadcast program as recorded.

9. Educational institutions are expected to establish appropriate control procedures to maintain the integrity of these guidelines.

Special Note: On January 17, 1984, the U.S. Supreme Court announced its opinion in the Sony case involving an action originally brought by Universal City Studios and Walt Disney Productions. The court ruled that off-air videotaping by individuals in their homes for their own private use does not violate copyright, especially in view of the fact that most individuals tape for delayed viewing or time-shifting. However, this decision has no effect upon off-air videotaping by schools, colleges, libraries, and like institutions or in any other situation where the circumstances involve a public performance as defined in the Copyright Laws (Publ. L. 94-553).

APPENDIX III

Learning Resources Program
User Satisfaction Survey Forms

Courtesy of Broome Community College, New York.

LEARNING RESOURCES CENTER
FACULTY AND STAFF SURVEY

The Learning Resources Center (LRC) is interested in learning something about how often, for what purposes, and in what different ways BCC's faculty and staff use the LRC. Your response is important to us since the results will be used to improve LRC materials, facilities and services. Thank you for your help. <u>*PLEASE CIRCLE ALL RESPONSES.*</u>

1. You are a
  a. BCC administrator or middle manager
  b. BCC full-time faculty
  c. BCC full-time adjunct
  d. BCC part-time adjunct
  e. BCC support staff
  f. non-BCC administrator, faculty or staff

2. If you are a faculty member at BCC, what is your rank?
  a. instructor
  b. assistant professor
  c. associate professor
  d. professor
  e. technical assistant

3. If you are a faculty member at BCC, how long have you been acting in this capacity?
  a. 2 years or less
  b. 3-5 years
  c. 6-9 years
  d. 10 years or more

4. If you are a BCC faculty member, in what area do you primarily teach?
  a. Business
  b. Office Technologies
  c. Dental Hygiene
  d. Medical Assistant
  e. Medical Laboratory Technology
  f. Medical Record Technology
  g. Nursing
  h. Physical Therapist Assistant
  i. Radiologic Technology
  j. Biological Sciences
  k. English
  l. History & Social Sciences
  m. Humanities
  n. Early Childhood
  o. Criminal Justice
  p. Fire Protection Technology
  q. Paralegal
  r. Chemical Engineering Technology
  s. Civil Engineering Technology
  t. Computer Studies
  u. Electrical Engineering Technology
  v. Engineering Science
  w. Mechanical Engineering Technology
  x. Mathematics
  y. Other

5. You are
  a. Male
  b. Female

6. How frequently do you use Learning Resources Center (LRC) services?
  a. 4-5 times a week
  b. 1-3 times a week
  c. 1-3 times a month
  d. less than once a month
  e. only when accompanying a class orientation
  f. other _____
  g. never use LRC services

7. How often do you use the LRC for the following purposes? (1=often, 2=sometimes, 3=not at all)

a. reviewing materials for your own instruction	1	2	3
b. reviewing materials for student use	1	2	3
c. reserving material for student reading assignments	1	2	3
d. gathering materials for other professional activities	1	2	3
e. conducting student orientations on LRC use	1	2	3
f. reading books avocationally	1	2	3
g. browsing magazines and newspapers	1	2	3
h. using audiovisual materials	1	2	3
i. socializing/relaxing	1	2	3

8. How often do you use the following equipment? (1=often, 2=occasionally, 3=never, 4=did not know equipment was available)

a. overhead projector	1	2	3	4
b. 16mm film projector	1	2	3	4
c. teleconference	1	2	3	4
d. video cassette player (with TV monitor)	1	2	3	4
e. audio cassette recorder	1	2	3	4
f. slide projector	1	2	3	4
g. camcorder	1	2	3	4
h. LRC studio & editing equipment	1	2	3	4
i. other _____	1	2	3	4

9. Generally, how would you rate the availability and performance of audiovisual equipment you use? (1=very satisfied, 2=satisfied, 3=tolerable, 4=dissatisfied)

a. ability to reserve and schedule equipment when needed	1	2	3	4
b. delivery of equipment	1	2	3	4
c. performance of equipment	1	2	3	4
d. quality of projected images	1	2	3	4
e. quality of sound	1	2	3	4

OVER, PLEASE

10. Please rate the following statements on a scale of 1 to 5. (1=always, 2-sometimes, 3=seldom, 4=never, 5=not applicable)

a.	The LRC has the books that you need	1	2	3	4	5
b.	The LRC has the books that your students need	1	2	3	4	5
c.	The LRC has the magazines that you need	1	2	3	4	5
d.	The LRC has the magazines that your students need	1	2	3	4	5
e.	The LRC has the audiovisual materials you need	1	2	3	4	5
f.	The LRC has the audiovisual materials your students need	1	2	3	4	5
g.	The LRC has the audiovisual equipment that you need	1	2	3	4	5
h.	You can rely on the LRC to provide audiovisual equipment when and where you need it	1	2	3	4	5
i.	You can rely on the condition and performance of audiovisual equipment	1	2	3	4	5
j.	You can rely on the audiovisual staff to respond quickly when malfunctions occur	1	2	3	4	5
k.	The reference staff is is helpful and efficient in finding information	1	2	3	4	5
l.	The circulation staff is helpful and efficient	1	2	3	4	5
m.	Procedures for placing materials on reserve are straightforward and reliable	1	2	3	4	5
n.	Requests to add materials to the LRC's collection are dealt with fairly and efficiently	1	2	3	4	5
o.	Photocopiers in the LRC serve your students' and your own needs	1	2	3	4	5
p.	The LRC is open when you want to use its facilities and services	1	2	3	4	5
q.	The LRC is open when your students want to use its facilities and services	1	2	3	4	5
r.	The LRC provides access to quiet study space to meet your and your students' needs	1	2	3	4	5
s.	The LRC helps me determine what instructional equipment I need and how to use it	1	2	3	4	5

11. What is the most positive statement you can make that describes your feeling about the LRC and the services it provides?

_____

_____

_____

_____

12. What is the most negative statement you can make that describes your feeling about the LRC and the services it provides?

_____

_____

_____

_____

13. In your opinion, how could the LRC improve its existing services to better meet your needs?

_____

_____

_____

_____

14. What additional services/facilities could the LRC provide to better meet your needs?

_____

_____

_____

_____

_____

15. How would you rate the LRC overall? (1=excellent, 2=good, 3=fair, 4=poor)   1   2   3   4

LIBRARY/LEARNING RESOURCES CENTER
STUDENT USE SURVEY

The Library/Learning Resources Center (LRC) staff is interested in learning something about you and how often and for what reasons you use the LRC. Your response is important to us since the results will be used to improve LRC materials, facilities and services. Thank you for your help. **PLEASE CIRCLE ALL RESPONSES.**

1. You are a
   a. full-time student at BCC
   b. part-time student at BCC
   c. student at college/university other than BCC
   d. high school student in early admit program at BCC
   e. BCC Community Education student
   f. local high school or BOCES student
   g. adult community member not currently in college
   h. other _____

2. If you are a full-time or part-time student at BCC, in which division are you registered?
   a. Business
   b. Health Science
   c. Liberal and General Studies/Career Programs
   d. Technology, Engineering, and Computing
   e. Non-matriculated

3. You are
   a. Male
   b. Female

4. Your age is
   a. 19 or under
   b. 20 to 21
   c. 22 to 24
   d. 25 to 29
   e. 30 to 39
   f. 40 or over

5. You normally attend classes
   a. Days (before 5 p.m.)
   b. Evenings (after 5 p.m.)
   c. Both days and evenings
   d. Weekender only
   e. Weekender and days or evenings

6. On average, the number of hours you work a week for salary or wages is
   a. 35-40 hours or more
   b. 30-34 hours
   c. 25-29 hours
   d. 20-24 hours
   e. 15-19 hours
   f. 10-14 hours
   g. 5-9 hours
   h. 4 hours or less
   i. do not work outside the house for compensation

7. How frequently do you use the Library/Learning Resources Center (LRC)?
   a. 4-5 times a week
   b. 1-3 times a week
   c. 1-3 times a month
   d. less than once a month
   e. only when assigned
   f. never use the LRC

8. How often do you use the LRC for the following purposes? *(1=often, 2=sometimes, 3=not at all)*
   a. studying your own material   1 2 3
   b. reading reserve material   1 2 3
   c. obtaining information for class assignments   1 2 3
   d. social reasons   1 2 3
   e. reading books for pleasure   1 2 3
   f. browsing magazines/newspapers   1 2 3
   g. viewing audiovisual materials   1 2 3

9. Do you find it easy to get help in *(please rate on a scale of 1 to 4 where: 1=always, 2=sometimes, 3=never, 4=never needed help)*
   a. using the card catalog   1 2 3 4
   b. using periodical indexes   1 2 3 4
   c. locating books on the shelf   1 2 3 4
   d. using reference services   1 2 3 4
   e. checking out/returning library materials   1 2 3 4

10. Please rate the following statements on a scale of 1 to 5. *(1=always, 2=sometimes, 3=seldom, 4=never, N/A=Not Applicable)*

	1	2	3	4	N/A
a. The library has the materials I need (books, magazines, newspapers, audiovisual materials)	1	2	3	4	N/A
b. The staff helps me find information	1	2	3	4	N/A
c. The staff helps me borrow/return materials efficiently	1	2	3	4	N/A
d. The LRC has the books I need for my assignments	1	2	3	4	N/A
e. The LRC has the magazine articles that I need for my assignments	1	2	3	4	N/A
f. The LRC provides an adequate number of viewing stations for videocassettes and other audiovisual materials for my needs	1	2	3	4	N/A
g. The LRC provides access to quiet study space for my needs	1	2	3	4	N/A
h. Photocopy services in the LRC serve my needs	1	2	3	4	N/A
i. The LRC is open when I need to use its services and facilities	1	2	3	4	N/A

OVER, PLEASE

11. What is the most _positive statement_ you can make that describes your feeling about the LRC and the services it provides?

_____

_____

_____

_____

_____

12. What is the most _negative statement_ you can make that describes your feeling about the LRC and the services it provides?

_____

_____

_____

_____

_____

13. In your opinion, how could the LRC _improve its existing services_ to better meet your needs?

_____

_____

_____

_____

_____

14. What _additional services/facilities_ could the LRC provide to better meet your needs?

_____

_____

_____

_____

_____

15. How would you rate the LRC overall? (*1=excellent, 2=good, 3=fair, 4=poor*)   1   2   3   4

**Please return at the next meeting of this class.
We appreciate your cooperation and assistance. Thank you.**

APPENDIX IV

Selected Position Descriptions

POSITION DESCRIPTION

Title: Dean of Learning Resources
Division: Learning Resources
Reports to: Vice President of Instructional Services

POSITION SUMMARY

Under minimum supervision, has the authority, responsibility, and accountability for the administration of the Division of Learning Resources, which includes Access Services, User Services, and Telecommunications Networking Services, ensuring the division is responsive to the needs of the college and the community at large within the confines of established policy and the available resources of the college.

SPECIFIC RESPONSIBILITIES

1. Plans, develops, coordinates, implements, supervises, and evaluates all learning resources programs and services.
2. Works in partnership with faculty and staff to improve instructional resources and assure quality programs and services.
3. Establishes and maintains linkages to the larger learning resources community, including local, state, and regional professional learning resources organizations.
4. Coordinates the learning resources program review and planning process ensuring the program goals and objectives relate to those of the college.
5. Informs faculty and staff of innovations and resources in information access, instructional support, and developmental education.
6. Makes recommendations for initial appointment, promotion, or termination of staff. Conducts annual performance appraisals. Ensures staff development.
7. Plans, prepares, submits, and implements Division budget with the input and cooperation of affected staff.
8. Serves on appropriate college, regional, and state committees.
9. Performs other duties as assigned by the Vice President of Instructional Services.

RELATIONSHIPS WITH OTHERS

Works with deans, directors, and vice presidents to provide LRP services. Also must be able to motivate and direct the Division's administrative, professional, technical, and clerical staff.

MINIMUM QUALIFICATIONS

Education: Masters in Library Science or Educational Technology or Information Science.

Experience: Five years progressively responsible experience in a learning resources center of a community college; administrative experience preferred; experience with automated library systems desired.

Skills/
Abilities: Oral and written communication skills;
Strong public service orientation;
Ability to work in a collegial environment;
Organizational skills.

POSITION DESCRIPTION

Title: Information Services Librarian
Division: Learning Resources
Reports To: Direct of User Services

POSITION SUMMARY

Provides information services for community college students, faculty, administrators, and broader college community, including general reference services, bibliographic instruction, collection development, and promotion of services and resources. In addition, holds leadership role in the implementation and promotion of electronic reference and microcomputer resources.

SPECIFIC RESPONSIBILITIES

1. Provides general reference services to students, faculty, administrators, and broader college community.
2. Conducts bibliographic instruction classes; creates point-of-use instructional aids and pathfinders; and provides individualized assistance with the use of learning resources.
3. Participates in collection development activities ensuring access to resources responsive to college needs.
4. Promotes LRP services and resources; serves as liaison with faculty for assigned departments; compiles bibliographies.
5. Coordinates the implementation and promotion of electronic reference and microcomputer resources.
6. Maintains an awareness of new information tools and technology to meet the needs of students, faculty, and staff.
7. Assumes appropriate responsibilities of a college faculty member and learning resources professional.
8. Performs other duties as assigned.

RELATIONSHIPS WITH OTHERS

Works under the general supervision of the Director of User Services. Cooperates in a collegial manner with LRP professional, technical, and clerical staff. Works with students, discipline faculty, administrators, staff, and broader college community.

MINIMUM QUALIFICATIONS

Education: MLS from an ALA accredited program;
               Appropriate specialized coursework desired.
Experience: Experience with electronic information resources
               and microcomputer required;

Information services experience in a community college preferred.

Skills/
Abilities:

Oral and written communication skills;

Strong public service orientation;

Ability to work in a collegial environment;

Strong interpersonal skills with faculty, students, and others.

POSITION DESCRIPTION

Title: Equipment Maintenance and Repair
              Technician
Division: Learning Resources
Reports to: Director of Access Services

POSITION SUMMARY

Under general supervision of the Director of Access Services, responsible for maintaining, testing, troubleshooting, repairing, designing, and constructing audiovisual equipment for use in campus facilities and to provide varied skilled technical services and information as requested.

SPECIFIC RESPONSIBILITIES

1. Maintains, repairs, calibrates, and trouble-shoots classroom audiovisual equipment, listening centers, multi-media installations. Documents in writing, repair and preventative maintenance work conducted on all equipment.
2. Assists supervisor in performing product searches of commercially available equipment.
3. Designs, constructs, installs, and maintains specialized audiovisual equipment. Documents in writing, operating and service instructions for all in-shop constructed equipment and facilities.
4. Maintains inventories of LRP equipment.
5. Provides back-up services for related College audio and audiovisual facilities as needed.
6. Performs other related duties as assigned.

RELATIONSHIPS WITH OTHERS

Works with other LRP staff and the college community. Conducts college business with external vendors and representatives.

MINIMUM QUALIFICATIONS

Education: Associate degree in electrical engineering or graduation from technical school.
Experience: One year audiovisual repair experience.
Skills/   Knowledge of solid state electronics including use of
Abilities: related tools and specialized equipment;
              Ability to work well with people under pressure;
              Strong public service orientation;
              Ability to work in a collegial environment.

POSITION DESCRIPTION

Title: Telecourse Coordinator
Division: Learning Resources
Reports to: Director of Telecommunication
                Networking

POSITION SUMMARY

Develops and administers telelearning programming delivered via cable, ITFS, fiber optic, and satellite transmission in consultation with the Director of Telecommunication Networking Services.

SPECIFIC RESPONSIBILITIES

1. Serves as chief operational administrator of telelearning programs. Administers telelearning budget. Negotiates relevant contracts.
2. Coordinates course selection with deans, faculty, and related departments.
3. Serves as primary communicator of telelearning programs to various campus groups and to the public.
4. Serves as contact person for public libraries, cable, and open-air television companies who assist with delivery of telelearning programming.
5. Conducts program evaluation and assessments. Reports headcount statistics. Maintains continuous program data and creates annual report.
6. Maintains accurate semester schedule information and develops telelearning distribution schedules.
7. Represents the college with regional and national professional telelearning organizations.
8. Performs other duties as assigned.

RELATIONSHIPS WITH OTHERS

Works under the general supervision of the Director of Telecommunications Networking Services. Works with deans, directors, and vice presidents to provide telelearning services. Coordinates closely with the Director of Community Relations and with area agencies for the delivery of telelearning programming. Cooperates in a collegial manner with LRP professional, technical, and clerical staff.

MINIMUM QUALIFICATIONS

Education: Bachelors degree in education or communication;
                Formal training in telecommunications and computer literacy desired.

continued

Experience: Experience with alternative education, telecommunications, and computers desired.

Skills/   Oral and written communication skills;

Abilities: Strong public service orientation;

Detail oriented with strong organizational skills;

Strong interpersonal skills with faculty, students, and others.

POSITION DESCRIPTION

Title: Library Technical Assistant
Division: Learning Resources
Reports to: Coordinator of Circulation Services

POSITION SUMMARY

Provides general LRP services to students, faculty, staff, and other LRP patrons. Responsible for specialized duties in the learning resources circulation area including charging and discharging materials, stack maintenance, processing reserves, audiovisual assistance, and other specialized duties.

SPECIFIC RESPONSIBILITIES

1. Provides general LRP services to students, faculty, staff, and other LRP patrons.
2. Charges and discharges materials; maintains overdue records; compiles statistics; and other circulation functions.
3. Maintains the LRP collections ensuring their access to patrons. Repairs LRP materials as necessary.
4. Processes materials onto and off of reserve ensuring efficient service.
5. Assists patrons with the operation of audiovisual equipment.
6. Performs other duties as assigned.

RELATIONSHIPS WITH OTHERS

Works with other LRP staff and the college community.

MINIMUM QUALIFICATIONS

Education: Associate degree.
Experience: Library or clerical experience desired;
                Computer experience desired.
Skills/   Oral and written communication skills;
Abilities: Cooperative, service-oriented attitude;
                Effective interpersonal skills;
                Accurate keyboard and clerical skills.

Index